# THE JEWS OF SAN NICANDRO

# THE JEWS OF
# SAN NICANDRO

JOHN A. DAVIS

YALE UNIVERSITY PRESS
NEW HAVEN AND LONDON

For information about this and other Yale University Press publications, please contact:
U.S. Office: sales.press@yale.edu    www.yalebooks.com
Europe Office: sales@yaleup.co.uk    www.yaleup.co.uk

Set in Minion by IDSUK (DataConnection) Ltd
Printed in Great Britain by the MPG Books Group

Library of Congress Cataloging-in-Publication Data

Davis, John A.
    The Jews of San Nicandro / John A. Davis.
        p. cm.
    ISBN 978-0-300-11425-6 (cl:alk. paper)
    1. Jewish converts from Christianity—Italy—Sannicandro Garganico.
    2. Jews—Italy—Sannicandro Garganico—History—20th century.
    3. Conversion—Judaism—History—20th century. 4. Sannicandro Garganico
    (Italy)—Religion. 5. Sannicandro Garganico (Italy)—Ethnic relations. I. Title.
        BM729.P7D38    2010
        296.7'140945757–dc22

                                                                2010020666

A catalogue record for this book is available from the British Library.

10  9  8  7  6  5  4  3  2  1

# Contents

# Illustrations and Maps

## Illustrations

## Maps

# Acknowledgements

My efforts to piece together the many different strands that make up the story of Donato Manduzio and the converts of San Nicandro have led me in many different and often unexpected directions, in the process incurring debts of gratitude to many individuals and institutions. The University of Connecticut has supported the project through a semester of sabbatical leave and an internal fellowship at the Institute for the Humanities (UCHI). Dr Gisèle Lévy, librarian at the *Centro bibliografico delle communità ebraiche italiane* (CBCEI, Rome), Dr Michela Procacci of the *Direzione generale per i beni archivistici*, (Rome), and Dr Renato Spiegel at the *Central Archive for the History of the Jewish People* (Hebrew University, Jerusalem) have all provided expert guidance on sources, while Zippi Rosenne, Director of the Oster Visual Documentation Center (Tel Aviv, Israel) helped to locate the photographs that appear in the text.

Alberto Cavaglion, Lisa Benaim, Joel Blatt, Ester Fano, Ken Gouwens, David Kertzer, Axel Körner, Amelie Kuhrt, Ross Miller, Elissa Papirno, Maria Gabriella Rienzo, Roberto Vivarelli, Desmond Ryan, John Sawyer, Umberto Gentiloni Silveri, and Anna and Stuart Woolf have all been generous with suggestions and information. Special thanks to Alessandro Visani who did a wonderful job tracking down documents in the Vatican Secret Archive and in the *Archivio Centrale dello Stato* in Rome. In San

Nicandro, Signora Giuliana Incoronata and Signora Lucia Leone kindly introduced me to their community and allowed me to copy their collection of photographs and records.

In preparing the book I have benefited greatly from the comments and questions raised by the audiences with whom I have had the opportunity to share the story, and I am most appreciative of the invitations to give talks extended by Wendy Heller (Italian Studies, Princeton), Bruce Laurie (History Department, UMass), the Columbia University Italian seminar in New York, Andreina Bianchini (UConn Program, Palazzo Rucellai, Florence), Carol Clark and Ruggero Raneri (Raneri di Sorbello Foundation, Perugia), K.E. Fleming and Gilles Pécout (directors of the joint NYU-ENS seminar in Paris), Marta Petrusewicz (CUNY Graduate Center, NY), and Alex Grab (History Department, University of Maine).

Michael Dintenfass, Bob Gross, Marta Petrusewicz and Sylvia Schafer generously gave of their time to read earlier drafts of the book: when it came to writing the final draft their comments proved to be constructive and helpful, as did those of the anonymous and eagle-eyed reader for Yale University Press. No praise would be too high for the professionalism, enthusiasm and commitment of my editor Heather McCallum and her colleagues, with whom it has been a pleasure to work.

While I am happy to have this opportunity to acknowledge the assistance I have received from all these individuals and from many others who must remain unnamed, it goes without saying that responsibility for the book and everything it contains rests solely and entirely with the author. My wife Elaine has followed the story from start to finish, and it is to her that the book is dedicated.

1 General Map of Italy

# Introduction

## The Prophet of San Nicandro

To mark the coming of Rosh Hashanah and the start of the Jewish New Year, in September 1947 *Time* magazine carried the curious story of an unusual conversion to the Jewish faith that had taken place in a remote part of southern Italy. The story had begun some twenty years earlier in the town of San Nicandro Garganico in Apulia, when Donato Manduzio, a 'dark-eyed, sallow' veteran of the First World War, decided to abandon the Catholic faith to become instead a self-proclaimed Jew. He was soon joined by others, all of them very poor, and within a few years the community of would-be converts numbered some eighty people. Somehow they managed to make contact with the Chief Rabbi in Rome, but he was reluctant 'to take the unusual group into the community until he had heard more about them'. Despite their repeated requests it was not until after the Second World War that the rabbinical authorities in Rome agreed to consider their case and finally consented to their formal conversion. The report ended with a question. Now that the converts had completed their 'arduous journey as far as circumcision is concerned', what next? They were now Jews, but how were they to live as Jews in a rural Italian town where there were no other Jews, no rabbi and no synagogue?[1]

The answer came two years later when the majority of the San Nicandro converts left Italy to emigrate to the recently founded

State of Israel. The founder of the community, Donato Manduzio, was not among them, having died two months before Israel was officially proclaimed. Some of the older members of the community, including Manduzio's widow Emanuela, chose to stay in San Nicandro, where there is still a small community of families who practise the Jewish faith. Of those who emigrated, the majority stayed in Israel, where they and their descendants remain to the present day.

The story of the Jews of San Nicandro has attracted much curiosity and speculation over the years. It is not only unusual; it would seem to be the only case of collective conversion to Judaism in Europe in modern times. Collective religious conversions are anything but uncommon in the contemporary world, of course, as is witnessed by the remarkable following that the Pentecostal Churches continue to attract in different parts of the Americas, Europe and Africa.[2] But, unlike the evangelical faiths, Judaism does not seek to proselytize. Potential converts are proverbially turned away up to seven times and while individual conversions to the Jewish religion are quite common, collective conversions are not. Even if the numbers involved in the San Nicandro case were never very large, there are no other examples in recent times of the conversion of a whole community. Dr Arnaldo Ascarelli, the surgeon who performed the ritual circumcisions on the male converts in San Nicandro in August 1946, later commented that although he had been involved in many cases of individuals converting to Judaism, nothing similar to the collective conversion of Manduzio's followers had occurred since biblical times.

No less curious is the timing. The small group of poor families in San Nicandro who decided to adopt the Jewish faith in the 1930s did so at precisely the moment when Jews throughout Europe were being targeted for persecution. Indeed, the San Nicandresi faced that persecution head on after 1938, when Mussolini's regime introduced the Racial Laws that excluded

Jews from the 'national community', as it was redefined by its Fascist masters. This was exactly when the small community in San Nicandro chose to become Jews and refused to hide their adopted identity.

The context in which all this happened is another puzzle. San Nicandro is situated in one of Italy's poorest and most remote regions. The town sits perched on the north-western edge of the Gargano promontory, a mountainous plateau that juts out into the Adriatic at some 900 metres above sea level to form the easily recognizable spur on the boot of the Italian peninsula. Looking northwards from the town, shallow sandy beaches map the contours of Italy's Adriatic coast, while the little cluster of the Tremiti islands lies in the foreground: today the islands are popular holiday resorts, but in the 1930s they were used as prison colonies for common criminals and opponents of Mussolini's regime. To the north-west the seemingly endless wheat fields of the arid northern Apulian plain stretch to the foothills of the Apennine chain, while to the east the land rises to the uplands of the Gargano plateau, which reaches its highest point on Monte Sant'Angelo.

Today the Gargano and its coastal resorts are thronged with tourists each summer, but fifty years ago this was still one of the least accessible parts of southern Italy. From San Nicandro it is about sixty kilometres to Foggia, the provincial capital, and 180 kilometres to the port of Bari in the south. But before the coming of the first railway branch line in the early 1930s travellers had to face a difficult journey that took them first across the malaria-infested swamps that separated the promontory from the mainland, and then along ancient and rutted highways that were often impassable and in any case impracticable for modern forms of transport.

In the period in which the story of Manduzio and his fellow converts took place, the Gargano plateau attracted few visitors other than travelling pedlars and the pilgrims and penitents who came to visit one of the many local sanctuaries and sacred sites. From the earliest times, however, the promontory had been an important site for pilgrimages and few Mediterranean regions could claim a richer patrimony of Catholic symbolism and mythology. According to legend Monte Sant'Angelo was where the Archangel Michael had come to Earth on the final day of Creation to survey and report on the Lord's handiwork. The site and other sanctuaries attracted medieval pilgrims from all over Europe, including crusaders who before setting off for the Holy Land to do battle with the infidels (following much the same route that the San Nicandro converts would take when they left for Israel in 1949) came to make their vows to St Michael. In the centuries that followed, the holy sites of the Gargano retained a special place on the sacred itineraries of the devout.

Although Manduzio often referred to San Nicandro as a 'poor mountain village' it was not small. In 1930 it had a population of some 17,000 souls and could boast a cathedral and three parish churches, a Norman castle, seven doctors, one veterinarian and three pharmacists. But like most rural towns in southern Italy at this time size was a measure not of prosperity but of poverty and overcrowding. The great majority of the town's inhabitants were agricultural workers. Some owned small plots of land, although these were never enough to sustain them or their families. Often the land they worked lay far from the town, so that every day they had long and tiring journeys to make backwards and forwards; normally on foot, although by the 1930s by bicycle too. There were many tradesmen, shopkeepers, shoemakers, tailors, seamstresses and the like, all competing for too few customers. The situation was exacerbated by the Depression, which in the 1930s hit all the Mediterranean economies – including southern Italy's – hard. For many families the large stone quarries on the outskirts of San Nicandro, for example, had been an important additional source of employment, but falling demand for building materials caused the quarry to close in the 1930s. The situation in the surrounding rural areas was even worse, and many families chose to move into the town in the hope of finding either work or assistance.

Economic conditions in San Nicandro deteriorated badly in the 1930s and became even worse during and after the Second World War. But the situation was new only in degree. For as long as anyone could remember there had been little work in San Nicandro, something to which people were accustomed. They knew that nothing was certain except uncertainty, hunger and hardship and that they had been born in a proverbial land of remorse from which there were few avenues of escape. But still they dreamed of escaping, and above all of emigration.[3]

The world that Manduzio and his followers inhabited was similar in many respects to the one immortalized by Carlo Levi in post-war Italy's first international best-seller, *Christ Stopped at Eboli*. Although the book was not published until after the war, it was based on his experiences in the late 1930s when the Fascist authorities had sentenced Levi to a brief period of 'internal exile'. He served his sentence under house arrest in a village in the southern province of Basilicata that was even more remote than San Nicandro. Levi was from Turin and this was his first encounter with the rural South. The experience left him with a deep respect for the dignity with which his rural neighbours faced the hardships of their lives. But the bleakness and poverty of their world filled him with horror and revulsion. In the opening passage of his book he described the South as a land that history had passed by, leaving it untouched by change and locked in superstition and ignorance so that even the elementary connections of cause and effect were still not understood.[4]

The peasant world that Levi described and which countless anthropologists have since sought to explain did bear many similarities to the world of Donato Manduzio and his followers. Yet in retrospect we can see that this world was also beginning to register the impact of important and irreversible changes that escaped Carlo Levi's otherwise attentive eye. Both directly and indirectly these changes had important bearings on the San Nicandro story. In the first place, although San Nicandro was remote and inaccessible, it was not isolated. Its inhabitants travelled far and wide in search of work, and many of them had taken part in the mass emigration to the United States before the Great War. The town had been closely involved in the often violent struggles between the landowners and the unions organized by farm labourers that had spread throughout many parts of the South and with special ferocity in the province of Apulia in the same period. During the war, thousands of young men like Donato Manduzio had served in the army. When those fortunate enough to have survived the battles on the Piave and the Isonzo fronts came home after the war, they found San Nicandro caught up in the upheavals and violence of the post-war years that in 1922 led to the collapse of Italian democracy and the Fascist seizure of power.

There were many other indications of change in a peasant world that Carlo Levi believed to be trapped in an immobile past. It is striking, for example, that not only Donato Manduzio but most of his followers could read and write. Indeed, without the ability to read the sacred texts unaided their story could never have happened. It is perhaps even more remarkable that the women, who in these peasant communities conventionally received scant education, were also able to read and write, and often much better than the men. The backgrounds of the would-be converts suggest that there were many ways in which poor southerners could become literate. The most obvious were the village schools, even though the children of poor peasants rarely attended beyond the elementary grades. Military service might offer other opportunities, as did participation in the labour unions and revolutionary political movements that found a strong following in rural Apulia before and after the Great War.

The steady growth of literacy in these rural communities was a symptom of much broader changes, however, many of which were associated directly or indirectly with emigration. The first great wave of mass emigration from the South had begun in the 1890s, starting in Sicily. After the turn of the century Italians from the mainland South began to follow and the great exodus from Apulia coincided with the major downturn in the economy in 1907 that lasted until the outbreak of the Great War. In those years thousands of young agricultural labourers left Apulia and the Gargano towns to cross the Atlantic, but although some settled permanently in the United States, for most of them the transatlantic crossing was just an extension of more traditional seasonal migrations in search of work. Once they had saved whatever they thought they needed to start up again, most came back. But when they returned the stories of their experiences of the New World had a profound impact on the cultural milieu of the rural South. Most of those who returned were soon reduced to the same poverty as everyone else, but nonetheless the *americani*, as they were known, personified what had become the great aspiration of most southerners.[5]

Its harsh realities masked by gilded myths and selective memories, emigration became the great hope of poor southerners. But once the Great War began the escape route was cut off and would not reopen until many years later; indeed not until after the Second World War. In 1915 those who had emigrated had to choose between returning home to fight for king and country or losing their Italian citizenship, while the obligation of military service made it impossible for others to leave. After the war there was no resumption of the earlier mass emigration, in part because the US government imposed new immigration quotas that discriminated deliberately against southern Italians, but also because once the Fascists came to power they declared emigration to be an affront to the dignity of the national community and a waste of human resources that were needed to build the new Italy and its empire.

When emigration ceased to be a practical possibility, the ideal became even more compelling until it was finally realized in the new great mass exodus from the rural South that began in the 1950s. This last emigration revealed how deeply the desire to escape had become fixed in the minds of poor southerners and this time few chose to return, and the post-war flight from the unrelenting poverty of the South was to be the final chapter in the long history of an ancient Mediterranean peasant world.

The San Nicandro converts who in 1949 emigrated to Israel were part of that narrative and were among the first of the thousands of southerners who set out to create new lives and new identities after the Second World War. From the very beginning their story revealed the legacies of earlier emigrations, which, among other things, had brought new religious movements to southern Italy in these years. Those movements were part of a more general revival in popular religiosity that occurred in many different parts of Europe after the First World War. That trend was very visible in Italy, and as economic conditions deteriorated in the 1930s the search for more intimate and direct religious experience seems to have intensified. The search took many different forms, and anthropologists, for example, were both struck and surprised by the revival of folk religions and by the continuing potency of magic in many parts of southern Italy. But the most pervasive examples of popular religious mobilization were the numerous and rapidly expanding Marian cults, which in Italy were actively promoted by both the Church and the Fascist dictatorship.

One of the most famous of these in the 1920s and 1930s was located just a short distance from San Nicandro in the town of San Giovanni. Its focus was a Capuchin monk known as Padre Pio, who claimed to have received the marks of the stigmata of the crucified Christ and to be able to perform miracles. Much later Padre Pio would become twentieth-century Italy's most popular saint, but in the early days his claims were treated with great suspicion by the Church. The cult that grew up around him in San Giovanni Rotonda owed less to popular acclaim than to a carefully devised marketing operation directed by a bizarre and not very spiritual group of politicians, entrepreneurs and fraudulent speculators.[6] Closer scrutiny reveals that the case of Padre Pio was an exception that does not easily fit into the broader pattern of popular religiosity in southern Italy. But although it had little in common with the more spontaneous search for more direct forms of religious experience that was evident in the cases of the evangelical communities and the San Nicandro converts, for example, enthusiasm for Padre Pio in San Giovanni Rotonda nonetheless reflects the growth in popular devotional movements in these years.

The story of the San Nicandro converts was certainly part of a wider search for more direct and unmediated forms of religious experience, but it had less in common with the popular Marian cults than with the forms of popular religion that returning emigrants had brought back to southern Italy from North America. While working in the United States, many Italian emigrants had converted to one of the evangelical faiths, and when they came home they brought their new faiths with them. Since the great majority of Italian emigrants were from the South, it is no surprise that these churches and communities were founded primarily in the South. Although the numbers were never great, after the end of the First World War communities of Pentecostalists, Baptists, Jehovah's Witnesses and Seventh Day Adventists were founded in Sicily and in many parts of the mainland South.

The presence of these evangelical communities played a direct part in Manduzio's story, and it was from Pentecostalists that he received an Italian-language edition of the Bible that set him on the path to his own religious epiphany. The presence of these evangelical communities in the heartland of Catholic Europe is another example of the ways in which emigration and its legacies were changing the world of the southern Italian peasant. But if the story of the would-be Jews of San Nicandro was deeply influenced by the cultural legacies of emigration, it has also to be set against the search for forms of religious experience that might in some ways mitigate the terrible hardships of the day-to-day life of the rural poor. Donato Manduzio made that connection very explicitly when he stated that his own search for spiritual guidance had been driven by a desire to understand why the world he inhabited was full of pain and suffering. Similar concerns may explain the receptive responses to the strong messianic content of the new evangelical faiths.

At a moment when physical emigration was a dream that could not be realized, passionate and individual forms of religious experience offered an alternative spiritual emigration. But if Manduzio's followers were by no means the only poor southerners who were seeking spiritual consolation for the unrelenting hardship of their lives, that does not explain why they chose Judaism or why they stuck to that choice through thick and thin, despite repeated setbacks and huge disappointments. In part, the answer to that question begins and ends with Manduzio. Had he simply become an evangelical Protestant, then his story would have disappeared into the short and largely neglected history of evangelical Protestantism in southern Italy in the interwar years. But as the *Time* magazine reporter noted, Manduzio had rejected the tenets of evangelical Protestantism because he was unable to believe that the Messiah had already come to earth in the form of Jesus Christ. It was his reading of the books of the Old Testament, in other words the Hebrew Bible, and his belief that the Messiah was still awaited that led him to the Jewish faith.

How had he come to this conclusion unassisted? There is no indication that anyone had led Manduzio or the others to the Jewish faith, nor is there evidence of any connection with other Jews or with the Jewish faith prior to their conversion. Indeed, Manduzio at first believed that the Jews had all perished in the biblical Flood and that he had been called by the Almighty to revive a faith that had long since disappeared from the face of the earth. The Jewish faith was something that the would-be converts discovered on their own, and it was Manduzio who insisted that such a discovery would have been impossible for an autodidact who had never been to school had it not been for the direct intervention of the Almighty. He had no doubt that his conversion was a miracle.

Obviously this spin on the story makes it not only simple and uncomplicated, but also inspirational. That is also how many of those who have written about it have chosen to interpret it. The unsigned report published in *Time* magazine in 1947, for example, was published on the same page as an account of an appeal launched by Pope Pius XII for a worldwide Catholic crusade against the evils of Communism. The editorial juxtaposition of the two reports neatly contrasted on one hand the menace of the new Cold War world and the threats posed by international Communism with Manduzio's simple but inspirational spirituality on the other.

Even before the story of the converts of San Nicandro had reached its conclusion, against the background of post-Second World War Europe, the gradual unfolding of the true scale of the Holocaust, the emergence of the new Cold War and the conflicts in the Middle East, their story easily became symbolic of a primal hope in unsullied spirituality and of the force of faith in the face of evil and adversity. Bringing out this broader symbolic meaning of the story was the explicit aim of the first detailed account of the conversion, written by Phinn E. Lapide, a pseudonym for Pinchas Spitzer, a Canadian Jew who had settled in Palestine and had met Manduzio and his followers in the spring of 1944 while serving with the British Eighth Army in Italy. Lapide presented the San Nicandro conversion as a biblical allegory. He was fascinated by the converts' story because he saw in it what he believed to be clear parallels with the history of the

Jewish people. Casting Manduzio in the role of Moses in Apulia, he rewrote the converts' tale as a modern-day version of the story of the Jewish people in their biblical exile. Although Lapide spoke some Italian and knew the converts well, his account is full of inaccuracies and passages of pure invention – he even claimed to have played a major role in the conversion. But the striking simplicity that the story took on in this telling was what many found to be inspirational.[7]

In Italy, by contrast, the story was seen rather differently. From the start it was less the conversion that attracted attention than the fact that the converts had soon afterwards been able to emigrate to Israel, where it was said that they had been given land by the government. At a time when the post-war exodus from the south had not yet started, the story quickly came to symbolize the great aspiration of most poor southerners and, as a young journalist named Giovanni Russo discovered, the news soon resonated widely. At the time, Russo was writing about the protests that had spread through the rural South after the collapse of the Fascist regime, when once again the South became the theatre for often violent confrontations between the peasants and the landowners. Different political parties, but primarily the Socialists and the Communists, were competing to give direction to the protest movements, arousing fears that southern Italy was poised to follow post-war Greece on the path to civil war and Communist subversion.

In this politically charged climate, the news that a group of peasant families in San Nicandro had become Jews, had been allowed to emigrate to Israel and had been given land by the Jerusalem government was a source of great interest. Wherever Russo went, people wanted to know whether the story was true and, if so, how they too could become Jews so that they could leave Italy and be granted land in Israel just like the people from San Nicandro.[8]

Despite Carlo Levi's belief that the relation of cause to effect was not understood in the South, that was exactly how other southerners connected the conversion of the San Nicandresi and their subsequent emigration. Russo himself thought that this was the most likely explanation, and out of curiosity he decided to visit San Nicandro, where he spent two days in conversation with Manduzio's widow and other remaining members of the community. But by the time he left the town the sceptical young journalist had come to accept that the collective conversion was authentic. He also believed that the key to this unusual story lay in the charismatic character of Donato Manduzio, whom he placed in the tradition of local prophets and faith healers in which southern Italy in general and the Gargano peninsula in particular were especially rich.

Giovanni Russo was convinced that the San Nicandro converts had purely spiritual motives. So too was Elena Cassin, an Italian professor of Assyriology at the Sorbonne, who knew many of the members of the Jewish communities in Turin, Florence and Rome that had been directly involved in the San Nicandro story both before and after the war. It was at the specific request of Raffaele Cantoni, the President of the Union of Jewish Communities in Rome at this time who had been in direct contact with the San Nicandro converts since the late 1930s, that shortly afterwards Cassin began to write her book, and it was Cantoni who provided her with access to all the documents and correspondence with various members of the Italian Jewish communities.[9] Her aim was to write a serious and documented account of the story that would correct the factual errors in Phinn Lapide's book and find a broader explanation for the conversion. As well as the copious correspondence between the converts and various members of the Jewish community, she drew extensively on interviews conducted in the early 1950s with community members in both Israel and Italy and on the more than 200 handwritten pages of the journal that Manduzio had kept.

Like Russo, Cassin believed that Donato Manduzio was the key to understanding how the conversion had taken place. She saw in his simple spiritual conviction, unbending commitment to his discovered religion and deep knowledge of the biblical texts the sources of the authority that he came to exercise over the rest of the community. She also placed him in a tradition of village seers and faith healers, and went on to argue that the converts were the modern-day inheritors of earlier traditions of peasant protest and banditry in southern Italy. Unfortunately Cassin does not offer convincing explanations for either how the story originated or how it developed. Nor is it clear in what sense Manduzio and his followers can be considered as examples of pre-modern peasant rebelliousness.[10] They rejected Catholicism, but unlike the evangelical Protestants they showed no desire to become independent. Indeed from the start their great ambition was to join the wider Jewish community and submit to its laws and regulations.

While Cassin's account meandered through the remote history of peasant protest in southern Italy, curiously she took only marginal account of many of the more direct and immediate protagonists. But she knew all about these dimensions of the story. She was very close to Raffaele Cantoni, a man who had been directly involved in the decision to approve the formal conversion of the entire community in 1946, as well as in the events that led to their emigration to Israel in 1949. Yet she not only deliberately played down the importance of these external interventions, but went out of her way to conceal them – even to the point of pretending to have heard of the story first during a visit to Israel in 1952 when she met with some of the immigrants from San Nicandro who had settled near Safed, in Galilee.

Why she should have played down the interventions of Cantoni and others remains unclear, although the omissions enabled her also to present the story as a simple and striking unmediated conversion.[11] But that is to leave unanswered many of the key questions that the conversion poses. How had the would-be converts been able to make contact with some of the most influential figures in the Italian Jewish community? Why had those people taken them seriously? How had the community survived the Racial Laws which forced most of the Jewish leaders to leave Italy after 1938? Why did the rabbinical authorities in Rome take the very unusual decision to accept the conversion of the entire community? How were the converts then able to emigrate to Israel at a time when there were thousands of Jewish war refugees in transit camps awaiting that very opportunity?

In reality, the story of Manduzio and his followers was neither straightforward nor autonomous. Although it took place in a remote part of southern Italy, it was not played out in isolation. From the very beginning what the would-be converts liked to refer to as 'our little story' intersected with bigger historical narratives that at every step shaped its outcome. The ways in which it developed were mediated by the broader histories of the Italian Jews in the 1930s, by the politics of the Fascist dictatorship and the Vatican, by the events that followed Italy's entry into the Second World War, and not least by the activities of the Zionist agencies in Italy during and after the war. In its final stages the story took new and often unexpected turns that caused it to overlap with that of the thousands of mainly Jewish refugees and Displaced Persons who found themselves trapped in transit camps in Italy after the war and with the networks that were engaged in organizing the post-war clandestine Jewish emigration to Palestine.

The story of Manduzio and his followers was woven into the post-war exoduses of both European Jews and the poor of Italy's South, crisscrossing major historical movements and acquiring a large and varied cast. As well as the converts themselves, the protagonists included evangelical pastors and Catholic priests, bishops and cardinals, rabbis and intellectuals, Fascists and anti-Fascists, German, Allied and Jewish soldiers, philanthropists, Zionists, agents of the Haganah and the Mossad, refugees, international charitable organizations, policemen, spies, informers, emigrants and immigrants, some villains but also some true heroes and heroines. The chapters that follow will explore how these multiple narratives converged and with what consequences for Manduzio and his followers.

# CHAPTER ONE

# Manduzio's Story

The fullest account we have of the origins of the story is provided by Manduzio himself in his Journal, which he began to keep in 1937. It is a rich and idiosyncratic assemblage of inconsistent entries freely interspersed with personal reflections, dreams, visions and prayers, which at times becomes a rather jumbled stream of consciousness. Though a reader might struggle to identify dates, names and facts, it is nonetheless crucial to understanding the community, the conversion and the man.[1]

To start at the beginning. Manduzio tells us that he was born in San Nicandro on 25 July 1885 and that he never attended school because his family was very poor. Other sources indicate that the only inheritance he had from his father was the unflattering nickname of 'Caccabra' ('shitface'), although to judge from an early photograph he seems to have been quite good looking as a young man. In 1910, at the age of twenty-five, he married Emanuela Vocino, whose background was very similar to his own. Manduzio was called up when Italy entered the Great War in 1915, and while serving with the 94th Infantry Regiment he fell ill with the disease that would leave him a cripple for the rest of his life. In the Journal he refers to his disability to explain why he could not move or travel unassisted, but he never describes the nature of the disease, or how it originated. However, it was during his long convalescence in military hospitals that he learned to read and write, from which was born what he called his 'great passion for literature'.

When he was well enough to travel, he returned to San Nicandro. He could no longer work, but he drew a veteran's pension which enabled him and his wife to get by. At first he was completely bedridden, but he continued to read voraciously, especially novels and melodramas. He particularly enjoyed the tales of the struggles between the Paladins and Saracens set at the time of the Crusades that were popular throughout southern Italy, but other favourites included Alexandre Dumas's *Count of Monte Cristo*.[2] That these texts were all available in cheap popular editions indicates that more reading went on in these rural communities than is often assumed. Since there were no lending libraries, the books would have been either inherited or bought from one of the travelling pedlars who were the main source not only of non-essential goods and small luxury items, but in the days before the radio of news as well.

Stories and legends were also communicated in the form of poems, songs and dramatizations, and in his Journal Manduzio described how he loved to organize presentations and recitals in his own house at the time of local festivals and holidays. Eagerly awaited by the whole neighbourhood, these performances played an important part in rural social life and were one of the ways in which the patrimony of local legends and myths was shared with those who could not read. In the Gargano communities this legacy was especially rich because over time the legends associated with St Michael had been grafted on to earlier Greek and Roman mythology to create an imagined past steeped in magic and mysticism.

Manduzio was familiar with these traditions and both his knowledge and the care that he devoted to the recitations that were staged in his house made him widely respected. But it was his growing reputation as a healer that made him a person of special regard. Faith healers were to be found in most rural communities,

1 The most widely circulated photograph of Donato Manduzio, taken in San Nicandro in 1929.

not only in southern Italy, since few people could afford doctors or medical treatment when they were sick, or even pay for a trained vet when their animals needed attention. There were folk remedies for virtually every affliction and eventuality. Most were handed down by memory, but when in doubt popular almanacs and astrological guides offered an abundance of practical advice and information. Most households had a copy of these almanacs that, like devotional manuals and catechisms, were mass-produced specifically for the rural poor. Updated every year, they contained calendars, lists of holidays and saints' days, as well as all kinds of practical information such as remedies for common ailments, information on the healing powers of individual saints and astrological information and lunar tables that could be used to predict the weather and anticipate natural disasters.

Even so, the portents and precepts were not always easy to interpret without the help of someone deemed to have special expertise. Manduzio enjoyed such a reputation and at first neighbours and then people from surrounding settlements came to him for advice. Some wanted his opinion about an illness or affliction, others wanted to know when they should move their animals from one pasture to another, when to sow or harvest their crops, or how to settle a dispute with a relative or neighbour. This meant that he was frequently called on to act as a mediator, but the respect and authority he had acquired were enhanced by the recognition of his powers as a faith healer.

The numerous successes attributed to him were carefully recorded in the Journal, and the entries illustrate clearly how the healer's credibility depended on the belief that sickness or misfortune was a form of divine punishment for a sin or crime committed either by the sufferer or by someone close to the sufferer. The skill of the faith healer lay in first identifying the sin that was the cause of the suffering or misfortune and the name of the sinner, and then in proposing an appropriate penance that might atone for the sin that was the presumed cause of the disease. Any form of medical intervention or physical medication was rejected as counter-productive: disease or misfortune was merely the physical symptom of divine displeasure, so that without spiritual repentance there could be no cure. If the cure did not work, this did not necessarily reflect on the powers of the healer, but was rather a sign that the sufferer had failed either to divulge fully the sins that had caused the complaint or to perform the indicated penance properly. Successes were needed to secure a good reputation, and by Manduzio's own account these had not been lacking. Indeed, many of his cures were considered to be little short of miraculous, making him by the later 1920s a well-known figure in his community where he was held in high regard.

By then Manduzio's reading had begun to take him beyond popular literature and astrology to study sacred texts. The ones that were easily accessible were the mass-produced devotional manuals and lives of the saints that were promoted by the Catholic Church and lay religious associations. The Bible was much less easily available, and then only in Latin. But Manduzio was able to acquire an evangelical version of the Bible in Italian from a neighbouring Pentecostalist, a member of one of the many evangelical communities that had been founded in southern Italy by emigrants returning from the United States before and after the Great War. By the late 1920s they had found their way to the Gargano promontory, and as well as small groups of Pentecostalists both in San Nicandro and in the neighbouring town of Apricena, there was also a community of Seventh Day Adventists in nearby Lesina.[3]

Manduzio later recounted in the Journal that when he started to study the books of the Pentateuch he came to understand that the novels and profane texts he had previously read were false: 'like a man who had been blind I now understood that all their fantasies were untrue'. His new studies also led him to ask questions of the religious creeds he saw around him. To his amazement, he came to the conclusion that both Catholicism and Protestantism were 'empty and vain in comparison with the true Creator of all'.[4] The turning point, so Manduzio claimed, had come on a Sunday when the Pentecostalists, who were trying to persuade him to join them, invited him to discuss their beliefs with them. After listening attentively, Manduzio asked for a copy of the Bible, from which he began to read aloud the Ten Commandments and 'how the Eternal One had sanctified Saturday as the Sabbath'. When he had finished, he turned to them and asked why Pentecostalists did not follow God's directive. They gave no reply.

The fact that the Pentecostalists did not observe Saturday as the sabbath led him next to the small community of Seventh Day Adventists in Lesina. Conveniently for Manduzio, whose mobility was still very limited, this was only a short distance from San Nicandro. The meeting proved to be critical because it finally made clear to him why the beliefs of all the evangelical Protestants were unacceptable: the sticking point for Manduzio was their belief in the Second Coming of the Messiah. From his own by now extensive readings of what he called 'the Five Books of Moses', Manduzio was convinced that Jesus had been a prophet but not the Messiah. His wife Emanuela later claimed that Manduzio's discovery of the God of Moses finally resolved the problem with which he had wrestled all his life. Why had the world been created? In the books of the Hebrew Bible he discovered a world of cruelty and suffering, of false prophets, false idols and false religions which he recognized as his own. If the Messiah had already come to earth, why did all this suffering and hardship still exist? From the books of the Pentateuch Manduzio had instead learned that salvation lay in following the Law of the God of Israel as it had been given to Moses on Sinai, that the Creator was one and indivisible and that there were no messiahs, only prophets. Those seeking salvation and comfort must therefore learn to observe the Law of the God of Moses, forsaking other gods and idols, and following the path of the righteous.

Without being aware of it, Manduzio had discovered the God of the Jews. The Journal contains two different and at first sight contradictory accounts of how that discovery became explicit. On the opening page he declared:

> A true event took place in the year 1928 in Southern Italy in a town called San Nicandro in the Province of Foggia, where God gave inspiration to a man he deemed worthy to establish the Jewish religion in this remote place. This man was Donato Manduzio and by Divine inspiration he was instructed to declare the Laws of the One God. In what follows, Signor Manduzio sets forth for you the true story as it happened . . . a small but luminous story that reveals how from Darkness came Light, a Light that reduced the darkness and the shadow of death.

In the second telling, the date of the conversion was moved forward to August 1930 and was oriented, in a fitting biblical style, around a dream. In his dream, Manduzio found himself in a 'dark place' where he heard a voice calling to him: 'I am bringing you a Light.' In the darkness he saw a man who was holding a lantern that was unlit. When Manduzio asked him why he did not light it, the man replied: 'I cannot because I have no matches, but you do and they are in your hand.' Manduzio looked down and saw that he was indeed holding matches that were already alight; so he took the lantern that was already filled with oil, primed it and trimmed it. When he then lit the lamp, the darkness vanished and the dream ended.[5]

Despite the contradictions in the chronologies, the biblical metaphor of the dream in the second account serves retrospectively to underline the exceptional nature of Manduzio's conversion. Aware, perhaps, that the story might test the reader's credulity, Manduzio warned that this was the 'Word of God' and that 'no one should besmirch this story in any way'. To emphasize the miraculous nature of the conversion, he also deliberately drew attention to his own lack of education, telling his readers to ignore the 'errors of spelling or grammar since its author had no schooling and no masters other than the Master of the Prophets, the Master who guided Abraham through Canaan'.

In ways that reveal a great deal about the man, Manduzio skilfully turned his lack of schooling into a strength. The fact that he had no formal learning and education was in itself now proof that the knowledge that had led to his conversion must have come from some other source. That source was the Almighty, who had chosen to speak through him. It was for that reason that Manduzio claimed to be a latter-day prophet: 'The Prophet of This Century' as he proudly wrote on the title page of the Journal, to whom the Almighty had entrusted the task of proclaiming 'the Laws of the One God'. In other words, Manduzio's conversion was more than a personal revelation: it was a mission that had been bestowed on him personally by the Almighty through dreams and visions. In one of the first of these he heard himself being addressed as Levi, from which he understood that the Almighty had decided that His Word, 'that no one had ever revealed', must go forth from Manduzio's house and that he, Manduzio – 'Levi' – should be his prophet.

Manduzio gives us a detailed, triumphant account of his own conversion, but strangely he never explains why the others accepted his divinely appointed role as prophet – although his Journal is full of the various transgressions they subsequently committed. None of his followers left accounts of why they joined Manduzio, so their motives remain obscure. Manduzio did, however, carefully list the names of the original members of the community and those who joined later (albeit with some confusion when it comes to the exact dates). Initially the group consisted of nineteen adults – eleven men and eight women – as well as thirty children. Not a large number, but not that small either given the broader implications of the decision to follow a faith about which none of them had any prior knowledge. The original converts were all from San Nicandro or neighbouring villages, and their backgrounds were similar to those of Manduzio and his wife. Nearly all were engaged in some form of agricultural work. All were extremely poor, but while none had more than elementary schooling they could read and write. Most were simple agricultural labourers, although the more prominent figures in the small community had a trade of some sort, as did some of the women.[6] In age they ranged from early thirties to mid-forties. Manduzio was forty-four years old in 1929, his wife Emanuela and Antonio Bonfitto were both thirty-nine, and the others were in their early thirties. Manduzio and his wife had no children, but most of the others were married with families, although there were also two single men: Matteo Cataldo, a widower, who died shortly afterwards, and Rocco di Paolo, a bachelor who was blind.

No other members of Manduzio's family joined the community and his brothers made it known that they thought he had gone mad. But many of the would-be converts were related to one another.[7] There was also a relatively high number of women without husbands, something that might be taken as a reflection of the many widows typically found in these rural societies. But in fact most of these women were neither widows nor were they unmarried; they appeared to be 'single' only because their husbands had not converted. For example, Lucia Gravina's husband and her children did not adopt the new religion, even though they all continued to live together in the same house. Concetta di Leo, who with her husband Antonio Bonfitto was one of the first converts, became one of the most prominent members of the group; but Antonio was the first to abandon his new faith when he refused to allow Concetta to give one of their children a Hebrew name.

These 'mixed households' were a constant source of problems, not least because they made the already difficult observance of

Jewish ritual – most obviously dietary laws – even more complicated. However, the number of women who converted without their husbands suggests that the movement had a special attraction for women, many of whom would prove to be its most committed members. The reasons for this are not clear, although women also played a prominent role in many of the evangelical Protestant communities and it may have been the opportunities to take such a role in the religious and social lives of the community that attracted them. Manduzio's wife, Emanuela Vocino, for example, was held in great respect and she took exclusive responsibility for ensuring that their house was properly prepared for the weekly prayer meetings. She also acted as Manduzio's principal intermediary with the other women, although Concetta di Leo, Giuseppa Iannone and Lucia Gravina were all part of the inner group and they too assumed a variety of functions and responsibilities.[8]

Although a number of women joined the community without their husbands, there were no cases of men joining without their wives. Manduzio's Journal records an endless litany of the transgressions committed by the women, who despite constant rebukes and sanctions seem to have been prepared to submit to his often quite severe authority. The male heads of households who joined the community were not so willing, however. One of the most recalcitrant was Francesco Cerrone, who with his wife Angela Pizzichetta moved to San Nicandro from the nearby town of Cagnano to join the community in 1932. Cerrone was a shoemaker by trade and he later claimed that he had moved to San Nicandro in the hope of finding work. He was known as 'lu Bruzzese', because after his marriage he worked for many years in the nearby province of Abruzzo, but the family's economic situation was desperate. When he and Angela joined the community, they had two sons and a daughter (Pasquale, Giuseppe and Emma). Another daughter, Giovanna, followed and then in 1932 Angela gave birth to twin daughters, the first children to be born since the community had been founded, who were ceremoniously given Hebrew names: Sara and Ester. Three more children, Nicola, Myriam and Gherson, soon followed, hence Cerrone's constant complaints about the family's unbearable poverty.

Costantino Tritto and his second wife Incoronata de Lelle joined the group in 1934. Tritto was also a shoemaker and was known for some reason as 'the Spaniard'. After the war he had briefly been a Socialist and had then joined various evangelical Protestant communities before being introduced by the blind man Rocco di Paolo to Manduzio's community. When he moved to San Nicandro, Costantino had two sons (Antonio and Nazario) by an earlier marriage, and another son, Samuele, followed.

Angelo Marrochella and his wife Grazia Rendina were among the last to join the community in 1938. They also lived a little way outside San Nicandro at Terranova, and Marrochella's work as a stone-cutter often took him quite far away when the quarry near San Nicandro was closed down. Born in 1911, he owned a small piece of land but was extremely poor and also had a large family. Before joining Manduzio's community he too had been involved in other religious movements and had briefly belonged to a group of 'Waldensian evangelists'.[9]

Francesco Cerrone, Costantino Tritto and Angelo Marrochella quickly became Manduzio's most vocal critics. None of these men had been introduced to the group by Manduzio, which became a cause of friction from the start. Cerrone and Tritto had both been introduced by Rocco di Paolo, and although in the Journal Manduzio commended Di Paolo for his good work in bringing these men and their families 'to the Light', he remained suspicious of their willingness to accept his authority. He also became suspicious of his old friend Di Paolo, whom he accused of committing a grave but unidentified sin that he had failed to disclose; as a result Manduzio claimed that it posed serious danger to Di Paolo's cousin, Concetta di Leo, who he believed also knew of the sin and had not divulged it.

Manduzio's Journal at times seems little more than a record of the disputes that wracked the small community. Not all of these related to religion, although resistance to Manduzio's attempts to assert his authority was the principal cause of discord. In practice, Manduzio's authority and the question of ritual observance were inseparable. He was both the interpreter of the Law and its enforcer, and made it a rule that only those who fully observed Jewish ritual, as the converts understood it, could take part in the weekly prayer meetings in his house. In practice none of the converts could follow even the most elementary precepts of Jewish ritual: they had to eat whatever food they could afford, abstention from work on Saturdays was for most virtually impossible, their children had to attend the village school where their religion was not acknowledged, and they had no access to a rabbi. But ensuring the community's observance of his rules – forsaking false gods, ridding their houses of false images, observing the sabbath and (as far as they could) abstaining from eating unclean foods – quickly became the daily test of Manduzio's authority. Characteristically, he turned his physical handicap into an advantage. Since he could not move from his house, he declared his knowledge of what was taking place in the houses of his followers through dreams and visions, which of course also confirmed his unique power to communicate directly with the Almighty.

Manduzio's authority was further enhanced by his continuing to practise as a faith healer. The beneficiaries were not always members of the community, and one of his most celebrated successes came when he cured the owner of the Café Trieste in San Nicandro of an illness that the man's doctors had diagnosed as terminal. Among his own followers the most spectacular demonstration of his healing powers involved Lucia Gravina, who with her mother-in-law, Giuseppa Iannone, had been among the first converts. Despite her best intentions, Lucia had it seems been guilty of many transgressions – Manduzio knew, for example, that pork was frequently eaten in her house and that she and her family often worked on the sabbath – and in Manduzio's eyes probably her greatest sin was that she had failed to persuade her husband Michele and their sons to convert. Nonetheless, Manduzio expressed great fondness for her in his Journal, and when Lucia was suddenly taken ill with severe internal pains in 1938, he at once knew the cause.

Lucia was taken to the hospital at San Severo, but when the surgeons made a preliminary examination they discovered an advanced tumour of the uterus and decided not to continue with the planned operation. Her husband was told that she had at the most just days to live. Manduzio first heard the news from his wife, who told him that word had reached San Nicandro that Lucia Gravina had died. But Manduzio knew that this was untrue and prayed for her to be saved. The following day Lucia woke up feeling better, and was shortly able to leave the hospital. The only explanation that the astonished surgeons could offer was that the tumour was benign. But everyone else attributed her recovery to Manduzio's intercession, including Lucia and her mother-in-law, who promised that henceforth they would meticulously follow the Law.

In his Journal Manduzio proudly noted that following the miraculous recovery of Lucia Gravina the whole neighbourhood now acknowledged that 'Truly their God is the True God.' But Manduzio was also prepared to use his powers of healing more coercively. He knew, for example, that the family of another member of the community, Leonardo Leone, were not observing the Law, and he warned that this would have dire consequences. When Leone's son fell ill, Manduzio sent Leone a message warning that the child would die if the family did not mend its ways. A year later Leone himself developed a serious chest infection and Manduzio let it be known that he had been 'struck down by the Almighty'. He sent Concetta di Leo as his emissary to tell the family that the illness was a punishment and that although the whole community was praying for his recovery the family must do the same. When she heard this, Leonardo's wife flew into a rage and demanded that Concetta leave the house immediately, but Manduzio's words had not been in vain and shortly afterwards Leone died.

As leader it was also Manduzio's task to mediate in the incessant petty disputes that dominated the lives of this small community, few of which had anything to do with their religion. Vincenzo di Salvia, for example, regularly beat his wife Costantina, whose relatives begged Manduzio and his wife to reconcile the couple. Manduzio's repeated interventions seem to have had little effect, however, and for this and other offences Vincenzo was eventually sent to prison for three months. The sentence was a disaster for the family, now deprived of their sole breadwinner, but the small community came to Costantina's aid. Manduzio however, did not miss the opportunity to warn Costantina that her husband's violence was a sign that they had failed to follow the Law. When Vincenzo was released from prison, the couple solemnly swore their observance forthwith, although it was not long before Costantina was the victim of domestic violence again.

Marital problems were not the only source of tension in the community. When Francesco Cerrone and Costantino Tritto joined the community they had been on good terms, and indeed Tritto often sided with Cerrone in challenging Manduzio's leadership. But when Cerrone decided to open his own cobbler's shop next to Tritto's on the principal street, Tritto became convinced that Cerrone was trying to steal his customers. The two men nearly came to blows, and when Manduzio tried to intervene Cerrone ceased to come to the weekly prayer meetings and for a while dropped out of the community. It was at the moment of Cerrone's temporary departure in 1938 that Costantino Tritto introduced Angelo Marrochella and his wife to the community. From the start Manduzio did not hide his suspicions that neither Marochella nor his wife was willing to observe the Law. Their constant questioning of why they should give up eating pork and abstain from work on the sabbath aggravated the situation. Manduzio retaliated by accusing Angelo's wife of transgressing the Law, after which she played little further part in the community.

The very bleak picture of this small community that recurs in the pages of Manduzio's Journal reflects the realities of everyday life in an impoverished rural township in these years, and the desperate insecurity of the small group whose members had nonetheless found a sense of hope in their newly adopted religion. From these accounts we get an often contradictory image of Manduzio. By some he was admired and even loved, but others appeared reluctant to accept his authority and it seems that he was ready when the occasion arose to use his power in forceful ways. But against this rather forbidding image we also have to set the recollections of the only surviving member of the community. Costantino Tritto's son, Nazario – who later changed his name to Eliezer – was one of the San Nicandro converts who emigrated to Israel in 1949.[10] Written much later in his life, Eliezer's recollections conjure up vividly the day-to-day life of this little community in the 1930s as seen through the eyes of a small boy. He was born shortly before his parents joined Manduzio's community, and his earliest recollections leave no doubt about the centrality of its religious faith and rituals.[11] His memories are dominated by the sequence of religious feasts and festivals, and the central role played by Manduzio.

Despite his severe physical disability, Manduzio was both the leader of the community and its omnipresent inspiration. It was Manduzio who first compiled a Hebrew lunar calendar so that the community could know the dates and times of all the Jewish festivals: Rosh Hashanah, Yom Kippur, Sukkot, Hanukkah, Purim, Pesach, Shavuot, Tisha Be Av. Eliezer also remembered that it was Manduzio who insisted that all members of the community must respect the sabbath, and woe betide any of the 'brothers and sisters' who broke that rule. It was Manduzio who demanded that every family destroy the images and false idols that were in their houses, and hence all traces of the Catholic religion, its saints, madonnas and icons.

In Eliezer's pages, Manduzio comes across as a gentle and caring man who was especially adored by the children. Eliezer fondly recalls how Manduzio would involve them in religious festivals and in theatrical performances of the biblical stories that were staged in his own house with the children taking all the parts. He remembered, too, the care with which he supervised every detail of the tabernacles that were built to celebrate Sukkot, and how they were filled with fruit and sweets on which the children were allowed to gorge themselves at the end of the festival. Eliezer could never forget the tantalizing aroma of the kid that was roasted for Passover, when no one was allowed to leave Manduzio's house before four o'clock in the morning and all the meat had been consumed. He recalled, too, that Manduzio used to organize Bible-reading classes for the children and made them learn passages of the sacred texts by heart, encouraging and praising them and giving prizes to those who learned their lessons best.

Since he was a cobbler and ran a small shop in the town, Eliezer's father was a little better off than the others, but the family was still very poor. Yet, although these were hard times, for the children at least it seems that these were also happy ones and Eliezer's account reflects the mutual support and security that bound the community together and gave them a sense of identity which set them apart from their neighbours in San Nicandro. Looking back on his childhood more than half a century later, Eliezer includes among his recollections many things that he probably learned only later. But although he could not be expected to have had any memory of the larger events that were dominating the life of Italy and Europe in the years he was describing, his account does nonetheless illustrate how the community's fortunes were constantly being shaped by its contacts with the outside world.

From his parents and other members of the community Eliezer heard many times the story that at first Manduzio had not been aware that there were other Jews in Italy. From his reading of the Bible Manduzio had concluded that the original Jews had all perished in the Flood and he thought that the reason for his dream was that he had been chosen to revive a religion that had long since disappeared. But once he learned that there were Jews in Naples, Turin, Florence and Rome, to name only the Jewish centres that he came to hear of, where there were rabbis, synagogues and other organizations, he worked tirelessly to contact them.

Eliezer also remembered the books and religious texts, ritual furnishings and manuals, as well as primers in Hebrew, liturgical music and hymns that began to arrive regularly in San Nicandro from Rome, together with copies of the monthly journal *Rassegna Mensile di Israel*. He was especially proud that his father, Costantino, who would later adopt the Hebrew name Chaim, was appointed as the local officer of the Keren Kayemet le-Israel[12] (The Jewish National Fund) with the title of fiduciary and that he organized small collections of money that were sent to Rome. Eliezer's childhood memories present the life of the community in ways that differ from the often more sombre accounts in Manduzio's Journal, but they also indicate that what he called 'our little story' was from early on being influenced by the contacts that were established with the outside world, first and foremost with the Italian Jews.

# CHAPTER TWO

# Jewish Encounters

It seems that Manduzio first came to hear that there were other Jews in Italy from one of the many travelling pedlars who visited San Nicandro. But once he knew of their existence he was eager to contact these Jews without delay. He wanted to communicate the special mission that had been entrusted to him, but he also needed to seek recognition of his own position as leader and negotiate the community's admission into the wider community of the Children of Israel. This, however, was no easy task. The would-be converts knew nothing about the Jews they wanted to reach and they had no intermediaries to help them. In this respect, at least, their situation was different from that of the neighbouring evangelical Protestants who were autonomous, independent of any ecclesiastical community. Manduzio and his followers, by contrast, not only had to negotiate a place within a well-established hierarchy but they also had to deal with people whose backgrounds were totally different from their own.

Indeed, in many respects the social and cultural gap between Manduzio's world and that of the Jewish leaders with whom he tried to communicate was even greater than the geographical distances separating San Nicandro from Rome. But geography was also a problem since, although land-bound, the Gargano was virtually an island. The principal roads were deeply rutted cart tracks that during the winter months were often impassable. An even greater obstacle was posed by the malaria-infested coastal swamps and lagoons that separated the promontory from the mainland plain, making the countryside uninhabitable and forcing the rural population to live in teeming 'agro-towns'. The completion of the first railway branch line from the city of Foggia in 1931 was for that reason greeted by the local population as an event of epic proportions. Mussolini's regime loudly boasted that with the construction of the new electric railway line from Foggia to Peschici in the north-east of the promontory Fascism had finally brought modernity to the Gargano.[1] To judge by the enthusiastic references made to it by Manduzio and his companions, that view was widely shared. By finally putting San Nicandro on the map and for the first time making it accessible to outsiders, the new railway would have its own important part to play in Manduzio's story. Although nearly all of those who over the next decade made their way to visit the would-be converts complained of the discomforts of the long, tiring and difficult journey, without the railway it is unlikely that Manduzio's story could have reached the outside world.

In any case, the first attempts to make contact with that outside world coincided with the arrival of the new railway line. In August 1931, Manduzio sent the first messages to contact others Jews, addressed simply to the 'Head of the Jewish Community' in Genoa, Naples and Turin. The messages were plain postcards with little more than the names of the would-be converts and an address scrawled on the back. But they did receive a reply. It came from Turin and advised the senders to contact the General Office in Rome. They did so immediately, but despite writing more letters by the end of September they had received no further response.

Manduzio wrote again. Like the previous letters, this one was addressed simply to 'His Excellency the *Commendatore* of the Jewish Community in Rome'. Manduzio began by excusing himself for his insistence, but explained that 'a fixed thought, a natural and spontaneous instinct drives us to beg for your help'. He said that he and his companions had no ulterior or evil motive for writing, but were simply responding to 'the inspiration of the Living God'. He went on to explain that 'inspired by a Celestial Vision and an Inner Voice' he and his followers had for some time become 'convinced and unquestioning believers in the existence of the One Living God, Who had led them to understand that they too were righteous Sons of Israel'. Had their previous letters gone unanswered because they had forgotten to include a pre-paid envelope for the reply? He had no way of knowing, but in any case Manduzio insisted that they had written only because they felt 'alone and almost lost'. On behalf of his companions he begged the *Commendatore* to act as a good father and shepherd and help them learn what they must do and what Laws they should follow 'because here we have no teaching to enable us to attain what we aspire to by the voluntary inspiration of the Supreme God who illuminates us and guides us on the right Path'.

Again there was no response, so in early November Manduzio wrote again to express his 'great dismay' that none of his letters had been answered. Was it because he had not listed the names of the would-be converts? If so, he now gave their names (eleven men and about twenty women), with assurances that, although their community was small, when God had created the world there was only Adam and Eve and so with God's help they too would grow in numbers and in spirit. But Manduzio also warned the 'Chief' that it was his duty to care for the sheep of the Living Lord and that as a good shepherd he must send them at once a book in which the Laws of Abraham were written down. They would of course be willing to pay for this, but they urgently needed this book so that they could learn from it and then pass on its teachings to other members of their community. He said that they dutifully followed the Ten Commandments and believed in the One God, but they had no temple and they needed someone to come from Rome to teach them what they needed to know.

In a rambling postscript Manduzio also asked the Rabbi whether they were right to pray for the 'lost people who are trapped in the fantasies of the false Catholic priests and should they instead let them know the fine and beautiful word that God teaches us in the Old Testament in the hope that they will return to the ancient but now forgotten faith'. He said that they had decided to send the letter by registered post because he was sure that his previous ones had gone astray, and he closed by saying that they were awaiting the words of the rabbi as anxiously as they awaited the Word of God.[2]

As if in answer to their prayers, a reply finally arrived shortly afterwards. The delay is not difficult to understand. Anyone reading the correspondence would immediately have been aware of the very humble background of the writers and would probably have suspected some sort of prank. As was common practice among the poor, Manduzio sometimes used a professional letter-writer, which produced communications that were in stilted but correct Italian. This was expensive, however, and a cheaper alternative was to use something similar to a child's hand-held printing block, or else to use cut-out letters pasted together to form whole sentences. Both these methods meant that the letters looked decidedly strange, but so did those in Manduzio's own spidery hand, written in an elementary syntax that was part Italian and part dialect, full of deletions, childish ink splodges, scrawly insertions and endless repetitions and postscripts. To add to the confusion, the first postcards carried no message, just the name and address of the senders. But the letters continued to arrive and they revealed that, whatever their grammatical or formal shortcomings, the writer did have a wide knowledge of the Bible, which was cited liberally. While there were also clear signs of the obsessive character that was evident in the entries that Manduzio made later in his Journal, in important

37

respects the tone of the early letters to Rome was quite different. Manduzio wrote simply as a spokesman for his 'brothers and sisters', whose determination to convert to the Jewish faith he attributed to 'divine inspiration'. The letters contained no reference to his later claim to be a prophet. On the contrary, they were simple pleas for help and guidance to enable the community to learn how to follow the Law and become true Jews.

Manduzio's unconcealed irritation when his letters went without reply was taken as a sign of sincerity, however, and together with the supplicant's underlying humility and evident lack of formal education finally persuaded the Chief Rabbi of Rome, Angelo Sacerdoti, to investigate the case more closely. He turned first for advice to a close colleague, Alfonso Pacifici, who at his request prepared a brief summary of the case. The letters, Pacifici explained, came from a small group consisting of some six or seven families who wanted to convert to the Jewish religion. They had initially been contacted by some Protestants who had given them an evangelical edition of the Bible, from which they had learned of Judaism, and were now observing the sabbath. Pacifici pointed out that there was no indication that the would-be converts had had any prior contact with other Jews and for that reason he recommended caution: 'This seems to be a rather dangerous topic but one to which we should certainly give serious consideration.'

That 'dangerous topic' did not allude to issues relating to the Fascist regime, since in 1931 its relations with Italian Jews were still good. What Pacifici had in mind probably reflected a suspicion that the story was some sort of practical joke designed perhaps to discredit the rabbi. But the letters kept coming and Pacifici mentioned that as well as those from Manduzio there had been one from 'someone called Cerrone' who also asked 'for help, support and advice so that they may become Jews and build a synagogue'. Such guidance could of course be easily provided, Pacifici commented, but he also wondered 'whether this isn't perhaps another unconscious case of *marranismo*'.[3]

*Marranos* is a Castilian term that has a more negative meaning than *conversos* or converts, because it refers specifically to those Jews and Muslims who had agreed to convert to Christianity after the Spanish monarchy decreed their expulsion in the fifteenth century, but secretly continued to practise their own faith.[4] There are to this day many Jewish families who allegedly descend from the original *marranos* from the time when southern Italy had been under Spanish rule and indeed, the question that Pacifici asked is the one that is invariably raised when people first hear of the story of the San Nicandro converts. But there is no evidence that this was or could have been the case. Neither Manduzio nor his followers had any prior contact either with Jews or with the Jewish religion and we know that they were themselves initially unaware that there were other Jews in Italy.

Pacifici went on to advise the Chief Rabbi to 'test the seriousness of these people', and it was on that basis that Sacerdoti finally replied to Manduzio in November 1931. He asked for more details about their religious beliefs and warned them that Judaism did not seek proselytes. Nonetheless, he was sufficiently interested in their case to ask a colleague, Giorgio Sessini, to go to San Nicandro and report on what was going on there. Sacerdoti still had his doubts, however, remarking to Pacifici that 'no one is better qualified than Signor Sessini to explain the difficulties that we put in the path of those who plan to realize certain projects'.[5]

Sessini's mission was probably designed to nip the whole business in the bud, but the news that the rabbi was sending someone to San Nicandro filled Manduzio with joy. He wrote to thank the 'Illustrious Gentleman' and to say how pleased his 'brothers and sisters' were to learn that someone from Rome would shortly come to instruct them in the Law of the Eternal Lord. He also pointed out that thanks to the new electric railway ('la ferovia letrice') the journey was quite easy and visitors could now come straight to San Nicandro. His state of excitement was even greater when he wrote again in January 1932 to say that, while he and his friends had been discussing arrangements for meeting the rabbi's emissary, they had heard someone asking for them in the street. It was none other than Signor Giorgio 'Sirsillo' (that is, Sessini), with whom they passed some hours in discussion before he took his leave.

'Sirsillo' promised the community some books, which Manduzio reminded Sacerdoti about in a letter that contained more pressing concerns. One of the Protestants had come to Manduzio's house and told him that if he and his followers did not believe in God the Father, God the Son and God the Holy Ghost but wanted to preach that there was only the One God he would need to obtain written authorization from the head of their religion. Manduzio requested that the rabbi send him the relevant certificate as well as musical accompaniments for the psalms that his followers loved to sing. Their dear brother Francesco Cerrone was a talented musician, he told them, and would know how to teach them to sing the appropriate melodies.

When three more weeks passed without a reply, Manduzio wrote angrily demanding an explanation and insisting that the would-be converts urgently needed the books that had been promised by Signor 'Sirsillo', as well as guidance on how to prepare for the celebration of Easter (by which he meant Passover). The would-be converts clearly still had some way to go in the search for their new faith and in his reply to them Rabbi Sacerdoti now also revealed a degree of irritation. He explained that he had taken a personal interest in the case, even though it was a complicated one, not least because of the remoteness of San Nicandro. However, he had no idea what Manduzio was referring to when he talked about a 'statute' or certificate. The copies of the psalms that he had asked for were available only in Hebrew, and they were sung to traditional tunes that were not written down and in any

case could not easily be adapted to be sung with Italian transla-
tions. However, he hoped that he would be able to come to San
Nicandro in person, and he wanted to invite one or more of
Manduzio's followers to visit Rome or Florence where they could
spend time 'in surroundings where it would be easier for you to
learn our ways so that you could teach the others what to do'.

Then nothing more until April, when a mysterious stranger
arrived in San Nicandro claiming to be a Jew who had been sent
from Rome. Manduzio was suspicious and a telegram was sent to
Rabbi Sacerdoti asking for confirmation. It turned out that the
young man, who also turned up in Rome, was a fraud or, as
Sacerdoti put it, 'mentally unhinged'. Who he was we do not
know, but the rabbi was clearly disconcerted by this episode. It
led him to suspect that something strange was going on in San
Nicandro, and he told Manduzio that he was concerned by what
he considered to be 'a strange atmosphere that has nothing whatsoever to do with the Jewish way of thinking' and that seemed to
have taken hold in the town.

In his next letter Sacerdoti took a sterner tone: 'You and your
companions have often expressed your desire to convert to
Judaism and I have always made it clear how much this amazes
me. I have asked you many times how you came to this conviction, since you have had no previous contact with Jews and know
very little about what Judaism is. I have also repeatedly told you
that to come to this knowledge requires long preparation and
deep study'. Sacerdoti said that he was concerned that Manduzio
and his followers had been seized by an 'obsessive haste' and he
referred to what he called 'spiritual tendencies that had nothing
to do with Judaism'. He warned them again that Judaism did not
seek proselytes and accepted converts 'only in cases of clear
necessity and when the aspirant converts were properly prepared,
mature and fully educated in the Jewish faith'. On all these issues,
the decision was made only by the 'religious leader' whose hand,
he warned them, could not be forced. He would, however, send

someone who could explain to them what Passover really meant for Jews.[6]

Sacerdoti's tone softened, however, as he told Manduzio that in every case of conversion that he had ever had to deal with his policy from the very first moment had always been to turn away potential converts. But in this case there was, he admitted, something different. He believed that Manduzio's letters conveyed an impression of deep sincerity and he was convinced that the group had experienced a true spiritual crisis, which was why he was prepared to take them seriously. But he warned them not to give him cause to repent his decision.

Despite frequent reminders from San Nicandro, however, there was no sign of the books and gramophone records of Jewish sacred music that had been requested. Then in October the would-be converts unexpectedly received their second Jewish visitor, Count Federigo Luzzatto, a leading member of the Association of Jewish Cultural Associations in Italy who was travelling with three friends to visit the Fiera del Levante, an international trade fair in Bari and one of the showpieces of Fascist colonialism. At Angelo Sacerdoti's request, the travellers had agreed to break their journey to visit San Nicandro, where they spent a whole day with Manduzio and his companions.

After his return to Rome, Luzzatto wrote the first full account of what he described as the 'pseudo-Jewish community' of San Nicandro. He said that it consisted of six to eight men, fourteen to sixteen women and a number of children aged from two to eight. All were 'contadini o artigiani' (peasants or artisans) by occupation; two were war invalids and drew a daily pension of eight to ten lire. One had been blind from birth and was supported by the families of the others. One was a shoemaker, and the leader of the group was Donato Manduzio, who lived at Via del Gargano.[7] Some had come directly from Catholicism, but others were first evangelized by a Protestant pastor who had a congregation nearby of about 120 followers. From their reading of the Bible given to them by this pastor (the Evangelical Bible published by the Bible Society of Piazza Venezia in the Italian translation by Diodato) they had conceived the idea of becoming 'followers' of the Jewish religion, which was previously quite unknown to them.

Luzzatto referred to their correspondence with Rome and he also mentioned that Rabbi Sacerdoti had sent them many Jewish texts in Italian. So, despite Manduzio's complaints, some of these must have arrived. The texts that Luzzatto alluded to included a Jewish Catechism (the 1846 Livorno edition), *The Book of the Family* (B. Artom's Italian edition), *Bene Zion* (published in Venice in 1828) and two more recent books: *A History of the Jewish People*, and *The Defence of Judaism* by Dante Lattes. In addition, Pacifici had also sent them an Italian version of the Pentateuch in ten lessons and some issues of the journal *Rassegna Mensile di Israel*. Luzzatto noted that the converts observed the sabbath strictly as well as certain dietary prescriptions, but although they 'abstain from eating pork and eel they buy their meat from the village butcher'. In the town they were known as *sabattini* or *sabattisti*, 'since their observance of Saturday as the sabbath is the most visible external sign of the group'. With their Catholic neighbours they seemed to have no difficulties, but the Protestants were more of a problem. 'They are well versed in both the Old and the New Testament, which enables them to carry on lively debates with the Evangelicals, of whom they frequently get the better – at least, that's what they say.'

The would-be converts believed that Jesus was a prophet or a preacher. Their religious functions took place on Friday evenings, Saturday mornings and Saturday afternoons.

These consist of each individual reciting in Italian and in a slow voice the Paternoster [although Luzzetto did not explain why the would-be converts still recited a Christian prayer]. One of those present then reads a passage from the Old Testament or one of the lessons from the Pentateuch on which the reader also offers an elementary commentary. Then with the women leading they sing various chants that have been composed almost entirely by one of the women in the group (a certain Concetta di Leo) to the tune of peasant melodies. The ceremony ends with an exhortation: Today is the Lord's Day, Let us go forth and Rejoice! After which they play patriotic anthems on the gramophone (such as 'God save the King of Italy' and the Italian National Anthem). Throughout the proceedings, the men remain standing with their heads uncovered (in fact before my visit they used to kneel to pray) while the women wear a veil or scarf over their heads.

The prayer meetings were held in Manduzio's house in a large clean room with walls painted white, the men seated on one side, the women on the other, to make a large circle. 'They have destroyed and burned all the pictures and images that they previously owned and on the wall there is only a handwritten version of the Decalogue . . . Concetta di Leo, as well as composing the chants sung at these meetings, has also woven the Decalogue on a white tablecloth.'

Luzzatto was particularly interested in the hymns and canticles that the would-be converts had composed, some of which he carefully transcribed in his report. He also noted that at 'Easter' the group had eaten the bitter herbs that had been sent by Rabbi Sacerdoti, and he added they wanted to have more instruction in the Jewish faith and had also expressed a desire for circumcision. Their most immediate needs, however, were for a Jewish calendar, a Hebrew–Italian educational primer, some short practical religious textbooks like those used in primary schools, and articles describing Jewish laws regarding marriage and the exemption of children from lessons in Catholic doctrine in school. They had also asked for gramophone recordings of sacred Jewish music or information on how to obtain them, and copies of the Italian journal *Rassegna Mensile di Israel*.

A month after his visit, Luzzatto received a letter from Manduzio acknowledging receipt of 'a sabbath lamp and a Jewish calendar' from Rome, but nothing else even though they had sent a postal order for a subscription to the journal *Rassegna Mensile di Israel.* Nor had they received replies to their letters and they complained that they had been abandoned by the Chief Rabbi. Luzzatto showed the letter to Pacifici, who said that only Rabbi Sacerdoti could take further initiatives, but he agreed that this was 'an extremely important matter'. It was not until late November, however, that Sacerdoti finally wrote again. He told Manduzio that he was still interested in their case and would send someone to investigate more closely before the end of the year. In the meantime he would be travelling to Palestine, but he promised to despatch more books and he recommended that Manduzio and his friends should carefully study the books of Genesis, Exodus, Leviticus, Numbers and Deuteronomy, learn and obey the Ten Commandments, practise virtue and honesty and avoid all forms of idolatry: 'I greatly admire your enthusiasm, but you must also be aware that we can arrive at the Truth only through study and time, which requires patience and tenacity.'

Expectations were high that the rabbi himself might soon come to San Nicandro and in December 1932 Manduzio wrote to advise him on practicalities. The best route from Rome, he said, was to take the Adriatic railway to Ancona and from there the line to San Severo where there was the connection with the 'electric train that comes directly to the station in San Nicandro'. The rabbi had asked about the risk of catching malaria, and Manduzio reassured him that no cases had been reported that year, but advised that before leaving Rome he should have his doctor prescribe an anti-malarial tonic.[8]

Rabbi Sacerdoti never made the journey, although the promised books and journals did finally start to arrive in San Nicandro. Manduzio's letters were now directed exclusively to Alfonso Pacifici, whom Manduzio began to treat as an equal. He commented on various items of news that he had read in the periodical *Rassegna Mensile di Israel*, and for example mentioned his approval of a speech made in Florence by 'His Most High Excellency, our Governor and great *Condottiere* Mussechini' (that is, Mussolini) that had raised their hearts. He continued to ask Pacifici for all sorts of practical assistance and information, such as the Italian metric equivalents for Jewish weights and measures. He also repeated the requests for the gramophone records that had never arrived and for additional copies of the books that had. The replies were always slow in coming, and in July 1933 Pacifici wrote from Florence to apologize, explaining that very few of the books Manduzio had requested were available in Italian. He suggested that the most appropriate for the children would be texts that had been specially prepared for use in schools like *Ricordi di tempi antichi*, *I primi tempi*, *Le otto fiaccole d'oro*, *Il Piccolo mondo ebraico* and *La Primavera ebraica*, and asked whether they already owned any of these.

Manduzio meanwhile continued to make new requests, asking now for language primers so that they could start learning basic Hebrew. Again there were no replies, on this occasion because in 1934 Pacifici had left Italy to settle permanently in Jerusalem. It was not until December that year that Manduzio came to know of this, and he at once wrote to send the community's best wishes for Pacifici's new life in the land of the Spirit where he would also be 'far from the unclean'. But he also expressed his outrage that the would-be converts had received no news from Florence or from any of the other Jewish centres in Italy, nor had they had any comforting words from Rabbi Sacerdoti, to whom they asked to be remembered. In closing, Manduzio begged Pacifici not to abandon them but to continue to act as a good shepherd towards his lost sheep.

Soon afterwards the would-be converts learned of the death of Angelo Sacerdoti, but their spirits were then raised by the arrival of another Jewish visitor, the renowned scholar and activist

Jacques Faitlovich. Faitlovich was a Polish Jew who after studying in Paris had spent long periods in Italy before and after the Great War when he settled in Palestine. He was known above all for his activities on behalf of the Ethiopian Falashas (also known as Beta Israel), whom many believed to be one of the lost tribes of Israel. Their discovery in the late nineteenth century had aroused much interest, and Faitlovich had emerged as one of their leading champions. In 1907 he had founded the Pro-Falasha Committee in Italy, whose aim was to support and protect the Falasha and find ways to enable them to resettle in Palestine. Between 1904 and 1946 he made eleven journeys to Ethiopia to visit the Falasha tribes, including one in the year before his brief visit to San Nicandro.[9]

What brought the leading champion of the Ethiopian Falasha to San Nicandro? The short answer is that in Jerusalem Faitlovich had learned about Manduzio and his followers from Pacifici, who had suggested that he might take the opportunity of a forth-coming journey back to Rome to visit San Nicandro. Since he was planning to travel by boat from Haifa to Brindisi and then by train to Rome, the detour, thanks again to the new branch railway line, was just a matter of making the connection for San Nicandro at San Severo.

Pacifici wrote to alert Manduzio to the imminent arrival of a distinguished visitor, so when Manduzio heard a knock at his door at about nine o'clock in the evening of 28 January 1935 he was not surprised. When he opened the door he found a stranger carrying a small suitcase: 'Are you by chance our brother Dr Luigi Falto [as Faitlovich is called in the Journal]?' To which Faitlovich replied: 'As you can see, my friend, I have come from Jerusalem to bring you greetings from Alfonso Pacifici and from all our brothers in the Holy Land.' Manduzio lost no time in calling his companions to greet their guest, who was impatient to hear all about their conversion. When he had heard them out, Faitlovich exclaimed: 'Your story is a true Miracle of the Creator who has brought to this place of Darkness a Light similar to the one he gave to Abraham who left his father and mother to follow the will of the Sacred One.' Faitlovich spent the whole of the next day with them, recounting what Manduzio described as many wonderful stories. He gave them some Hebrew texts, as well as some books 'about the African tribe that he had visited', and promised that he would send some elementary language text-books so that they could start to learn Hebrew. He also suggested that they should send one of their boys to a college where he could study the language.[10]

Faitlovich's visit had far-reaching consequences for Manduzio and his followers. He was the first non-Italian Jew to visit San Nicandro, and his international prominence ensured that their case would become more widely known. But Faitlovich had specific reasons for wanting to know more about the would-be converts of San Nicandro that were connected with his work on behalf of the Falashas. He certainly never thought of the San Nicandro converts as European equivalents of the Ethiopian Jews. Manduzio and his followers were gentiles seeking to become Jews, while for Faitlovich the Falashas were unrecognized Jews seeking recognition. But what connected the two cases was Faitlovich's broader conviction that Jews should actively encourage and promote proselytism and that the Land of Israel would be the site for a general ingathering of Jews from all over the world and of all backgrounds.

These were very much minority opinions, and although Faitlovich may have connected his ideas with the Zionist project for a return of the Jewish people to the Land of Israel, his views on prosyletism were not shared by many other Zionists, let alone most Jews. Nonetheless his visit made it clear that the Jews who had shown an interest in the would-be converts in San Nicandro were open, albeit cautiously, to the principle of conversion. They were all prominent figures among the small minority of Italian Zionists. Alfonso Pacifici was the leading exponent in Italy of what he termed 'integral Zionism'. Angelo Sacerdoti as Chief Rabbi of Rome had also actively promoted the Zionist cause among Italian Jews and also with Mussolini's government. Even though relations between the regime and the Italian Jews would change dramatically a few years later, down to the mid-1930s they were good and Sacerdoti saw Zionism as a way of strengthening links with Italian Jews overseas.[11]

This should not be taken to mean that the discovery of Manduzio and his followers formed part of a broader Zionist agenda. Ten years earlier Sacerdoti and Faitlovich had been involved in a very public disagreement over an issue related to the Falasha, and subsequent events show that Pacifici also disagreed with Faitlovich specifically with regard to Manduzio and his followers. Nonetheless, the curiosity about the San Nicandro case that all three men showed, as well as their openness in principle to the possibility of conversion, marked them off from the mainstream of Italian Jewish opinion at the time. That curiosity was perhaps also nourished by the fact that Manduzio and his followers were part of that 'other' Italy that was in many respects hardly less distant from the Roman and Florentine worlds of Sacerdoti and Pacifici than was the Ethiopia of Faitlovich's Falashas.

Faitlovich's visit to San Nicandro illustrates how the 'discovery' of Manduzio and his followers was linked to much broader developments in the cultural and political worlds of Italian Jews in these years. But Faitlovich was not only an internationally renowned and respected figure and the first non-Italian Jew to visit them; he was also the first to greet them not as would-be converts but as true converts. Indeed, he had told them that their conversion was a true miracle. And that was not all. Faitlovich, as well as entrancing them with his stories of the Holy Land, had been the first actively to encourage them to emigrate.

The impact of Faitlovich's visit became apparent immediately after he had left. Francesco Cerrone wrote to Alfonso Pacifici in Jerusalem to tell him what joy Dr Faitlovich's visit had brought them all, adding that he had now decided to emigrate to Palestine at once and asking Pacifici to help him obtain immigration permits. He said that Dr Faitlovich had been deeply moved when he saw the poverty in which he and his family were living: 'we are poor, we own nothing and have barely any clothes'. At this time he had seven children, which meant that with himself and his wife there were nine mouths to feed, 'or ten if you counted the rent for the house as another mouth to be filled'. As Signor Pacifici well knew, Cerrone continued, in Italy there was 'a terrible crisis and an interminable shortage of work'. Before the visit of their noble-hearted guest, Cerrone had not known where to turn, but thanks to Dr Faitlovich he now understood that 'for us Jews there is no other land to take us but our own, the Land of Israel, the Land of Benediction and of Peace'. He was writing 'with fraternal love and indescribable joy and in the hope that this request will not be refused especially since at this moment there are very few who are able to emigrate from Italy'. Cerrone had heard that hardly any permits for emigration were being issued by the Italian authorities, although he thought that it might be easier for them since they were Jews and 'the Italian Jews are held in high esteem by our government'.

The problem was his dire poverty, which he knew would make things difficult for them and was why he needed help. But he added that another reason for emigrating was that his older boys were growing up and he did not want to lose them to 'the world of the pagans and idolaters . . . You will I am sure understand that there are many brutish people here and I want above all to bring up my little ones in proper surroundings and have them study their true mother tongue.' He also wanted practical information: how much would it cost for the whole family to move to Palestine? Should he come first with the two boys and wait for his wife and the others to follow, or would it be better for them all to make the move together? What should they bring with them by way of furniture and possessions?[12]

Cerrone's letter received no reply, and in April Manduzio wrote to Pacifici with a new tone of authority. Why had they received no reply, he demanded angrily? They were deeply saddened by the news of the death of Angelo Sacerdoti, but they felt lost and betrayed. He then went on to say that not only Francesco Cerrone and his family but the entire community now wanted to emigrate to Palestine. They expected that Pacifici would by now have obtained the necessary permits for them all, and they had all agreed that the first to leave should be those most in need. That meant Francesco Cerrone, his wife and seven children, and Antonio Bonfitto, with his wife and one son. He added that Cerrone was a shoemaker by trade, but because there was little work he also did general building work, while Bonfitto was a farm labourer who was used to working on vineyards.[13] In closing, Manduzio told Pacifici that their only desire was to escape the poverty to which they were condemned 'so that our innocent little ones might have the chance of a better life'. They had read in the Italian Jewish journals they now received that in Palestine there was a great shortage of manual labourers. This was work for which they were well qualified and he did not wish that it should be done by the Arabs 'who are truly unworthy to receive the bread of God while we are left to go hungry'.[14]

Again there was no reply from Pacifici, but in the meantime Francesco Cerrone had been following up another of the suggestions made by Jacques Faitlovich, who had offered to contact his friend Dr Ascher, head of an institute for Jewish children at Bex-les-Bains near Lausanne in Switzerland, to ask if it would be possible for one of Cerrone's boys to attend the school. Cerrone had written to Ascher and on 23 September 1935 received a reply in which Ascher, after apologizing for his poor Italian, explained that 'My friend Dr Faitlovich told me to accept for the time being just one, and preferably a boy aged 11 or 12, although later it may be possible to think of more.' The problem, he said, would be getting the boy to Switzerland and satisfying the border and customs regulations. Who could accompany the child to the border at Domodossola–Brig and ensure that he met all the requirements of the Swiss police and customs officials? He said that he would write to Dr Pacifici (who was now in Jerusalem) to find out whether he knew anyone who could accompany the boy.

In December, Ascher wrote again to say that Pacifici had not replied and warning Cerrone that the 'Swiss police are very demanding and rigorous: to cross the border the boy would need not only a birth certificate and a passport, but also a visa issued by a Swiss consular office in Italy'. In January 1936, Ascher sent another letter inviting Cerrone's son Giuseppe 'to come and study at my institute which is also a College. I wish to provide everything necessary for the boy and you will incur no expenses.' When he wrote once more two months later, Ascher's tone had changed and he was much less encouraging. He warned Cerrone that 'emigrating is no easy matter and it is useless that you should entertain false ideas. Our country prohibits immigration for foreigners seeking work, because there are also many people in Switzerland who have no jobs and like everywhere else there is an economic crisis here too you know.' Given the problems, he suggested that they both write to Dr Faitlovich (who was now back in Palestine) to find out whether it would be possible to emigrate to Eretz Israel ('The Land of Israel'). He added that sadly 'even emigration to our Holy Land Palestine requires a lot of money: much more than you or I possess, dear Signor Cerrone', and he could only advise him to trust in the Lord.[15]

The growing sense of exasperation among the would-be converts is evident in Cerrone's correspondence with Dr Ascher, but it was even more explicit in Manduzio's letters to Pacifici in Jerusalem. He wrote to Pacifici in September to upbraid him for failing to reply to his earlier letters: 'You have given us no reply: why not?' Only Dr Faitlovich had honoured them with a visit, when he had brought them joyful news. He alone understood them and their aspirations, he alone remained mindful of them and even from faraway America Faitlovich had sent messages showing his sympathy and support. For this they were very appreciative and grateful, but they would be even more grateful to have news from time to time from Jerusalem, 'the city of our God that we too now deeply desire to visit'. Manduzio begged Pacifici to despatch some trusted friend to visit them in San Nicandro and sent best wishes and a cordial *shalom* from 'my little community'.

Pacfici's reply when it came was lengthy and judicious. He thanked Manduzio for the 'large number' of letters he had sent and said that before replying he had consulted with Dr Faitlovich and with 'a learned friend of mine here in Jerusalem'. After careful consideration, he was writing to say that what they saw as neglect and abandonment was in fact just a way of testing and proving their faith. Since this had been going on for many years now, there could no longer be any doubt about their sincerity and desire to convert. This was something that gave him great pleasure, 'especially at a time when the enemies of Israel and of God have increased in the world and when we must thank the Lord with all our spirit for every heart that is open to His truth and willing to enter His service'.

There was, he said, no longer any doubt that Manduzio and his followers should be recognized as 'brothers in the service of the one God'. But, having reached this point, they had a choice to make. Since the Lord had willed that they had been born 'outside Israel' they could if they wished simply follow the Pact that the Lord had made with the Sons of Noah, who recognized the One God and followed the Ten Commandments. To clarify the distinction, however, Pacifici pointed out that the Sons of Noah had to acknowledge that God had chosen the Sons of Israel as His firstborn, and that the requirements and obligations placed on the Sons of Israel were of a different and much greater order. The Sons of Israel must know and follow every precept of the Torah, the religious instruction given to Moses on Mount Sinai, since to disobey even one of these precepts was to violate the Pact with God and risk His curse. Because Manduzio and his companions had been born 'outside Israel' they could become Sons of Noah, but if they wanted to become Sons of Israel they should be aware that this was a much more serious undertaking, one that required a discipline that had to be observed every day of their own lives, and of the lives of their children and their children's children. They should also be aware that:

Israel has transgressed and continues to transgress gravely and for that reason has brought down on itself the curse of the Lord which is why in so many countries today Israel is overthrown, oppressed and tormented so that the blessed Torah is vilified or prohibited (in Germany and in Russia our brothers have been forbidden on pain of death to follow the Torah). We see that Israel is scattered in many different lands and that the Return to the Land of Our Fathers is difficult and that even here [Palestine] there are obstacles of every sort, dangers and threats, and all because Israel has broken the Pact as it was predicted.

Why should Manduzio and his colleagues voluntarily take on the guilt and the responsibility for the sins of Israel, which would be borne also by their children and their children's children for ever? If they really were fully aware of what the Pact involved and what they were committing themselves to, then the answer would be that:

the Lord is willing to call you and we will send you teachers and books so that you may learn the duties of the Sons of Israel and if after long study you hold firm to your commitment we will be willing to welcome you with joy into the Pact of Israel sealed by the blood of circumcision. But if, on the other hand, you feel that this is too onerous, we will say to you: 'Be not troubled because even as Sons of Noah you can bring benediction to the world and comfort to your brother Israel.'

The choice, dear brothers, is yours but we would advise you to ponder carefully on these matters before you reply.[16]

When the reply came, it must have surprised Dr Pacifici. Manduzio thanked him for his 'good advice', but went on to say that he and his colleagues were 'amazed to hear that we are not Sons of Israel . . . We know by Divine Revelation that we are more than Israelites, we are descended from the third branch of Jacob and directly from Levi. We find ourselves here outside Israel only because of the sins for which we have been driven out and persecuted by the enemies of God.' But as Jeremiah said, 'the Lord will send fishermen to bring you back. He and his brothers and sisters had indeed been bought back from the Dead, and the Lord had rescued them from Darkness.' Manduzio insisted that if what they practised and knew was in some respects lacking, it should be remembered that none of them had 'studied at a Rabbinical college or was a Rabbi, because everything we know has been taught to us by the one God who is the only Teacher and Shepherd'. He ended on an uncompromising note: 'If you say that we are outside Israel, then this is a sign that you do not recognize the Divine Revelation with which we alone have been favoured.' The only thing they now lacked was a knowledge of the Hebrew language and the study of the Talmud (the compilation of Jewish civil and ceremonial law and legend), yet neither of these things impeded their communications with the Lord who knew all languages and all things, and the only reason that they needed to learn Hebrew was to make it easier for them when they realized their great dream which was 'to emigrate to Eretz Israel'.[17]

There is no record of any further correspondence with Alfonso Pacifici. Meanwhile, Cerrrone's attempts to have one of his boys study in Switzerland with Dr Ascher came to nothing – according to Ascher, because Pacifici had refused to help. So by the beginning of 1936 the high hopes that had been raised by the visit of Jacques Faitlovich had been disappointed, the ambitions to emigrate to Palestine had made no progress, and there was every sign that Pacifici was rapidly losing interest in the case.

It was at this moment that an unexpected and potentially disastrous event took place. One morning in February 1936 (Year XIV of the Fascist revolution) two officers of the criminal justice court in Foggia appeared in San Nicandro and delivered to the house of Donato Manduzio an official notification that he had been found guilty of committing a criminal violation of the Decree of 18 November 1935, which made it illegal to hold religious meetings or maintain a house or oratory for such purposes without the prior authorization of the state. There was a fine to be paid for the violation and a court order instructing that no further meetings for prayer or other religious purpose be held in Manduzio's house until the appropriate permissions had been obtained. The court's ruling therefore threatened the existence of the small community. The fine was small, 250 lire plus 30 lire taxes, but still a burden. The greater problem was that without the legal authorization they could not continue to meet and pray in Manduzio's house or anywhere else without incurring further fines and even more serious penal measures.

This was the most serious crisis to confront the community since its inception. But how had the authorities become aware of their presence, and who had taken the initiative? It was at this point that the 'little story' of Donato Manduzio and his followers was unexpectedly caught up in the larger narratives of Mussolini's regime and the relations between Fascism and the Catholic Church in Italy.

# CHAPTER THREE

# The Duce and the Pope

What brought the officers of the criminal court in Foggia to Manduzio's door in February 1936? After a decade of Fascist rule, Italians had grown accustomed to living under the watchful eyes of the state and its representatives, not to mention a faceless army of informers and spies. The arrival of the court bailiffs was an indication that the activities of the would-be converts had now come to the attention of the authorities.

The crisis of parliamentary government and the passing of the liberal order in Italy had not gone unmarked in San Nicandro. In the years after the Great War, like most of the rest of Italy, Apulia had been caught in the spiral of violence that led to the Fascist seizure of power in 1922. In San Nicandro there had been a revival of the violent pre-war confrontations between the unions of agricultural labourers and the landowners. Faced with this resurgence of militancy, most Apulian landowners had been quick to throw in their lot with the recently formed Fascists. While in many respects the objectives of the political movement that Mussolini had founded in 1919 were unclear, there was no uncertainty when it came to identifying its enemies. Fascism was born as a response to the Bolshevik Revolution and to the fears that the revolutionary events in Russia had raised throughout Europe even before the war to end all wars was over. In an Italy that the war had left deeply divided, Mussolini's followers appealed to their fellow countrymen to join the crusade against Bolshevism and to destroy those who seemed determined to bring the perils of revolutionary socialism to Italy.

The Fascist programme proved attractive to landowners everywhere in Italy, and not least to those in Apulia who been trying to destroy the agricultural labourers and their unions long since the start of the century. So when the war ended and the conflicts resumed with even greater force, thanks to the Fascist programme the landowners could now claim that in fighting the labourers' unions they were rescuing Italy from the global threat of Bolshevism.[1] Apulia now became one of the most violent epicentres of the unrest that overwhelmed Italy and once assured of the landowners' support, the Fascists embarked on a campaign of terror directed against the labourers' unions and socialist associations. The police and the army either looked on impassively or actively collaborated, as when the Fascist counter-revolution in Apulia reached its climax in August 1922 and Blackshirt squads led by the local Fascist boss, Giuseppe Caradonna, occupied the city of Bari. They ransacked the Socialist Party offices before running riot in the working-class districts of the city, where they shot and beat their opponents with impunity. After this brutal display of force, the remaining towns in Apulia that were controlled by Socialist administrations chose not to resist. Well before Mussolini's March on Rome in October 1922 symbolically set the seal on the Fascist seizure of power in Italy, therefore, the Fascists were already securely in control of Apulia and its main cities. Three years later, constitutional government in Italy came to an end and the Fascist dictatorship began. It aspired to create a system of totalitarian government, and lasted until the fall of Mussolini and Italy's military defeat in 1943. Until then, the Duce's regime was to be the ever present backdrop to the story of Donato Manduzio and his followers.

San Nicandro itself had witnessed its share of Fascist cruelty. When the town's labourers staged a strike to protest against Fascist violence in March 1922, the Fascists responded with customary brutality. One protester was shot dead and others were savagely beaten. The San Nicandro labourers seemed undeterred, however, and even after the March on Rome they dared to stage another protest demonstration. They paid a heavy price. Two demonstrators were killed, and dozens more badly wounded. Similar violence occurred in neighbouring towns, and in San Giovanni Rotonda labourers who had dared to denounce the Fascists were beaten to death on the street. Even priests who had shown them less than full support were threatened.

After Mussolini had seized control of Italy, San Nicandro witnessed the purging of all those who had opposed the Fascists on their bloodstained path to power. Even though shortly after Mussolini's coup in 1925 the Prefect of Foggia could proudly state that in his province all forms of opposition to the 'National Government' had been destroyed, San Nicandro figured prominently among the list of exceptions.[2] This was an indication of the strength in the town of the labour movement, which would play a leading role in the protest movement that spread through southern Italy after the fall of Fascism. But after 1922 any form of political opposition or dissent became impossible. Once in power, the Fascists kept a close watch on real and supposed enemies. Italians at risk of attracting the attention of the authorities learned to keep their heads down and to show those outward signs of conformity that some historians mistake for consensus.

In this respect, at least, Manduzio and his followers seem to have been typical. Apart from Costantino Tritto, who had very briefly been a Socialist after the war, none had a history of political activism. All the members of the group went out of their way to avoid attracting attention and to maintain at least the appearance of political conformity. When Federigo Luzzatto visited San Nicandro in 1932 he noted that the group's weekly prayer meetings ended with them all singing the National Anthem and the hymn to the monarchy. Indeed, there is no reason to suppose that they were not attached to the new regime. In his correspondence with Angelo Sacerdoti and Alfonso Pacifici, Manduzio made a number of laudatory references to the Duce, while other members of the group frequently suggested asking the Duce to intervene on their behalf. In 1935, for example, Francesco Cerrone told Pacifici that, since the Fascist regime was known to be particularly well disposed towards the Jews in Italy, the Duce would certainly look favourably on their desire to emigrate. Indeed, at this point Mussolini still courted Italian Jews and even claimed to support the Zionist project for a Jewish homeland.[3]

Manduzio's followers paid lip service to the regime, but there is no indication that they had any interest in politics of any sort. Their disobedience was limited to their decision to abandon the Catholic religion at a moment when this risked placing them outside what the Fascists termed the 'national community'. But the very fact that they appeared to be ordinary law-abiding citizens, yet still attracted the attentions of the authorities, proves that very little went unnoticed in Fascist Italy.

There was nothing coincidental about the timing of the bailiffs' visit. By 1936 Mussolini's regime had launched Italy's new imperial enterprise and was at the peak of its prestige, both at home and abroad. Ethiopia had been invaded in the previous year, and in May 1936 the Duce would proclaim the founding of a new empire that was to restore to Italy the glories of Ancient Rome. Although this imperial mission would soon bring about the regime's decline and fall, it was accompanied by major changes at home and in particular attempts to realize the broader ambitions of the Fascist revolution. That in turn meant mobilizing, regimenting and disciplining Italians in ways that emphasized the cohesiveness of the national community. It was no longer enough not to be an opponent: Italians were expected to demonstrate their active commitment, and the regime's suspicions were directed against any activities or behaviour deemed to be 'unItalian'. These included religious deviation, and the launch of the imperial project coincided with the high-point of the alliance between the regime and the Catholic Church and the regime's efforts to make Catholicism a defining quality of national identity.

The alliance between the Catholic Church and the Fascist dictatorship had been formally established in the Concordat of 1929. Although the alliance was never an easy one, the Lateran Pacts (of which the Concordat was part) had finally brought to an end the long disputes that had divided the state from the Church in Italy since the time of the Risorgimento and Italy's political unification in the mid-nineteenth century. The Risorgimento had forced Pope Pius IX to abandon Rome and deprived him of all the territories that he and his predecessors had ruled as secular monarchs since the early Middle Ages, save the Vatican City. No longer a pope-king (*papa-re*), he was divested of his powers as a temporal ruler and became solely a spiritual leader. In response, the Pope condemned the new Italian state, which he described as the 'negation of God', and excommunicated its ruler, King Victor Emmanuel II. With his cardinals, he withdrew from the Quirinale palace in the centre of Rome to take up residence across the Tiber river where he described himself as 'the prisoner of the Vatican'.[4]

Little progress was made in healing the rift between Church and state until the eve of the Great War, which generated new appeals for national solidarity. But as the war drew to an end, Bolshevism provided the Catholic Church and Italian nationalists with a common foe. The spur to action was provided by the miraculous apparition of the Madonna to a group of peasant children in the Portuguese village of Fatima in 1917, during which the Madonna had allegedly told the children that she would return only when the ruling family had been restored in Russia. The Vatican's swift recognition of the miracle was seen as a clear signal that the Church was ready to lead the post-war crusade against Bolshevism. This also meant that the Catholic Church would play a critical role in the political crisis that developed in Italy after the war. As the Church sought to mobilize the faithful in the crusade against international Bolshevism, emphasis was placed on the essential role of Catholicism in defining Italian national identity. As the partnership between the Vatican and the Fascist dictatorship grew closer, non-Catholic Italians as a result found themselves at risk of being excluded from the new national community. This would have potentially serious implications not only for Italy's small non-Catholic Christian minorities but for all religious dissidents, including Manduzio and his followers in San Nicandro.

Despite his own fiercely anti-clerical background, Mussolini was a political realist and pragmatist who could not fail to be impressed by the Church's unique capacity for mobilizing the faithful. Ever since the turn of the century, the Church had adopted a variety of new strategies explicitly designed to engage all sections of Italian society. In particular, the Church had taken a strongly proactive role in promoting a range of popular devotional movements, especially those dedicated to the Virgin Mary that flourished in many parts of Italy, above all in the South. In the past these had often been treated with some suspicion by the Church hierarchy, not least because they were largely autonomous. But the Vatican now came to acknowledge that these devotional associations offered important opportunities for regaining control over forms of popular religiosity that in the past had had little contact with the established Church, and at the same time for energizing and expanding the Church's popular base.[5]

The wartime Pope, Benedict XV, was an enthusiastic promoter of the cults of the Sacred Heart and Christ the King, while his post-war successors, Pius XI and Pius XII, were strong devotees of the newly founded cult of the Virgin of Fatima. Under Pius XI the Church took up the task of promoting and expanding such movements with even greater determination. Many long-forgotten saints were rehabilitated and long-abandoned sanctuaries were re-established and reconstructed. The devotional associations were also reorganized, given new support and funding and encouraged to develop a wide range of social, recreational and sporting programmes as well as religious activities. They began to publish newsletters that kept their members informed of their activities, to organize social outings and sports events and appeals for funds. As the networks expanded they often came to include emigrants too, for whom they became an important means of keeping in touch with relatives back in Italy. The devotional associations were engaged in a range of patriotic activities and demonstrations that were sponsored not only by the Church hierarchy but by senior members of the government and the royal family, and had a part to play in the attempts to 'nationalize religion' that came to have an important role in the Fascist dictatorship.

One striking but by no means unique example of this was the immensely popular mountain sanctuary of the Madonna of Montevergine, near Avellino, south of Naples. The original medieval site was completely transformed into a basilica capable of receiving thousands of pilgrims. New roads were built to facilitate access, and a winter sports complex, first-class restaurants and hotels that were patronized by members of the royal family and the Fascist hierarchy were erected around the basilica, whose façade could be seen for miles around spelling out DUCE in electric lights. In addition to the calendar of events in honour of the saint, the remodelled sanctuary became a favoured site for soldiers to receive a blessing before leaving to serve the Duce overseas or to give thanks for their safe return. Increasing numbers of pilgrims flocked to Montevergine and other sanctuaries such as those of the Madonna of Pompeii and the Madonna dell'Arco near Naples. At the time of Pentecost in 1900, some 200,000 pilgrims and penitents had made the arduous ascent on foot to the sanctuary at Montevergine. Thirty years later the number had risen to 300,000. Religion and nationalism were close partners.[6]

The Fascists admired the Catholic Church's capacity for mobilizing the masses and soon sought to bury Fascism's association with anti-clericalism and went out of their way to woo the Church. The first Fascist Minister of Education, Giovanni Gentile, abruptly reversed the regulations of pre-Fascist Italy by ordering crucifixes to be restored to the wall of every school classroom in Italy. The year in which Mussolini proclaimed the end of parliamentary government in Italy, 1925, was also a Holy Year which offered further opportunities to reassure the Church of the new regime's intentions. To signal the central role that the Catholic religion would play in the new Fascist Italy, Mussolini ordered the reinstatement of many religious holidays and offered state support for many popular devotional associations. The project of making Catholicism a platform for a new 'national religion' took a further step in the following year, the 700th anniversary of the death of St Francis of Assisi, whom the Fascist sympathizer and poet Gabriele D'Annunzio had called 'the most Italian of the saints, and the most sacred Italian'. Church and state vied to outdo each other in celebrating what became a symbolic fusion of religion and nationalism, and both claimed the credit when over a million and a half pilgrims visited Assisi.[7]

The collaboration between Church and state in promoting Catholicism as the essence of Italian national identity was greatly enhanced by the Lateran Pacts of 1929. But it has not often been noticed that the Concordat struck a major blow against the noble tradition of religious toleration that had been one of the fundamental guarantees protected by the constitution of Liberal Italy. Indeed, it was the promise of religious toleration that had encouraged many members of Italy's tiny religious minorities to play roles that were quite disproportionate to their numbers in the struggles for national independence and unity. For that reason, too, the Risorgimento had found many of its most dedicated supporters among Italy's small Protestant, Greek Orthodox and Jewish minorities.

The Vatican had always regarded the freedom of worship for non-Catholics that was first established in Italy by the Piedmontese constitution of 1848 and then guaranteed by the Risorgimento as a defeat for the Church. The advent of the Fascist regime, whose leader had been hailed by Pope Pius XI as 'a man sent by Providence', finally offered the opportunity to reverse that defeat. The critical concession that enabled the Vatican to limit religious toleration in Italy came from a seemingly anodyne clause in the Concordat referring to the status of non-Catholic religions in Italy. As had been the case in the existing Italian constitution, the new law recognized the Catholic Church as the 'sole religion of the State' and it went on to acknowledge that other religious communities were permitted to practise their faith 'in temples and oratories authorized for that purpose'.[8] But authorized by whom?

There lay the rub. It soon became evident that the purpose of the new law was severely to restrict the rights of non-Catholic religious communities to meet and worship especially those that were not part of a recognized church with an established hierarchy. These intentions were made clear when the Vatican began to urge the Italian government to enforce the new law and require that non-Catholics obtain official permission before holding religious meetings or ceremonies. The principal targets of these measures were the Protestants, and especially the new evangelical Protestant Churches that were particularly vulnerable because by choice they had no established hierarchy and were decentralized, largely independent and self-governing.

The Church's antipathy towards the evangelicals was fully shared by the Fascists. As their leading historian has noted:

the individualism of the evangelical congregations, their very emotional and spontaneous religious experience and their lack of hierarchy combined with a fundamentalist reading of the Bible, their total personal commitment, the extreme rigidity of their customs and an explicit desire to distance themselves from politics and the State, and millenarian belief in the Second Coming meant that these movements were not easily reconciled with the demands of the fascist regime.[9]

Indeed, even before it was prompted by the Vatican, Mussolini's regime had on its own initiative begun to target religious dissidents. In 1925 the authorities had closed a Pentecostal meeting house in Melfi in the province of Basilicata, and the Interior Ministry subsequently ordered the closure of others. In the meantime, Protestant pastors and preachers were being arrested on a variety of pretexts, including charges of blasphemy.

In April 1927 the regime's campaign against the evangelical communities took a further step when Mussolini's Chief of Police, Arturo Bocchini, instructed the prefects in each province to provide him with regular reports on their activities and membership. A year later he contacted the Italian Embassy in Washington to ask for further information about the Pentecostalists, particularly concerning the possibility that they might be Communists or Communist sympathizers. An Embassy official replied that it was not believed that there was any connection between Pentecostalism and Communism, but in his opinion these sects were nonetheless dangerous because they 'attract persons who become so obsessed with their faith that they neglect all other duties, work and interests'. A few months later Bocchini again warned the prefects throughout Italy that the police were aware that a number of new Pentecostalist communities had been established in certain towns in Sicily. They were a threat to Fascism and should be kept under close surveillance. Bocchini warned that they should be considered 'not as religious communities but as sectarian associations'. He also instructed Professor Osvaldo Zacchi, an eminent Roman psychiatrist, to prepare a 'medical–psychiatric report' on the consequences of the Pentecostalists' collective rituals and trances.[10]

The Vatican did not consider that the authorities were being sufficiently energetic in this cause, however, and once the Concordat came into effect it began to call for more vigorous action by the state and more tangible results. Its concerns were fully set out in a memorandum that was submitted to the Italian government in June 1930 on the subject of 'The Current Conditions of Evangelical Cults and Organizations in Italy'. In the report the Church made clear not only its alarm at the new evangelical faiths, but its 'serious apprehensions with regard to the marked revival in the Protestant movement in Italy'. It claimed that the number of Protestants in Italy had risen by nearly 25 per cent between 1911 and 1925, so that 'they now embrace perhaps as many as 200,000 individuals'.[11] These figures were almost certainly wild exaggerations, but they accurately reflected both the Vatican's fears and its irritation that the regime was failing to take more effective action. For that reason the Papal Nuncio in 1934 sent Mussolini's government a further memorandum on 'The Problem of Protestant Proselytism in Italy'.

Without drawing distinctions between Protestants, evangelicals, Pentecostalists and others, the Vatican document warned specifically of the serious dangers posed by the 'trembling Pentecostalists'. In the course of their worship, the report claimed,

> 'the adherents of these sects get into a state of agitation that leads to a trance, which poses great danger especially for women and children. To verify these facts it will only be necessary to send a psychiatric practitioner unannounced to carry out an on-site investigation at their meeting house at Via Adige 20 [in Rome].'

Without giving any source, the report went on to claim that 'other Evangelicals have told us that the true aims of the Pentecostalists seek to promote free love, immorality, spiritualism, hypnosis, false healing and collective insanity'.

The memorandum then specifically referred to the new law that subjected all non-Catholic religious gatherings to prior approval by the authorities and reminded the government of its responsibilities: 'Since Italian Law permits religious cults other than the Catholic Church provided that they do not profess principles or follow rites that are contrary to public order and public decency, it is difficult to understand why the cult of the Pentecostalists continues to be tolerated in Italy.'[12] The government forwarded the memorandum to the Chief of Police. He in turn passed it to his trusted assistant, Carmine Senise, who dutifully dug up the psychiatric report made by Dr Zacchi in 1928. This was sent to police chiefs throughout Italy, who were instructed to keep detailed records on all the evangelical sects and their followers.

A year later, a further ministerial circular of 9 April 1935 explained why more severe measures needed to be taken against non-Catholics. The instructions appeared under the name of the Under-Secretary at the Interior Ministry Guido Buffarini Guidi, but they had been written by Bocchini himself and they clearly reflected the broader changes taking place in Mussolini's regime as Italy embarked on its new imperial project. The language of racism and the notions of 'racial integrity' that had first been developed in the Italian colonies were now used to define and identify internal enemies of the new national community. The circular instructed the prefects in each province that the 'pentecostalists, or Pentecostals, or pneumatics or shakers, as they are variously known' could no longer be tolerated. Further, it stated that these individuals engaged in 'religious practices that must be considered contrary to the social order and harmful to the physical and psychological integrity of the race'.[13]

Giorgio Rochat was the first to point out that this claim marked a very significant innovation in the racist rhetoric of Italian Fascism that anticipated the language of the later Racial

Laws against the Jews of September 1938. In the opinion of the exiled writer Ignazio Silone, the circular was 'the most serious measure of religious intolerance in Italy since the Risorgimento: indeed, it put the clock back to the spirit of religious intolerance that had dominated Italy from the Counter-Reformation to the Risorgimento'.[14] The 1935 ministerial circular was a clear state- ment of the regime's determination to 'nationalize religion' as part of the broader project of creating a true Fascist state. In every province the police were again instructed to draw up lists and keep detailed records of all the evangelical communities. The communities were consequently exposed to constant harassment and interference by the police and the clergy, who now enjoyed a simple and effective legal weapon: the new law that required all non-Catholics to obtain prior authorization before holding religious meetings or ceremonies.

This was the law that resulted in the arrival of the agents of the Foggia court at the door of Donato Manduzio in San Nicandro in February 1936. In the document Manduzio was described as a Protestant pastor, and an identical indictment was delivered to a nearby Protestant pastor, who was also fined for holding reli- gious meetings without official permission.[15] Manduzio and his followers had unwittingly placed themselves outside what both the regime and the Catholic Church now defined as the national community. When the Duce launched Italy's new imperial project they were thus increasingly at risk. But there is more than a degree of irony in the fact that the would-be converts' first contact with official Italy was because they had been mistaken for evangelical Protestants. The legal injunction had nothing to do with the fact that they had chosen to become Jews, with whom at that moment Mussolini's regime had no quarrel. They had fallen foul of the law more simply because they had chosen not to be Catholics.

But long before the officers of the criminal court in Foggia made their visit, the activities, movements and contacts of

Manduzio and his followers were being closely watched by the police. Their mail was intercepted and their identities were investigated, as were those of the mysterious visitors who came to find them. Although the community may have had some inkling of this, it is unlikely that they could have known, or even guessed, that soon afterwards both the Duce's Chief of Police and the Pope's Secretary of State would be receiving regular reports about them.

# CHAPTER FOUR

# The Man from Milan

The 250 lire fine imposed by the Foggia criminal court was not large, but it posed major problems. The fine had to be paid at once to avoid incurring further penalties, but the bigger problem was that the group was now banned from using Manduzio's house for their weekly prayer meetings. Instead, each family would have to meet in their own houses to pray, something that was neither practical nor desirable since they depended on Manduzio's leadership and guidance in their worship. An additional problem of which they were unaware is that Jewish prayer requires, if at all possible, the presence of a quorum of ten males over the age of thirteen.

So what was to be done? This was not at all clear. The law required that Manduzio's followers obtain authorization from their religious leaders, so that the police could in turn issue the permission they needed to worship together. But they found themselves in a similar situation to the Pentecostalists and Seventh Day Adventists against whom the law was specifically directed, because there was no established religious authority for these would-be Jews to turn to since they had not yet been admitted into the Jewish community.

They first thought of appealing to the Ministry of Religious Affairs for guidance, and Manduzio decided that one of them should go to Foggia to make inquiries. Because of his own disability, he could not go in person, but choosing a representative posed delicate problems. He knew that by delegating this important task he risked jeopardizing his leadership. Once again, the jealousy with which he asserted his own unique role of leader was made plain when, after calling them together to select an emissary, he reminded the group that 'he alone had descended from Mount Sinai'.

Manduzio's chosen candidate was Antonio Bonfitto. But Bonfitto refused, explaining that 'he did not want to get into trouble with the authorities'. That was not unreasonable, but it infuriated Manduzio and confirmed what had been revealed to him in a vision some months earlier, that Bonfitto was the 'rotten branch'. Bonfitto's wife Concetta di Leo, who was one of Manduzio's closest and most loyal supporters, then told the others of Manduzio's dream, and agreed that her husband's behaviour revealed that Manduzio had truly prophetic powers.[1] The dispute between the couple worsened when Concetta gave birth to a son and refused to name the child Vincenzo, after her father-in-law, because it was not the name of a Hebrew prophet. Bonfitto flew into a rage and threatened Concetta with a knife, and it was only thanks to the timely intervention of Manduzio's wife, Emanuela, that tragedy was averted. Although he grudgingly agreed to have his son named Giuseppe (presumably a compromise since this is not the name of a Hebrew prophet), he announced that he wanted nothing more to do with Manduzio or his followers. Since Concetta remained loyal to the group, her household was now effectively split in two.

Division now threatened the whole community. Without consulting Manduzio, Costantino Tritto had been writing directly to Alfonso Pacifici, who had sent him a set of lessons from the Talmud. When Tritto received it he began to read passages aloud to Manduzio, who quickly realized that these texts and their interpretation posed a serious challenge to his own authority, and above all to the status of the dreams and revelations that were the sign of his special line of communication with the Almighty. Manduzio countered by describing a vision, warning that the Talmud contained passages 'that were unsuitable reading for a weak-spirited child of the One God'. He instructed Tritto that he should on no account continue reading the instructions from the Talmud 'because you are still not strong in the faith of the One God, so that you may bring harm to yourself and your children'. Outraged, Tritto and Manduzio's most persistent critic, Francesco Cerrone, wrote to Rome to protest against what they saw as Manduzio's ill-informed interpretations of the Jewish faith.

At this point the group of would-be Jews seemed destined to share the fate of most isolated communities of religious converts and disintegrate. That this did not happen owed much to the appearance of Raffaele Cantoni, a prominent and influential figure in the Italian Jewish community, who would be the most significant outsider to become involved in the story. In March 1936, Manduzio had written to the new Chief Rabbi Davide Prato to explain the situation following the court ruling, pleading with 'the gentlemen in Rome' to come to their aid 'as a matter of the utmost urgency', since the authorities 'have decided to destroy our Cult and to force us to abandon our religion'. But despite repeated letters and requests from San Nicandro, little came in return except reassuring words and it was not until a year later, in July 1937, that Manduzio received a letter from Florence informing him that a certain Signor Raffaele Cantoni would shortly be coming to help them sort out their problems.[2]

Cantoni duly arrived at Manduzio's house on the appointed day, 9 July, and to everyone's surprise immediately recognized the blind man, Rocco di Paolo. He had recently seen Di Paolo in the synagogue in Florence in the company of Giorgio Sarfatti, one of Cantoni's friends. Di Paolo's visit was probably connected with his admission to the National Institute for the Blind in the city, which was shortly to take place. But the fact that Di Paolo had independent contacts with members of the Jewish community in Florence, which was one of the most important and influential in Italy, suggests that the story of the would-be converts of San Nicandro was becoming well known to wider circles of Italian Jews.

Cantoni explained that the reason for his visit was to find out what they needed. Manduzio told him that many people had promised to help, but nothing had ever come of it. Cantoni insisted that 'my words are not empty and will not vanish into the air', and Manduzio replied that all they wanted was to be left in peace to carry on their meetings without being disturbed by the police. In that case, Cantoni declared, the matter could be quickly resolved. The San Nicandro community came under the jurisdiction of the Jewish community in Naples, and it would be easy enough for them to obtain from Naples the letter of recognition required by the law.

The next day was the sabbath, and Cantoni joined them for their weekly prayers in Manduzio's house, which seem to have resumed despite the court injunction. On the following day, Cantoni went with the others to look for a property that could be used as a permanent meeting house or oratory. A suitable house was soon found; Cantoni paid the owner a deposit and agreed to settle the balance of the annual rent (450 lire) by September. They then returned to Manduzio's house where Cantoni talked about aspects of the Jewish faith and told them that as well as the story of the flight from Egypt they must read about the Jews' return to the Promised Land. He also suggested that a boy from their community should attend one of the Jewish summer camps that had been organized in northern Italy, and agreed to pay the costs. Finally he raised the issue of circumcision, advising them that they should make the necessary arrangements as soon as possible, and promising to make inquiries on their behalf.[3]

The following day Cantoni left San Nicandro, and shortly afterwards sent Manduzio two bound copies of the royal decree law relating to non-Catholic worship and religious assembly, and a pamphlet entitled *The King, the Duce and Israel in Italy* which presumably explained the legitimacy of the Jewish faith in Fascist Italy. He told Manduzio to send copies to the police headquarters in Foggia and also to the Podestà (the Fascist official who replaced the formerly elected mayors) of San Nicandro. There were some other books that dealt with aspects of the Jewish faith and the Italian Jews, and he also enclosed a postal order for 200 lire to pay the expenses of Antonio Tritto, who had been chosen to attend the Jewish summer camp and who set off shortly afterwards.

At the end of August, an excited Antonio returned full of stories about the warmth of his reception at the camp where he had spent two weeks with a group of Italian and non-Italian Jewish boys. Unfortunately Cantoni's visit had not yielded any other happy results. The owner of the house they had planned to rent refused to allow it to be used as a religious meeting place, and there was no sign of any letter of recognition from Naples nor of authorization from the police in Foggia. Further urgent letters were sent to Cantoni, who after a number of last-minute cancellations finally turned up again at Manduzio's door on Friday 22 October. His return was a cause for great rejoicing, especially among the children with whom he had developed a very affectionate relationship during his first short visit. When the would-be converts were all gathered together, Cantoni opened his suitcase to reveal twenty-one prayer shawls (one for each of the males), a large sabbath candelabrum with eight candle-holders and also a smaller one, and a kiddush cup. When Manduzio inquired after the letter of recognition from Naples, Cantoni admitted that he did not have it yet, but said that the Chief Rabbi of Rome had agreed to contact Naples on their behalf, so it should arrive soon. As far as the police permission was concerned, he suggested that they should all go at once to the nearby police in San Nicandro.

Francesco Cerrone accompanied Cantoni to the police station, to find that only the public security officer, who was also the Podestà, was qualified to take care of the matter and he was not on duty that evening. Cantoni proceeded to another house that had been chosen for the prayer meetings, and after it had been properly cleaned and prepared, he led the prayers. Each male wore one of the shawls that he had given them. Afterwards Cantoni returned to the police station where he finally met the Podestà, who assured him that permission to hold religious meetings in the house had already been granted. The paperwork had not yet arrived from Foggia, but it was expected any day.

When Cantoni returned alone to Manduzio's house, he seemed disturbed, although Manduzio was not sure why. Cantoni asked him a number of times whether he would be prepared to go to the new prayer house, and Manduzio repeatedly insisted that he would do so willingly, except that his disability made it impossible for him to leave his own house without assistance. Cantoni must have been well briefed on the internal disputes in the community, and he clearly understood that the choice of a place to hold the prayer meetings had important implications. He knew that Manduzio's leadership would be seriously undermined if the weekly assemblies were held in a place that he was unable to attend. Manduzio was undoubtedly aware of this too. He nevertheless suggested that it might be appropriate for one of the others to lead the prayer meetings, as he himself had not attended school for so much as a day while others had completed the fourth grade and in one case even the fifth. Cantoni flatly refused. He had by now developed a strong personal affection for Manduzio, but he also had begun to have doubts about the sincerity of some of the others. Indeed, Alfonso Pacifici had complained to him about the behaviour of Cerrone and Tritto during their visit to Rome, and during his two brief visits to San Nicandro Cantoni himself had seen that many members of the community smoked on the sabbath. Both Manduzio and Cantoni had noticed that Cerrone had started selling ice creams from his house, even on the sabbath.

Although frustrated by Manduzio's insistence that it was impossible for him to leave his home to go to the new prayer house, Cantoni agreed to stay another day as Manduzio's guest. The following day, except Manduzio the whole group and all the children accompanied him to the railway station to see him off. Cantoni was clearly still concerned about Manduzio's position as leader, and while making his farewells he warned them 'to take care not to displease Manduzio in any way'.[4]

Cantoni would never return to San Nicandro again, but from the time of his first visit in July 1937 he played a decisive role in the story. The interest that he developed was both personal and emotional and it reflected the fascination and curiosity that drew many Italian Jews to the case of Manduzio and his followers in these years. In Cantoni's case there was also something more. He was born in 1896 and came from a wealthy Jewish family from Venice. He was neither an intellectual nor even an especially religious person. He did have a wide range of humanitarian interests and commitments, however, which also now came to embrace the would-be converts. His friend Gualtiero Cividalli later insisted that it was his broader experience and the fact that he did not come from an orthodox background that made him particularly open to 'understanding the primitive spirit of these people who were in every respect so far removed from the world of the Italian Jews but who nonetheless had found their way to the Jewish faith'.[5]

By profession Cantoni was an accountant who in the early 1930s he had become involved in a number of Italian Jewish charitable undertakings, especially in the work to assist the growing numbers of foreign Jewish refugees who were coming to Italy from Nazi Germany, Austria and the central and eastern European states. Most were in transit to other destinations, but many needed accommodation and support while they waited to leave. Cantoni threw himself energetically into the task, demonstrating not only excellent managerial and negotiating skills but also a capacity for fund-raising that astonished all those who knew him. His contacts soon ranged outside Italy, and as a result of his frequent travels on business he quickly built up an international network of contacts.

Initially, the efforts to assist foreign Jewish refugees in Italy were supported by Mussolini's government. Indeed, after Hitler came to power Mussolini saw opportunities for Italy to benefit materially from the Jews who were leaving Germany. He invited the Chief Rabbi of Rome, at that time Angelo Sacerdoti, to help the government promote the attractions of the Italian ports of Genoa, Naples and above all Trieste for those en route to either Palestine or the United States. In 1933 a Committee to Assist Jewish Refugees from Germany had been created in Milan and two years later Raffaele Cantoni was appointed its director. As a result, Cantoni soon found himself working with international organizations responsible for dealing with the rapidly growing numbers of Jewish refugees, the most important being the American Jewish Joint Distribution Committee (JDC), known as the Joint, founded in the US in 1914. He attended a meeting of the Joint in Paris in 1935, and a year later he also participated in the World Jewish Congress in Geneva where he met and became a close friend of Saly Mayer, the organizer of the Swiss Union of Jewish Communities.[6]

These activities enabled Cantoni to expand his already extensive network of international personal contacts in Europe, the United States and Palestine. In Italy his work for the foreign Jewish refugees brought him into close contact with the small group of Italian Zionists – especially Angelo Sacerdoti, Alfonso Pacifici and Davide Prato – who in these years held very influential positions, particularly in Rome and Florence. In contrast to the others, however, Cantoni's Zionism was above all philanthropic and humanitarian. His friend Augusto Segre remembered him as an impulsive and impatient man who wanted everything done immediately. He spoke in a heavy Venetian dialect that most Italians found difficult to follow, and if he did not get his way quickly he had a disconcerting habit of smashing chairs and other pieces of furniture. He was a man of action, and it followed that his commitment to the Jewish cause took a practical rather than a religious or ideological turn – hence his enthusiastic involvement in the project for establishing summer camps for Jewish boys and girls in Italy.[7]

Similar projects were being launched all over Europe in the 1930s, with many different aims. Some of the camps were religious, while others were more purely educational or simply recreational. In Italy, for example, Alfonso Pacifici was an enthusiastic advocate of the Jewish summer camps, which he believed offered an excellent opportunity for Italian Jews to 'live an integral Jewish life, albeit only for a short period each year'. Some were for children while others provided an opportunity for adult Italian Jews to return to a full religious life and prepare themselves for the *aliyah*: the return to the Promised Land. Dante Lattes, the most influential of the Italian Zionists, shared that view, as did Enzo Sereni, who in 1927 with his wife Ada Ascarelli would be the first Italian Jews to found a kibbutz in Palestine.[8]

For Cantoni the summer camps were also a means of providing temporary accommodation for some of the foreign Jewish refugees who were in transit after leaving Nazi Germany and Austria, and to offer basic agricultural training for those planning to settle in Palestine. The agricultural training camps, or *hakhsharà*, were very informal with no specifically religious goals. Once again, Cantoni's remarkable organizational skills were soon evident. He himself had considerable experience in estate management and he knew many landowners (some, but not all, of whom were were Jewish) who agreed to make land available for short periods in the summer. By 1938 some forty camps had been established in different parts of northern Italy.

Most were for foreign Jews, but others were for Italian Jews, like the one at Sesta in the beautiful Pusteria valley in the South Tyrol where Antonio Tritto stayed for two weeks in August 1937.

It is probably more than a coincidence that all of the Italian Jews who at one time or another were directly involved in the story of Manduzio and his followers were sympathizers with the Zionist cause. Alfonso Pacifici, Davide Prato and Enzo Sereni were all leading figures among the small group of Italian Jews who were Zionists, while Raffaele Cantoni had become involved with the San Nicandro community at the express request of Davide Prato. The common thread was not so much their Zionism, since each had his own interpretations of the Zionist project, as a greater openness towards the principle of proselytism than prevailed among their more orthodox fellow Jews, and hence their willingness to explore the case of the would-be converts of San Nicandro without preconceptions. To that curiosity, we should add the remarkable impact that the prospect of the Jewish faith finding converts in this remote and unlikely setting exercised on the minds and imaginations of those Jews who came to know Manduzio and his followers at first hand.

There were other reasons, however, why Cantoni's appearance on the scene would mark an important moment in the affairs of Manduzio and his followers. Although he was known to Mussolini's police primarily for his work for Jewish charities, Raffaele Cantoni was also regarded as a potentially dangerous opponent of the regime. In fact, he had a record of anti-Fascist political activities and in 1930 he had narrowly escaped being convicted as a traitor and a terrorist. His first encounter with the police had come when he was arrested in Venice in February 1915 for causing public disorder during a demonstration demanding Italy's entry into the war. He was later acquitted, fought in the Great War as a volunteer, was briefly taken prisoner and then wounded. In October 1919 he joined Gabriele D'Annunzio whose followers had occupied Fiume (now Rijeka in Croatia) a month earlier in protest against the Peace Treaties that had left Italy with a 'mutilated victory'. But he was quickly disgusted by D'Annunzio's entourage and left Fiume for Turin, where he became a Fascist 'of the First Hour', as the earliest members of Mussolini's movement were called.

Cantoni's flirtation with Fascism was brief. Again in disgust he abandoned the Blackshirts and instead joined a militant anti-Fascist movement in Turin called Italia Libera. To make matters worse (in the eyes of the Fascists) he was also an active Freemason, an organization that the Fascists claimed was a mortal enemy of the national community. After the Fascist seizure of power, in Milan Cantoni joined what soon became one of the principal clandestine opposition movements in Italy, Giustizia e Libertà (Justice and Liberty), which had been founded in Paris in 1929 by two leading anti-Fascists, Carlo Rosselli and Emilio Lussu.

The organization was soon infiltrated by an informer, Carlo De Re, who revealed the names of its members and their plans to the Italian police. As a result, in December 1930 Raffaele Cantoni was one of fifteen people arrested in Italy by the Fascist secret police, the OVRA, and charged with treasonous conspiracy against the state. His co-defendants included Ernesto Rossi and Riccardo Bauer, two of the leaders of Italian anti-Fascism. With them Cantoni appeared before the notorious Special Tribunal for the Defence of the State. Rossi and Bauer were found guilty and sentenced to twenty years' penal confinement for plotting against the state. Unlike the others Cantoni, who was also charged with 'attempting to reconstruct a Masonic lodge in Milan', was acquitted on grounds of 'insufficient evidence', and after a forced public declaration of his loyalty to Fascism and to the Duce he was released. Nonetheless, the acquittal was conditional and he remained on police bail and was under permanent police surveillance.[9]

It was not long before Cantoni's appointment as director of the Milan Committee for German Jewish Refugees came to the notice of the Chief of Public Security, Carmine Senise, Chief of Police Arturo Bocchini's right-hand man. Senise warned the Foreign Ministry in August 1936 that Cantoni was 'not a suitable person to be in that position'. He had previously been arrested for anti-Fascist activities, and although acquitted he was still under suspicion. 'According to confidential reports' ('secondo notizie fiduciarie', a formula much used by Mussolini's police to indicate information acquired from one of the regime's army of anonymous spies and informers), Cantoni was travelling all over Italy on the pretext of visiting German Jewish refugees. But his real purpose was 'to spread defamation and defeatism against the Regime'. For those reasons Senise asked the Foreign Ministry to withdraw Cantoni's passport, although this did not happen.[10]

Because of Senise's intervention, however, Cantoni was forced to resign as director of the Milan Committee for German Jewish Refugees. But despite losing his formal title he remained the prime mover in the Committee's activities as it struggled to deal with a steadily rising number of Jewish refugees coming into Italy. It was in the midst of these commitments that he agreed to Davide Prato's suggestion that he combine a planned journey to the South with a visit to Manduzio and his followers. As he probably well knew, the police were following every step.

The records also reveal, however, that Manduzio and his followers had been under routine police surveillance since the time of Jacques Faitlovich's visit in 1935. The fact that this group of impoverished families should receive visitors would have been unlikely to escape the attention of the authorities or their spies, but when the visitors also included a foreigner of some apparent distinction their curiosity must have been particularly aroused. In any case, since 1935 regular records had been kept both of the members of the community and of their visitors. The police knew, for example, that the group consisted of some nine families, all of whose names were recorded and had been checked. They knew that the group had been in existence for about seven years and that it met once a week in the house of Donato Manduzio, son of the late Giuseppe, 'aged fifty who lives at Via del Gargano No. 56'. The earliest report stated that 'All the families in the group know one another and are of the Hebrew faith. They meet more or less frequently for prayer, rituals and to discuss various aspects of the religion they profess.'

The police believed that Francesco Cerrone, not Manduzio, was the leader because it was Cerrone who had contacted the Union of Jewish Communities in Rome in 1937 and Cerrone who made the application for permission to open an 'oratory for the Hebrew Religion' in October 1937 (after Cantoni's second visit). But ever since Faitlovich's visit in 1935 Cerrone's mail had been systematically opened and read by the post office police. His police file contained copies of his correspondence with Dr Ascher in Bex-les-Bains about the possibility of one of his sons attending the school there. A postal order for fifty lire that Ascher had sent Cerrone had been confiscated because 'it violated the law banning the introduction of foreign currencies into the Kingdom from abroad', and Cerrone's application for a passport had also been rejected.[11]

The confiscation of the postal order must have alerted the would-be converts to the fact that they were being watched, which may explain why the police missed much of their correspondence. The police files tell us a great deal about the day-to-day surveillance and petty harassments that were the fate of many Italians under Fascism. They also reveal how much information on its citizens was routinely stored by the Fascist state and how effectively bureaucratic regulations could be used to thwart otherwise perfectly legitimate activities, including the right to follow a religion other than Catholicism. Whoever wrote the police report could not conceal his amusement over the difficulties that the verdict of the Foggia court in 1936 had created and the hopeless attempts made by the would-be converts to find a way out of the impasse. Yet, despite all the information that had been gathered about the group, the reports repeatedly stated that it posed no threat, that they were all 'peasants and artisans', that they were desperately poor and barely able to support themselves, although it was also noted that none was a member of the PNF (the National Fascist Party). But the main concern was the contacts that the group had somehow managed to establish outside San Nicandro.

Faitlovich's visit first triggered the alarm, but the suspicions of the authorities were further heightened by the appearance of Cantoni – 'a notorious Opponent [of the regime]'. Indeed, Cantoni's first visit in July 1937 had been deemed sufficiently important to warrant a full report from the senior government officer in the province, the Prefect of Foggia, to the Interior Ministry in Rome. The report indicates that the police were well informed and suggests that there were spies in San Nicandro who provided information. The authorities knew that the main purpose of the visit in July had been to 'found a Jewish temple' and that since the group had not located anywhere suitable Cantoni had promised to return. The police also knew that the would-be converts planned to establish an oratory or temple where they could meet regularly to hear commentary 'on sections of the Pentateuch by a pastor chosen from the ranks of the Jewish Community in Naples which has jurisdiction for Jews in this territory'. After Cantoni's second visit, at the Interior Minister's request the Prefect wrote again to confirm that the visit had again been 'subject to close surveillance'. A copy was enclosed of the petition for authorization to rent and open 'a venue suitable for use as an Oratory for practising the Jewish Religion, as is required by the Royal Decree Law 30 October 1930 1731', which had been signed by Francesco Cerrone.

After Cantoni left San Nicandro in October the police carefully intercepted his correspondence, as a consequence preserving a series of letters that give a clear insight into Cantoni's commitment to the would-be converts and his efforts to help them. We can see from the letters that Cantoni was a man of his word. Determined to find some way of removing the ban on their prayer meetings, and realizing that as non-Jews they would not be able to obtain a letter of recognition from a rabbi, Cantoni decided that they should be circumcised as soon as possible. He promised to arrange this after his July visit, and soon after leaving San Nicandro he wrote to an old acquaintance, Enrico Emilio Franco, who was a fellow Jew and a professor of anatomical pathology at the University of Bari, asking for his help. Franco was very disappointed not to have heard anything about the 'unusual event that has taken place at San Nicandro during the five years I was living in Bari', but since he had now moved to Pisa he regretted that he could not personally perform the operation. He offered to put Cantoni in contact with a urologist and former medical colleague in Bari named Dr Tullio Zapler, who would probably be able to assist.

Having intercepted these letters, the police turned their attention first to Dr Zapler, a German-Romanian Jew who had moved to Italy and settled in Bari in March 1928. There was already a long police file on him. When he first arrived in Bari his activities had given rise to concern 'because he was known to frequent local elements of doubtful political allegiance'. That concern grew when in 1930 Zapler married the daughter of a certain Signor Carlo Sciascia, who was in retirement but 'before the advent of Fascism had been a militant in the Socialist Party'. Zapler remained under close surveillance and the police knew he was an active member of an organization known as Keren Kaimet Israel which they believed to be 'politically dependent on a council made up of leading Freemasons from all over Europe'.

Because at this time the Fascist police were obsessed with Freemasonry, the fact that Zapler was a Jew attracted no special comment. In 1934 the police noted, however, that Zapler was in regular contact with the many Polish and German Jewish refugees who were studying at the University in Bari. After he was appointed director of the Municipal Clinic of Dermatology in the main hospital in Bari he twice (in 1935 and 1936) applied for Italian citizenship, but his applications were rejected 'because he could show no good reason why he deserved it'. Although the police considered him to be someone who needed to be carefully watched, he was not listed as an individual who posed any specific danger as he had not been reported making any open criticisms of the regime. The police also followed up on Professor Franco, an apparently blameless and distinguished man on whom they nonetheless already had plenty of information. They knew that he had been in close contact with both Zapler and the Jewish students at the University during his five years in Bari, during which time he too had been watched, even though the file acknowledged that 'our information suggests that he led a very private life and had no friends'. He was not a member of the PNF, but 'he was not a person who gave rise to suspicion for political reasons'.

Although they had little to show for their energetic devotion to the case, the agents in the Bari police station continued to follow the correspondence and soon picked up the letter in which Professor Franco introduced his friend Cantoni, whom he described as 'one of the most meritorious Italians working for the Jewish cause and one of the most outstanding for his efforts on behalf of those Jews who have come to Italy from other lands'. Franco told Zapler that Cantoni would write to ask for his professional assistance in connection with 'a group of about forty persons who have decided to make the formal passage to become Jews'. The policeman transcribing the letter thought it necessary to add with some pride a brief explanation on the side of the page: the unspecified favour Cantoni was asking Zapler was to 'perform on the men, boys and infants of the group the *brit mila*' – that is, circumcision.

Cantoni's letter to Zapler, dated 12 July 1937, was also intercepted and contains the fullest account of Cantoni's own reason for taking up the cause of Donato Manduzio and his followers, and for his commitment to helping them achieve their great ambition to become Jews. Cantoni explained that the purpose of his letter was to 'ask your assistance in a Jewish work [in Italian, *opera*] which your professional skills as an urologist make you particularly qualified to perform'. He informed Zapler that there were some forty individuals in the town of San Nicandro who for some years now 'have desired to become Jews in the full sense of the word. For some time they have been studying our language and praying our prayers and now they want to be circumcised as a first and irrefutable mark of their faith. You will already have guessed what I am trying to organize, which is to ask you to go to San Nicandro and perform this "good deed" for these people, an act that in this case will be all the more meritorious since it is from us that these people are awaiting the Light of Truth.' There were six adult males in the group and about fifteen boys, 'some of whom are of the most tender age'. Cantoni closed by thanking Zapler in the name of 'your good friend and mine, Professor Franco, and also Dr Kutsceroff, both of whom were full of praise for the work that you have done for the Jews down there [in Bari] and I am confident that you will assist me with the needs of those of San Nicandro'.[12]

Cantoni returned to San Nicandro in October, but there was no further information about Zapler, and the circumcisions were not performed. Nor, as we have seen, was the problem of the authorization to hold religious ceremonies resolved; indeed, the authorities had already decided against this. The police remained vigilant for further contacts and were now convinced that they had got to the bottom of the whole business. As they could not believe that Manduzio and his followers had the wit to have come up with the project of conversion on their own, they could only assume that someone must have put them up to it, probably for money. This, they now believed, had been the reason for Faitlovich's visit and certainly for Cantoni's: 'since he has large financial resources he might well be able to convert some of those in Nicandro Garganico because they live in very straitened economic circumstances'.

So that was it. The goings-on in San Nicandro were not about religion and there was clearly some more subversive project afoot. Very soon after this correspondence ended, however, Mussolini's regime decided to adopt anti-Semitism formally as a policy of state. As a result, the official view of the San Nicandro conversion took a new and more sinister turn.

# CHAPTER FIVE

# Persecution

During the period of Raffaele Cantoni's visits to San Nicandro in 1937, political changes were taking place that would have important consequences for the would-be converts and above all for the Italian Jews who had taken a close interest in their case. It was not until the following year that Mussolini's regime defined Judaism as 'an international conspiracy of anti-Fascism', but the decision to expel Italian Jews from the Fascist national community was preceded by a violent campaign of anti-Semitism that began in the second half of 1936. Attacks on Italian Jews by the Fascist press reached a climax with the publication of the Manifesto of Racist Scientists in July 1938. This declaration of the racial principles adopted by the regime was the rationale for the specific measures against foreign and Italian Jews that followed. Between September and November a series of laws and decrees were introduced, known collectively as the Racial Laws, which made 'racial anti-Semitism on the German pattern . . . an integral part of official Fascist doctrine'.[1]

The Fascist Racial Laws were harsh. Non-Italian Jews were required to leave Italy within four months, while those who had become Italian citizens since 1919 were stripped of their citizenship. Severe exclusions were imposed on Italian Jews as well, including a general prohibition on holding public office or any form of state employment, such as teaching in schools or universities and serving in the armed forces in times of war or peace. Italian Jews were prohibited from marrying what the Fascists now defined as 'Aryans' and they were disqualified from owning or running businesses. Jewish children could no longer attend either state schools or private non-Jewish schools. The use of textbooks by Jewish authors in Italian schools was banned. There was an element of uncertainty about how rigorously the regime intended to enforce these measures, however. Many thought that the anti-Jewish laws were just another example of the Duce's duplicitous opportunism, motivated by a desire to please Italy's ally in the Axis pact, Nazi Germany, rather than by a deeper ideological commitment to anti-Semitism. There were also certain exemptions; for example, for Jews who had been honoured for service in the Great War or who had been among the first members of the PNF. In practice these exemptions were rarely granted, but most Italian Jews did not believe that the regime seriously intended to apply the new laws.

In the long run that view proved to be dangerously optimistic, but this optimism was strengthened by the government's failure to make preparations for putting the new laws into operation. By the time Italy went to war in 1940, little of the grandiose plan for excluding Jews from the national community had been implemented. This not untypical failure meant that when some 30,000 applications for emigration permits started to flood in, the bureaucracy was unprepared and unable to process them. Although some left voluntarily, few of the estimated 4,000 foreign Jews who were in Italy at the time of the expulsion order were forced to leave.[2] Bureaucratic ineptitude cannot be taken to signify an absence of deeper intent, however, and at the time many saw in the regime's anti-Semitic turn the final revelation of essentially racist principles that had never been far from the core of Fascist ideology. The Duce's imperial illusion enforced openly racist policies in the Italian colonies, and the Buffarini-Guidi circular of April 1935 had defined religious dissidents as threatening the 'racial integrity' of the national community. Now in September 1938 the regime was invoking the same logic to exclude Italian Jews.

While the strength of racist thought in many sections of the Fascist regime has in the past been seriously underestimated, interpreting the regime's stance on the Jews is complicated by apparent contradictions. Inconsistency was a hallmark of Mussolini's dictatorship and a major source of irritation for the regime's allies and enemies alike. When it came to the Italian Jews, international Jewry and Zionism, Mussolini's inconsistencies were egregious but also more apparent than real. Public statements were frequently contradicted in private conversations and interviews in ways deliberately intended to create confusion. As the Israeli historian Meir Michaelis has argued, the regime's position on the Jews accurately reflected its changing relations with Nazi Germany. When Mussolini felt superior to Hitler, as he did immediately after the Nazi seizure of power, he took pleasure in proclaiming his support for the Jews to irritate the Führer. But when Italy moved closer to the Third Reich, as it did in the wake of the invasion of Ethiopia, Mussolini and the regime became more hostile to the Jews.[3]

Contrary to what self-serving Fascists later claimed, there is no evidence that Fascist anti-Semitism was imposed on Mussolini's regime by its German ally. Italian anti-Semitism was home-grown and the German alliance allowed figures who enjoyed the Duce's favour to orchestrate an increasingly vocal and public campaign against the Italian Jews in the two years preceding the introduction of the Racial Laws. This campaign was accompanied by important shifts in the regime's international relations. Following the decision to send Italian troops and equipment to support General Franco and the nationalists in the Spanish Civil War, Italy became more closely aligned with Nazi Germany, while its relations with Britain deteriorated. The Duce stepped up his verbal attacks on British imperialism, and declared Italy's support for the Arab revolt against British rule in Palestine that had been authorized by the League of Nations in 1922. Whereas the regime had previously supported the Zionist cause, Radio Bari, the regime's mouthpiece in North Africa and the Middle East, now adopted increasingly shrill anti-Semitic tones.[4]

Meanwhile at home influential sections of the Fascist press were raising the alarm about the internal 'Jewish Bolshevik threat'. In a widely discussed pamphlet published in September 1936, a prominent supporter of the regime, Alfredo Romanini, claimed that the Jews were the most dangerous enemies of both Fascism and Roman Catholicism, while in the semi-official *Regime Fascista* Roberto Farinacci responded to the appeal made by Joseph Goebbels, Nazi Minister of Propaganda, for a new solidarity against the international Jewish menace. The Rector of the University of Perugia, Paolo Orano, took up the campaign in his book *The Jews of Italy*, which not only denounced Italian Zionists but also questioned the loyalty of pro-Fascist Jews. In May 1937 the journalist Telesio Interlandi ('Mussolini's unofficial mouthpiece') also launched a vicious campaign against Italian Jews and Zionists that was conducted both in Mussolini's *Il Popolo d'Italia* and in Interlandi's own paper *Il Tevere*.[5]

These attacks divided Italian Jews, many of whom insisted on their loyalty both as Italians and as Fascists. Public mobilization of Jewish support for the regime had begun in 1934 when Ettore Ovazza, a committed Fascist and a Jew, had founded a journal called *Nostra Bandiera* in Turin. Ovazza's main concern was to respond to rumours that had begun to spread after sixteen men were arrested at Ponte Tresa near Turin and charged with organizing an anti-Fascist conspiracy. All were acquitted, but the fact that fourteen of the suspects were Jews gave rise to speculations in sections of the Fascist press. In response, Ovazza launched his journal with the aim of demonstrating the devotion of Italian Jews to Fascism, and denouncing Jews who opposed Fascism.[6]

A prime target was the small but influential group of Italian Zionists. Zionism did not have strong support among the majority of Italian Jews, few of whom were attracted by the idea of the return of the Jewish people to the Promised Land. From the time of the Dreyfus affair in France at the end of the nineteenth century, most Italian Jews – like Jews in many other western European states – had thought of Zionism primarily as a humanitarian project. They felt sympathy for fellow Jews in states where they were victims of persecution; they were willing to help them and they thought that a Jewish homeland might offer a solution for them. But Italian Jews themselves showed little interest in leaving Italy. Most considered themselves as much Italian as Jewish and for that reason were wary that the Zionist project might create tensions between their dual identities as Jews and as Italians.[7]

Many have argued that Zionism failed to attract support because Italian Jews considered themselves to be well integrated into Italian society. They formed a very small minority, as is evident from the census data which indicate that in 1938 the number of Italian Jews fell a little short of 48,000. As a religious minority the Italian Jews were thus even fewer than the estimated 60,000 Italian Protestants. Furthermore, Italian Jews – like other Italians – lived lives that were highly regionalized and localized, so that the already modest aggregate number was in reality broken up into a multitude of even smaller local Jewish communities, each with its own history, customs, kinship network, food and distinctive identity. While Jews could be found in all strata of Italian society, nearly all were townspeople and most belonged to the commercial and professional rather than the working classes. Except for Rome, where the tradition of the papal ghetto (closed only in 1870) had created a rather different community, few Italian Jews were strictly orthodox in their practice (as distinct from formal adherence) and the incidence of marriage with non-Jews was more common than in Jewish communities elsewhere in Europe.[8]

The influence of the small group of Zionists had increased, however, partly as a result of the Fascist government's decision in 1930 that every city with a sizeable Jewish community should establish a Jewish Union, which would in turn be affiliated to a national Union of Italian Jewish Communities. In both Rome and Florence members of the small Zionist minority consequently found themselves in important positions. In Rome, for example, the Chief Rabbi, Angelo Sacerdoti, had played a leading part in setting up the new Jewish Union. These institutional changes applied not only to Jews but to all non-Catholic religious minorities and reflected both the corporatist reorganization of the Italian state and Fascism's obsessive urge to centralize. At the same time, they reflected the new limits on religious toleration that had been established in the Concordat of 1929.[9]

For Manduzio and his followers, the existence of the Unions was a real stroke of luck. Had it not been for the creation of the administrative structures of which the Unions were a key part, Manduzio and his followers might never have made contact with the 'leaders' of the Jewish community. Each Jewish community had its own self-governing institutions, and the Union in Rome represented only the Jewish communities in the capital and the surrounding area. In fact, San Nicandro came under the jurisdiction of the Jewish community in Naples, even though the individuals who took an active part in the story were all associated with the Jewish communities in Rome, Florence and Milan. That was because the would-be converts had by chance first established contact with Rome rather than Naples. From the start this meant that their Jewish interlocutors were the small group of Zionists who were especially prominent in Rome and Florence.[10]

None of these men were Fascists, but until 1937 their relations with the regime had been good. The Duce had even on occasions declared his sympathy for the project for a Jewish homeland. He had met with Chaim Weizmann when the President of the World Zionist Organization visited Italy in 1923, and again in 1926 and

1927 after the dictatorship had been established. In the years that followed, the Duce responded positively to the efforts made by the Chief Rabbis Sacerdoti and Prato to strengthen ties with the Jewish communities in Tripoli, Alexandria, Salonica and Rhodes, believing that they might have a part to play in Italy's broader expansionist aims in the Mediterranean and North Africa.

For similar reasons, after the invasion of Ethiopia the Duce decided that for Italy to take an interest in the cause of the Ethiopian Jews would palpably demonstrate the humanitarian concerns that supposedly inspired Italian colonialism. In 1936 he therefore asked Davide Prato to organize a mission to report on the situation of the Ethiopian Jews and their place in the new Italian empire. Prato assigned the task to a prominent pro-Zionist colleague, Carlo Alberto Viterbo, who headed the Italian mission that travelled to Ethiopia a year later.

For the regime, of course, this was little more than an exercise in propaganda and in any case Mussolini was about to turn on the Jewish leaders. The Italian government instructed the Union in Rome to send two delegates to London to protest against the limited sanctions imposed on Italy at Britain's request by the League of Nations following the invasion of Ethiopia. When, as was to be expected, the protests of the Italian Jewish delegates went unheard, they immediately became the target of vicious attacks in the Italian Fascist press acting on behalf of the regime.[11] The campaign against the Italian Zionists now focused on Prato, who after a long and harsh campaign conducted both by Interlandi's newspaper *Il Tevere* and by the pro-Fascist Jews was forced to resign as Chief Rabbi of Rome in 1938. Soon afterwards he left Italy for Palestine, where he would remain until the end of the Second World War. Alfonso Pacifici had made that move three years earlier, but after Prato's departure Dante Lattes, Augusto Levi (President of the Italian Zionist Association), Umberto Nahum and other leading Italian Zionists followed. Carlo Alberto Viterbo and others remained in Italy, but their lives were made increasingly difficult.

Of the group of Italian Jews who had befriended the San Nicandro would-be converts, by the spring of 1938 Cantoni was the only one left in Italy. But even his ability to assist them was now severely limited. Following the annexation of Austria to the German Reich (*Anschluss*) in March, the numbers of Austrian and eastern European Jews in transit through Italy grew, while the foreign Jews who were temporarily living in Italy were also ordered to leave. As many as 4,000 foreign Jews were estimated to be seeking passage from Italy to other destinations, and about a thousand more were in need of temporary accommodation, while a similar number were waiting to leave Austria. Cantoni's work on behalf of these refugees was relentlessly demanding. At the same time, he faced mounting attacks from pro-Fascist Jews owing to his association with Davide Prato and the Italian Zionists. Then just weeks before his first visit to San Nicandro, he was deeply affected by the news that Carlo Rosselli (founder of Giustizia e Libertà) and his brother Nello had been assassinated in Normandy by French Fascists acting on orders from Rome.[12]

Opposition from pro-Fascist Jewish organizations in 1938 forced Cantoni to abandon public involvement in his work for the Milanese Jewish Refugee Committee. In collaboration with Giuseppe Fano in Trieste he then founded the Committee for Assisting Jews in Italy (COMASABIT), but a year later the police closed that down because of Cantoni's involvement. Thanks to vigorous protests by the new President of the Union of Jewish Communities in Rome, Dante Almansi, the Fascist Chief of Police Bocchini personally agreed to the establishment of a new charitable organization. This was the Delegation to Assist Emigrating Jews (DELASEM), in which Raffaele Cantoni and Carlo Alberto Viterbo, the leader of the Italian mission to Ethiopia to investigate the Falasha, were the key players. Cantoni again took a particular interest in the organization of camps for the foreign Jews in need of temporary accommodation. As well as helping foreign Jews in transit, by 1940 DELASEM claimed to have assisted nearly 3,000 foreign Jews in leaving Italy, mainly from Trieste.[13]

Although the attitude of the Fascist authorities towards Cantoni was inconsistent, his activities and movements were now being followed ever more closely by the regime's secret police. Their reports kept referring to his trial by the Special Tribunal in 1930, claiming that he should have been shot and that his acquittal had been the result of intervention by 'mysterious' protectors whose identities were not known. The prime suspect was his sister Pina (Giuseppina) who lived in Florence and was described as being wealthy and 'one hundred per cent Zionist'. She was suspected of making bribes on her brother's behalf to unknown persons high in the regime. One suspected 'protector' was the former 'intransigent Secretary of the PNF', Roberto Farinacci, who had also been a leading figure in the campaign against the Italian Jews.[14]

The language now used in the police reports on Cantoni clearly indicated how the regime's preoccupations had changed. In the earlier files he was always referred to as a 'notorious opponent of the regime and a Freemason'. By 1938, however, the fact that he was 'dangerous in every respect and especially because of his skill in evading detection' was linked instead to the fact that he was 'a crafty, scheming and unscrupulous Jew'.[15] According to 'confidential reports' (that is, information from spies), Cantoni was engaged in a massive operation to swindle Jews of their property and jewels. The police alleged that he persuaded unsuspecting wealthy Jews to part with their valuables and money, which he claimed he would send abroad to avoid seizure by the government. He was accused of fraud, of spreading false information, of openly criticizing the regime and of being a defeatist (even though Italy was not yet at war!). Yet, despite repeated requests, the authorities in Milan, Venice and Florence were unable to come up with evidence to substantiate any of these claims.

Cantoni must have known that the net was closing in on him, however, because in 1940 he applied for a passport to emigrate to Palestine. The request was at first refused, and then unexpectedly approved – but on the very day it was issued the passport was revoked on the personal instructions of Chief of Police Bocchini, whose brief handwritten note on Cantoni's file simply stated: 'Enough of this! Time to lock him up.'[16] Cantoni was arrested in June 1940, two days after Italy entered the Second World War, removing the last Jewish friend of the would-be converts of San Nicandro.

News of these events would reach San Nicandro only very slowly. It was the last thing that the community wanted to hear. Their situation had been gradually deteriorating ever since Cantoni's last visit in October 1937, which had not only failed to heal the rifts in the community, but had provoked new ones. No sooner had his train left than Costantino Tritto's wife complained that it was an outrage that Cantoni had stayed at Manduzio's house and had refused her invitation to be their guest. Despite various attempts at reconciliation, relations between Manduzio and Francesco Cerrone also deteriorated, exacerbated by the latter – in desperation – continuing to work on the sabbath. In an attempt to assert his authority, Manduzio insisted that both Cerrone and Leone (who also worked on Saturdays) should relinquish the prayer shawls that Cantoni had given them until such time as they were prepared to observe the rules and rituals properly. This order was the source of further wrangles and bad feeling.

Nor had the eagerly awaited official permission to hold prayer meetings materialized. Cerrone finally decided to go to Foggia to make inquiries, but was astonished to learn that, despite the information they had been given at the police station in San Nicandro, no authorization had ever been issued, nor was there any correspondence or request from the Podestà of San Nicandro on the subject.[17] When Cerrone came back with this news the community was thrown into consternation. More letters were written to Cantoni, to Rome and even to Naples, but there were no replies. Manduzio again wrote to the Chief Rabbi Davide Prato and to Carlo Alberto Viterbo in Rome, but they did not reply. Nor until early in 1938 was there any word even from Cantoni, who finally sent a brief letter to apologize for the delay. Without further explanation he said that Rabbi Prato was visiting Palestine, but that as soon as he returned he would assuredly take up the matter. Shortly afterwards ten copies of the Hebrew Bible (in translation) and ten copies of the Book of Psalms arrived from Florence.

Fears that they had been abandoned intensified after Manduzio received a letter from the community in Naples informing him that, because they had not been born Jews and their conversion was as yet not recognized, neither the Jewish community in Rome nor that in Naples could officially take them under their jurisdiction. More letters were written to Rome and Florence, but after a long delay only Cantoni replied. He apologized again for not writing sooner and again without going into further details he told Manduzio that 'the whole world has been turned upside down and even the Chief Rabbi is in danger because of his recent visit to the Holy Land'.[18]

Manduzio and his followers remained under regular police scrutiny. All their mail was still being intercepted, and Cerrone, whom the police still believed to be the leader of the group, had been called in for questioning. He was asked specifically whether he and his co-religionists were receiving money from the Union of Italian Jewish Communities in Rome. Cerrone denied this categorically, although he acknowledged that five years earlier when his wife gave birth to twins he had received a money order for 100 lire from the community in Rome. He denied that Cantoni had given anyone in San Nicandro any money during his visits in 1937, and added that it was not until the rite of circumcision had been performed and their conversion fully acknowledged that the group could expect to receive any financial assistance.[19]

From their interview with Cerrone, the police rightly concluded that 'the Jewish movement in San Nicandro is of very limited significance'. Nonetheless, the would-be converts remained under close watch. Meanwhile in 1939 police action against members of other religious minorities was also being stepped up. In the neighbouring town of Lesina, for example, Michele Parigino, a thirty-nine-year-old farm labourer and evangelical Protestant, was arrested in March for 'making blasphemous statements against the religion of the State' ('vilipendio contro la religione dello Stato'). The incident took place on the eve of the town's principal religious festival, when 'after drinking too much wine' Parigino had paraded around the town holding a banner on which was written 'Turn to Christ and you will have Eternal Life'. Then he started tearing down posters for the celebration of the local patron saint on the following day, crying out in loud voice, 'This is all rubbish' ('fesserie'). He was denounced to the police by the parish priest and arrested under article 402 of the Penal Code and an official noted that: 'The arrest has produced an excellent effect in the town, since Parigino's unseemly behaviour had provoked much public indignation.' In Cerignola, a town near Foggia, charges were brought by the local parish priest against Sabatino Doria, a thirty-one-year-old labourer who was accused of proselytizing on behalf of a 'religious sect know as the "Skakers" (presumably Shakers)'. In this case, however, the police decided that the claims made by the parish priest were false and probably malicious. Doria 'did nothing more than read the Evangelical Bible at home and in fact only rarely attended the meetings held in the church of the Waldensian Protestants'.[20]

The campaign against religious dissidents in general was becoming more intense at the very moment that the regime chose to target the Jews. When the first Racial Laws were introduced in September 1938 the government decided to open a formal inquiry into the case of the Jewish converts in San

Nicandro and, through the Italian Embassy to the Holy See, forwarded a memorandum to Cardinal Eugenio Pacelli, the Pope's Secretary of State and future Pope Pius XII, requesting information about them. The San Nicandro case was now brought to the attention of the highest officials in the Fascist dictatorship and in the Vatican of Pius XI, and the language used by both the state and the Church authorities in the exchanges that followed is highly revealing of the attitudes they shared when it came to religious and racial minorities. But the exchanges also demonstrate the deep tensions within the project for nationalizing religion in Italy.

The Italian government's memorandum was marked 'classified'. Based on the police reports previously sent to Rome by the Prefecture of Foggia, its purpose was to inform Cardinal Pacelli about '*a strange phenomenon of Jewish proselytism that has occurred in the town of San Nicandro Garganico, with specific reference to the conversion of persons of the Italian race to the Jewish religion*' (all underlined in the original).[21] The report stated that for about seven years some seven families had been practising the Jewish religion in San Nicandro under the guidance of the general community of Jews in Rome. They were also in communication with a Jewish accountant named Raffaele Cantoni. The families recognized as their leader a shoemaker named Francesco Cerrone. 'None of the group or their relatives own land, they all live in very lowly economic conditions, none of them are members of the PNF and their religious activities are limited to meeting every Saturday in the house of Manduzio, Donato, in Via del Gargano No. 56.'

Flatly contradicting earlier police reports, and without giving reasons, the memorandum claimed that all had previous convictions and one of them, Vincenzo di Salvia, had been sentenced to twenty-two years' imprisonment for desertion. Before their conversion to the Jewish religion – 'to which they must have been drawn by some promise of financial gain' – they had all been practising Catholics. It appeared to be the case that some months before some of them had wished to submit to circumcision, but this had not happened. The report concluded with a request: 'The Minister will be pleased to know whether the Ecclesiastical Authorities can provide any information on this subject.' Cardinal Pacelli's office forwarded the memorandum to Monsignor Giuseppe di Girolamo, the Bishop of Lucera. Before replying, the Bishop consulted the parish priest in San Nicandro, who confirmed that for several years there had been a group of 'delinquent fanatics in that town who camouflage themselves under the name of *sabattini* and who claim to be followers of the Jewish religion'. According to the priest, their leader was a certain Cerrone, 'a shoemaker of lowly extraction, who is lame and a petty crook', and they received alms and encouragement from outside. However, he acknowledged that the group was 'very small and did not engage in any activity, other than to meet in private houses'.

The parish priest went on to say that he had frequently reported these people and their activities to the Carabinieri, who had taken no action. The Bishop seized on this to voice his own complaint that 'the same was true when the police were asked to take action against the Protestants'. At the parish priest's urgent request a police officer had finally been sent to investigate, but reported that he had only found what he described as 'four wretched, dirty and irresponsible creatures'. It seems that the police could see no reason for pursuing the matter further. The Bishop went on to reassure the Cardinal Secretary of State that everything had been done 'to repress this sect, using the same measures that we have adopted to combat the Protestants'. But he also expressed the hope that the government's new interest was a sign that 'the clergy will now finally have the support from the government that they have so often called for, and with which their actions may now finally prove effective and lead to positive results'. The Bishop closed with a further complaint: 'despite everything that has been done to combat the Protestants, the Prefect of Foggia still allows them to practise their cult'.

In relaying this message to the government, Cardinal Pacelli's office decided to tone down the original, replacing the reference to the 'group of delinquent fanatics' in San Nicandro, for example, with the more neutral phrase 'certain persons'. However, the complaints against the failure of the state authorities to support the clergy in their campaign against the religious minorities and above all the Protestants went forward without modification.

The government's interest in the converts of San Nicandro did not end there. In 1939 and again in 1940 the Interior Ministry asked the Prefecture of Foggia to provide further information, and the case finally came to the personal attention of the Duce's vigilant Police Chief, Arturo Bocchini. From the start Bocchini had been personally involved in the measures taken against the religious minorities. As we have seen, in 1935 he had been the author of the notorious Buffarini-Guidi circular and in 1939 he was on the warpath again, whipping up the campaign against Pentecostalists, Seventh Day Adventists and Jehovah's Witnesses, whose destruction was now entrusted to the regime's secret counter-espionage agency, the much feared OVRA.

On 22 August 1939 he issued another circular on the dangers posed by 'The Religious Sect Known as Pentecostalists and Others'. Stating, quite wrongly, that there was no difference between the Pentecostalists and Jehovah's Witnesses, the memorandum claimed that both were religious cults that had 'no roots in Italian society' and had been imported from abroad, notably from the United States, with subversive intent. It was 'common knowledge' that the evangelicals covertly criticized and attacked the government, capitalism, war, the clergy and above all the Catholic Church. In their worship, they assumed 'ecstatic poses and give themselves up to prolix invocations, lamentations, cries and screams as well as gestures that cause their whole bodies to shake (hence they are often called "shakers")'.

Although they never openly attacked the government or discussed politics, they were always actively proselytizing their faith: 'It is therefore evident that spiritually they are rebellious against all forms of law which makes them by definition anti-fascists who consider themselves to be above the law'. With a heightented sense of alarm the circular went on to state that when members of these cults were enlisted they refused to touch firearms or weapons, making them 'in many ways even more dangerous than political subversives because they act on the religious sentiment of individuals, which is very much deeper than any political sentiment; they are capable of inspiring true forms of fanaticism and are invariably unwilling to accept any reasoning or regulation'. The followers of the evangelical sects acknowledged no religious authority and they practised 'individualism even with regard to politics'. Given the danger these doctrines posed for the existing order 'it is legitimate to suspect that these aforementioned doctrines have been spread by foreign agents or at least by means of foreign money with the purpose of challenging our political regime, demoralizing the national spirit and propagating anti-militarism'.

For those reasons, the police and OVRA agents began to arrest members of these banned Churches, many of whom were given harsh prison sentences or periods of confinement on one of the islands off the Italian coast that were used as penal colonies by the regime. In these operations, the police and the OVRA agents could rely on full and enthusiastic assistance from the clergy and the bishops.[22] In this climate of severe repression, it was an ominous sign that Bocchini should have taken a personal interest in the would-be converts of San Nicandro. The day after an apparently convivial dinner in Rome in June 1940, during which the Police Chief had chatted with his old friend Cavaliere Dolfino, who had recently been appointed prefect of Foggia, Dolfino wrote to thank

Bocchini ('cara Eccellenza') for the excellent meal and to respond to his 'verbal inquiry about the so-called Jews of San Nicandro Garganico'.

The Prefect ran through the now familiar information in the police files, claiming that the leader was 'a certain Francesco Cerrone, a shoemaker born in Carpino but domiciled for some time in San Nicandro'. Dolfino now offered the additional information that Cerrone had converted to the Jewish religion 'at the suggestion of a brother who has emigrated to America, mainly we can assume because he hoped to draw some material advantage from this'. He went on mention the visit by the notorious anti-Fascist Raffaele Cantoni in 1937, but stated that since then 'the Jewish community of which we speak has remained static and lives a rather lean life, while no one else in the town seems even to know about them'. He concluded that 'although the adherents are not members of the Fascist Party, they live in very wretched economic conditions and their conduct does not give grounds for concern. In any case they do not attempt to proselytize or indulge in any form of propaganda.' Nonetheless all their mail was inspected and they were subject to regular checks and questioning by the officers of the police headquarters and by the Carabinieri.[23]

The authorities' belief that he was the leader had already caused the unfortunate Cerrone a lot of trouble. In a letter to Rome in 1940 he complained that the Podestà of San Nicandro was conducting a personal vendetta against him. Despite the fact that he had been out of work for years, had eight children and a wife who was now pregnant again with their ninth child, his name had been removed from the provincial list of 'destitute and deserving' families, which meant that he had lost the small subsidy that came with this.[24] Even worse, the Podestà had told him that under the Racial Laws of September 1938 he and his family, being Jews, could not continue to reside in an Aryan neighbourhood and would be evicted from their house. For the same reason, his children could no longer attend the village schools and his sons were no longer eligible for service in the army.

Cerrone had again been questioned by the police and when they asked him whether he was a Jew, according to the story that was subsequently often retold, he replied that he was an Italian but also a Jew, and that he observed the sabbath just as Mussolini had ordered. This respect for the Duce was not feigned, and in his correspondence Cerrone frequently invoked Mussolini's authority, claiming for example that he read the Bible because the Duce had declared that it was the most beautiful book ever written. In their letters to Rome both Cerrone and Manduzio had suggested that the Union should ask the Duce to intervene personally to obtain the permission they needed to worship. In 1940 Cerrone also suggested to Raffaele Cantoni that the Union of Italian Jewish Communities should personally inform the Duce of the ways in which he and his fellow co-religionists in San Nicandro were being mistreated.[25]

Cerrone's belief that Mussolini might come to their rescue is an interesting illustration of the imaginary representation of the Duce at this time. But Cerrone was not the only member of the group to face harassment by the police. Costantino Tritto was brought in for questioning by the police on at least two occasions, and like Cerrone he was asked to state whether he was an Italian or a Jew. Costantino's son, Eliezer, in his later memoir remembered that he and the children of the other members of the community now faced problems at school: 'They were all Fascists, the teachers, the headmaster and the others, and they told us Jewish kids that we could not come to school any more because they said that we did not make the sign of the Cross at the time of prayer – and in fact like the other Jewish children I was not able to stay at school after the Third Elementary Class.'[26]

Understandably, the would-be converts felt abandoned and were increasingly apprehensive. Even before his community learned of the Racial Laws, Manduzio in his letters to Rome had become increasingly querulous. He repeatedly demanded to know why their messages had received no replies and why they were still without authorization to meet and pray together. When news of the laws against the Jews did finally reach them in the early months of 1939, the San Nicandresi still could not understand why they were not getting replies from Rome and they were also still unaware that Rabbi Prato and the others had been forced to leave Italy. Despairing at the lack of news from Rome, Manduzio asked Cirò di Salvia to find out what was going on. When he arrived in Rome, Di Salvia was treated with great courtesy by Israel Zolli, the Polish-born rabbi from Trieste who had recently been appointed to replace Prato as Chief Rabbi. But in reply to his request for guidance Di Salvia received only comforting words: they must follow the Law. When Di Salvia returned to San Nicandro, Manduzio again wrote to Rome to protest at their abandonment, but he finally received a firm reply. The Chief Rabbi told the would-be converts that they had no reason to fear: 'You are not Jews because you were neither born Jews nor has your conversion ever been legally completed'.

The rabbi's words were intended to reassure the would-be converts, but Manduzio was outraged. He and his followers were not concerned that they might be in danger because of the new laws against the Jews. Their concern was quite different. They were worried precisely because the Jews in Rome still refused to recognize them as Jews – as was made explicit in the rabbi's letter. For over a year, Manduzio insisted, he and his followers had been actively asking for recognition and above all for circumcision, without which (as was now clear from the Rabbi's letter) their conversion was still not recognized. He added that they had all undergone the 'circumcision of the spirit', and he was utterly confounded to learn now that this was not enough.[27] At this point even Manduzio seems to have become uncertain about his faith. As he had done before, he now went back to meet with the group of Seventh Day Adventists in nearby Lesina. The encounter, however, reconfirmed his belief that the Jewish faith was the only true religion.

Nonetheless, his leadership was again under threat, and his leading critics, Angelo Marrochella and his wife, were now the most recent recruits to the small community. From the start they had been a problem. First they wanted to move the meeting place to their own house despite the fact that they lived a little way outside San Nicandro. Then they repeatedly questioned the dietary rules imposed by Manduzio; they claimed not to understand why they should not eat pork. Moreover, Manduzio knew that despite their repeated denials, Marrochella's wife, a seamstress, worked on the sabbath. There were other disputes that remained unsettled and constantly threatened to disrupt the small community. Vincenzo di Salvia, for example, continued to beat his wife and served another term in jail. Antonio Bonfitto and his wife Concetta di Leo still lived under the same roof, but he – and now his eldest son – refused to associate in any way with the group. In the meantime Costantino Tritto and Francesco Cerrone had broken off their friendship after Cerrone's attempts to lure away Tritto's trade, which at least divided Manduzio's critics.

Things did not augur well for the small community. Its wounds were unhealed and the regime's attitude towards non-Catholics was becoming increasingly repressive. Despite all this, Manduzio somehow kept his faith and continued to write angry and insistent letters to Rome, all of which went unanswered. He finally received a brief letter from Raffaele Cantoni stating that he had been arrested and had just arrived in the penal colony on the Tremiti islands, almost in sight of San Nicandro, where he had been sent to serve his sentence. Manduzio was saddened to learn of his friend's arrest and imprisonment, but Cantoni's letter also gave him new hope. The long silence and the lack of replies to his letters did not mean that the community had been forgotten and abandoned by its friends in Rome. He understood now that they were fellow victims of persecution, and this news gave him reassurance and strengthened his faith.[28]

By then Mussolini had declared war on France and Great Britain, setting a course that would soon result in disaster for Italy and also bring unexpected new turns in the story of the would-be converts of San Nicandro.

# CHAPTER SIX

# Falling into the Net

Italy declared war on France and Britain on 10 June 1940, two days before the arrest of Raffaele Cantoni. The war was slow to reach San Nicandro, but when it did finally come to the remote Gargano promontory it would transform the story of the would-be converts. A critical part in that transformation was played by an encounter with a group of Jewish soldiers serving as volunteers in the British Eighth Army there. This meeting was the more remarkable because No. 178 General Transport Company of the Royal Army Service Corps was one of only a handful of units made up of Jewish volunteers from Palestine serving with the British army at the time. To understand who these volunteers were, how they came to be serving in the army and what they were doing in southern Italy we must first retrace the events that brought Mussolini's war to San Nicandro.

When Italy entered the war, Mussolini's generals launched offensives against Greece (October 1940) and against the small force of British and Commonwealth troops that guarded Egypt. In contrast to those in the Balkans, the Italian operations in North Africa at first proved to be quite successful, until the initial Italian gains were swiftly reversed by the counter-offensive by British and Commonwealth troops known as Operation Compass. By the end of February 1941, the Italians had retreated

800 kilometres, abandoned Cyrenaica and left some 130,000 of their men and no fewer than twenty-two generals as prisoners.

By then Italian forces were also facing serious difficulties in Greece, forcing Hitler to come to the Duce's aid. In February General Erwin Rommel arrived to take command in North Africa, and under his leadership the military position of the Axis partners was quickly restored. By the summer of 1942 there seemed little to stop the Germans invading Egypt and Palestine, and so gaining control over the entire Middle East. But that was not to happen. In Russia, which Hitler had invaded in June 1941, the German offensive was blocked at Stalingrad, while in North Africa General Bernard Montgomery's victory at the second battle of El Alamein (October–November 1942) proved to be decisive and in Churchill's words marked for Britain 'the end of the beginning' of the war. The entry of the United States into the war following the Japanese attack on Pearl Harbor in December 1941 had already shifted the potential military balance decisively. By the spring of 1943 the Allies were fully in control of North Africa. The next step would be the invasion of Italy, beginning with the landings in Sicily in July 1943.

The invasion of Sicily led to the temporary fall of Mussolini, who was deposed on 25 July by a coup orchestrated by the King, senior members of the Fascist regime and a number of generals. The Duce was arrested and bundled out of Rome, but shortly afterwards he was rescued by German paratroopers and installed as head of a puppet Nazi satellite government in northern Italy. With Nazi support the revived Fascist government – the Italian Social Republic, or more simply the Republic of Salò – survived until April 1945.

On 8 September 1943, the day before the Allied landings in the Gulf of Salerno began, the Italian government's surrender was finally announced after long prevarication. Accompanied by his ministers, courtiers and senior military advisers, King Victor Emmanuel III secretly and under cover of night fled from Rome, shamefully abandoning the armed forces and the Italian people to their fate. The royal entourage made its way first to Ancona and then by sea to Bari, which became the temporary seat of the royal government headed by General Badoglio. Italy's former ally, Nazi Germany, not the royal government in Bari, now determined the fate of the Italian people. Anticipating the Italian surrender to the Allies, Hitler had reinforced German defensive positions in Italy and, before the Allied landings, had moved major reserves of armour and troops to the peninsula. When the Allies landed, the German commander, Field Marshal Albert Kesselring, was well prepared and it would take twenty long months before the Allies finally reached Milan on 25 April 1945, just five days before Hitler's suicide in Berlin.

From September 1943 to April 1945 Italy was cut in two. As soon as the King fled from Rome, the Germans occupied the Eternal City and all of central and northern Italy fell under the control of the Nazis and their Italian Fascist collaborators. The territory under Nazi and Fascist control diminished only very slowly. Rome was liberated in June 1944, Florence in August of the same year, while Bologna, Genoa and Turin remained, like Milan, under Fascist control and Nazi occupation until the following spring.

During these long months the civilian populations in the occupied zones were exposed to the dangers of military operations and to repeated Allied strategic bombing raids. There were severe shortages of food and other necessities, and civilians were at risk of being caught in the crossfire of an increasingly fierce civil war waged between Italian Fascists and anti-Fascists. Many became victims of the savage reprisals wreaked by the German army. For both Italian Jews and the foreign Jews who found themselves in the occupied territories this was a time of extreme danger. The Nazis lost no time in implementing the Final Solution. Between 18 and 23 October 1943, some 1,680 Jewish men, women and children were rounded up in Rome and deported to the death camps. Similar actions followed in other

Italian cities under German control, and it is estimated that nearly 8,000 Italian Jews were killed between 1943 and 1945.[1]

The South of the country escaped some of these horrors, but was far from unscathed. From the moment that North Africa became a major theatre of combat, Allied bombers had targeted the principal southern Italian cities and ports, partly to undermine civilian morale, but above all to prevent supplies reaching the Axis forces in North Africa. The southern ports were easy and largely unprotected targets. Naples soon earned the unenviable title of being Italy's most frequently and heavily bombed city, but (in Sicily) Palermo, Messina, Catania and Gela and (on the mainland) Salerno, Bari and Manfredonia all suffered repeated attacks and high civilian casualties.[2]

After the invasion of Sicily, the bombing raids on the mainland intensified and the war now moved closer to San Nicandro. Because a number of airfields were situated close by, and above all because it was the main hub for the Adriatic railway system, Foggia was the target for three especially heavy air raids in August 1943, the last of which continued for two days and resulted in an estimated 20,000 civilian deaths. When the raid ended one eyewitness declared that 'the city of Foggia no longer exists'. Long afterwards, Eliezer Tritto could still recall the horror when the news of what had happened in Foggia reached San Nicandro. But neither San Nicandro nor the other towns of the Gargano peninsula were bombed, and locally many attributed this to the intercession of Manduzio's neighbour, Padre Pio, the popular stigmatic monk of San Giovanni Rotonda. The story was that as the RAF pilots flew their bombers towards the Adriatic they were met by a vision in the sky in the form of a bearded figure in a monk's cowl. In his outstretched arm he held a crucifix, and the pilots heard a voice begging them to turn away and spare the towns below.[3]

A more convincing explanation is that there was nothing of military or strategic significance on the Gargano peninsula.

Nonetheless, the war did not leave San Nicandro untouched and many of the younger men had joined the army either as volunteers or because they had been conscripted. Of Manduzio's followers, Angelo Marrochella had volunteered in 1940, while Eliezer's elder brother Antonio and one of the Di Salvia boys had been conscripted. Antonio was captured by the Germans near Bolzano in 1943, although he later managed to escape. His companion never returned.

Eliezer Tritto remembered that it was in the weeks immediately before the Allied landings that the first German armoured columns were sighted in San Nicandro. The town authorities were sufficiently alarmed to warn Eliezer's father that he should remove the Star of David badge that he liked to wear on his lapel, since it might provoke serious German reprisals against the whole town. The most worrying incident was when some German officers, who were strolling down the main street, decided out of sheer curiosity to enter Manduzio's house. Like everyone in San Nicandro, during the hot days his doorway was covered only by a screen of dried reeds. When the officers entered the house they found Manduzio seated at his table, but their attention was immediately caught by the Hebrew scripts, the Ten Commandments and other Hebrew insignia including the Star of David on the walls. They were there for over half an hour, during which time the news of their visit spread around the entire neighbourhood, throwing everyone into a state of panic. When the Germans came out they did not say a word, but simply carried on their stroll, never to return. Eliezer took this to be a sign that God had protected the little community in this moment of grave danger.[4] The arrival of Allied forces in September 1943 spared the people of San Nicandro from further danger, although like the rest of the population of southern Italy they would have to endure two more years of desperate shortages of food, fuel and other necessities.

The Jewish soldiers appeared in San Nicandro early in 1944. They were part of Eighth Army, whose units had liberated what remained of Foggia at the end of September 1943. After landing near Reggio Calabria on 3 September, Eighth Army's mechanized units had joined forces with an airborne division near Taranto before pushing northwards along the Adriatic coast. Despite dogged German resistance, they reached Foggia on 28 September, Manfredonia on the 30th and San Severo on 3 October.

Two days earlier the main body of the invasion force had entered Naples, but soon afterwards the Allied advance stalled. Under Kesselring's command the Germans had taken up strong defensive positions along a chain of fortifications known as the Winter Line that ran from Gaeta in the west to the Sangro river in the east. During what proved to be an unusually long, wet and cold winter the Allies repeatedly but unsuccessfully tried to break the heavily fortified German line, and it was only after heavy loss of life in the offensives against the German positions at Monte Cassino that they finally succeeded. At the cost of further heavy casualties, the Allies had meanwhile managed to establish fragile beach-heads further north around Anzio. When General Kesselring decided to pull back from the Winter Line the Allies were finally able to break out. On 4 June, two days before the start of Operation Overlord and the Allied landings in Normandy, US and Allied troops entered Rome as the Germans withdrew.

Except for those that were recalled to England to prepare for the Normandy landings, the Eighth Army units that had reached Foggia in September 1943 stayed there until the following spring. Meanwhile in December they were joined by No. 178 GT Company RASC, a motor transport unit that had recently shipped from Egypt. Its commander, Major Wellesley Aron, set up his operational HQ in Foggia in January 1944. The Company's task was to support the military units stationed throughout the province of Foggia and along the Adriatic coast, and its transports carried a wide range of supplies. These included timber needed for military construction, for which the best source was the ancient forests on the tip of the Gargano promontory. As a result, the lorries of No. 178 Company travelled regularly along the Gargano Provincial Highway, which took them directly past the house of Donato Manduzio in San Nicandro.

As well as their regimental and divisional markings, the lorries also carried the six-pointed Star of David, and it was not long before they were noticed. Early one morning as the drivers approached the bend in the road they saw a group of men and boys who were holding up a hastily improvised banner displaying the Star of David. The drivers stopped and came over to investigate, and Eliezer Tritto, who at the time was fourteen years old, later described what followed:

> There were a lot of soldiers and officers, and they came over and asked us what we wanted from them. We told them that we were Jews. They were astonished to discover Jews in the mountains of the Gargano and they immediately entered Manduzio's house where he quickly told them our story. After that day, their visits to Manduzio were frequent and they always brought candies and chocolates for us kids.[5]

The encounter was reported to Major Aron. Curious to learn more, he asked one of his NCOs, Corporal Pinchas Spitzer (also known as Phinn Lapide), who spoke some Italian, to accompany him and act as interpreter.

Major Aron's men were not the only Palestinian Jews serving with Eighth Army, however, and news of the San Nicandro encounter travelled fast. Out of curiosity many visitors now made the journey to San Nicandro, among them Major E. Aronov, commander of the 1st Jewish Camouflage Company (Royal Engineers), and the senior Jewish chaplain in Eighth Army, Captain Ephraim Elimelech Urbach. Corporal Spitzer acted as interpreter at all these meetings, since none of Manduzio's followers spoke either Hebrew or English. Most of the Jewish visitors reacted with astonishment to the discovery of a group of families who at this moment wanted to become Jews. They were also fascinated by the ways in which the would-be converts had improvised Jewish festivals and rituals, although there was some scepticism. Rabbi Urbach in particular was far from satisfied by the answers he received when he quizzed Manduzio about his beliefs, and above all about his visions and dreams.

This might well have been little more than one of those chance but transitory encounters thrown up in the chaos of war, had it not been for the backgrounds of the Jewish soldiers and the reasons that had brought them to southern Italy with the British forces. While there were Jewish volunteers from Palestine serving in other units of Eighth Army, Wellesley Aron's Company was one of only two units that was composed exclusively of Jewish volunteers. This was no accident. Major Aron's RASC Transport Company had its own remarkable story.[6] Its origins were rooted in the complex relations between the British and the Palestinian Jews, and above all in the long-running controversy over the proposal for the creation of a Jewish army that began when Britain went to war with Germany.

Soon after the war started the British government came under strong pressure both at home and abroad to create a Jewish combat force to fight the Germans. Chaim Weizmann, the President of the Zionist Organization, was a leading advocate of the project, which was strongly supported by the principal British spokesmen of the Zionist Organization, such as the historian Lewis Namier, Lord Rothschild and Lord Strabolgi. From the start the proposal was fiercely opposed by the British military and colonial authorities. In military terms a separate Jewish combat force would be anomalous and impractical, they claimed, but above all their objections were political. The creation of a Jewish combat force, they insisted, would be seen as a hostile move throughout the Arab world, whose support Britain desperately needed because of its precarious military position in the Middle East and in North Africa. There was also concern that such a force might be used to resist British rule in Palestine.

Hostility to the British authorities was also running high among Palestinian Jews, whose hopes had been raised when in 1937 a Royal Commission headed by Lord Peel had recommended that Palestine be partitioned into separate Jewish and Arab states. Those hopes were dashed in May 1939 when Neville Chamberlain's government published a White Paper that severely limited Jewish immigration to and land purchase in Palestine and proposed the eventual establishment of a mixed Jewish and Arab state. This change of policy reflected the British government's recognition that war with Germany was now almost inevitable. For that reason the government was especially concerned about the dangerous weakness of Britain's military position in the Middle East, which made it imperative to maintain good relations with the Arab rulers and avoid further Arab unrest in Palestine.[7] The White Paper was a placatory move. For most Zionists, however, it was a disgraceful betrayal of Britain's commitment to establishing a Jewish home, which had been proclaimed in the Balfour Declaration of 1917. They were all the more indignant because during the Arab revolt against the British mandate in Palestine that had started in 1936, the Jewish population had co-operated with the British authorities, and had been allowed to create militias that operated under the direction of the British army.

Against a background of rising tensions in Palestine, the Zionist leader David Ben Gurion declared: 'We shall fight the White Paper as if there were no war, and we shall fight the war as if there were no White Paper.' Although this was not a formula that all Zionists felt they could support, it raised the issue of a Jewish combat force. To discuss this, Moshe Shertok, the head of the Political Department of the Jewish Agency in Palestine, met General Archibald Wavell, at that time commander of the British forces in the Middle East, in Cairo in September 1939. Wavell told him bluntly that the political repercussions in the Arab world would far outweigh any military benefits such a combat force might have. The Arabs, he said, would see it as a sign of British support for a Jewish military take-over in Palestine after the war. Reporting to the War Office after the meeting, Wavell warned that every effort should be made 'to try to keep the politicians from any rash measures or promises'.[8] British military intelligence sources in the Middle East supported the generals. The strength of the reactions to the 1939 White Paper raised fears that the more extreme Jewish underground organizations might be used against the British authorities in Palestine. The intelligence reports also warned that, were a Jewish combat force to be created, it would be little more than an extension of the Haganah, the underground armed Zionist defence force.[9]

The fall of Chamberlain and the formation of Churchill's government in May 1940 raised Zionist hopes again since the new Prime Minister was known to be sympathetic to the creation of a Jewish combat force along lines similar to the Free French, Polish and Czech armies. In January 1941 Chaim Weizmann met the Colonial Secretary, Lord Lloyd, and proposed the creation of a more limited Jewish combat force of 10,000 men, of whom 3,000 would be raised in Palestine. Lloyd's reply was that the government favoured the project, but could not yet commit to a specific date. When he heard of Weizmann's proposal, Wavell again thundered that the project 'would cause a great deal of trouble in the Middle East'. Churchill dismissed his protests: 'General Wavell, like most British senior officers, is strongly pro-Arab . . . I am not in the least convinced by this stuff.' But he gave instructions that 'the Jewish Army project must be put off for six months . . . The sole reason to be given should be the lack of equipment'.[10] But it was not until three years later, in July 1944, that the War Cabinet finally gave its approval to the formation of a Jewish combat force, which in any case fell far short of the project for a Jewish army. In its place a Jewish Brigade Group (JBG) was formed in Italy in September 1944 with a strength of 330 officers and 6,500 men.

Many of those who joined the newly formed JBG had previously served as volunteers in different units of Eighth Army, including Major Aron's Company. The reason for their presence was the seriousness of Britain's military situation in North Africa in 1941, which led the government to start recruiting both Jewish and Arab volunteer forces to defend Palestine against a German invasion should Egypt fall. Some of these recruits were also sent to Egypt, but only in non-combat roles.[11] That was how Wellesley Aron's No. 178 GT Company (RASC) came into being. But it had never been the intention of the British army that this should be a unit composed exclusively of Jewish personnel. That was Major Aron's doing.

Wellesley Aron was a remarkable man whose background perfectly equipped him to play a part in the story of Manduzio and his followers. He was born in London in 1901 to German Jewish parents who returned to Germany in 1914 just before hostilities broke out. After brief internment they spent the war in Switzerland. In 1918 they returned to England and while a student at Cambridge Aron became a convinced Zionist and moved to Palestine. In 1928, at the request of Chaim Weizmann, he returned to London to act as assistant political secretary of the World Zionist Organization. While in London he founded the Jewish youth movement, Habonim. He returned to Tel Aviv in 1930 where he ran a successful commercial advertising agency. He knew most of the leaders of the Zionist movement in Palestine and in 1937 had sent General Wavell a plan for mobilizing resources in the event of war.[12]

When the war broke out in 1939, Aron was the first Palestinian Jew to be commissioned in the British army and he quickly made a name for himself in North Africa, where his transport company won admiration for its performance, reliability and remarkable engineering and mechanical skills. His repeated requests that it be designated a Jewish unit were always turned down by the military authorities, and it was solely because of his own initiatives that the Company became an exclusively Jewish unit. No. 178 GT Company performed its duties in North Africa with courage and thoroughness, but Major (at that time Captain) Aron and his men had their own missions as well. In 1942 the army had sent Aron back to Palestine to raise more recruits. As he explained in his memoirs:

> many of us had intimate connections with the *Haganah* in the years preceding the war, and it was now decided that a certain number of *Haganah* personnel be recruited to the British Forces not only for formal military training and experience . . . but also to ensure that wherever possible the units be encouraged to perform their duties in the dedicated spirit of the Jewish Defence Force in Palestine.[13]

As British military intelligence had rightly forecast, the Palestinian Jewish recruits were likely to include many who were part of the Haganah and had their own mission to accomplish. This was certainly true of Wellesley Aron's men, who took a leading role in assisting the Libyan Jews who had suffered during the lengthy Italo-German siege and occupation of Tobruk, creating temporary accommodation for them and using their transport to bring food and supplies. In these humanitarian operations they were working as part of a wider network that included British Jews serving in other units, Jewish military chaplains and Palestinian Jewish volunteers. Aron was also in close contact with Moshe Shertok and the Jewish Agency, as well as with leading figures in the Zionist organizations in Palestine. But Aron acknowledged in his memoirs that one of the objectives of the Haganah agents among his men was to acquire arms and ammunition 'for use by the *Haganah* in defence of the *Yishuv*' (the Palestinian Jews). Once Rommel's forces fell back from Tobruk, large quantities of captured Italian weaponry and materials began to find their way back to the Haganah leaders in Palestine with the help of Wellesley Aron and his men.[14]

When No. 178 Company was transferred to southern Italy at the end of 1943, therefore, Wellesley Aron and his men already had their clearly defined agenda. They were soon to discover that Italy offered even broader opportunities for assisting Jewish refugees than North Africa. Many Jews were already trying to escape from the Nazi occupation in northern and central Italy and attempting to reach the Allied lines in the South, among them three young Florentine Jews whom Raffaele Cantoni had told to make their way to San Nicandro in September in the hope that Manduzio would shelter them. As well as those from northern Italy, Jewish refugees from the Balkans were trying to reach the safety of southern Italy. Like the Italian Jews, their principal destination was the port of Bari, which was accessible from many points on both sides of the Adriatic Sea, although the journey was always hazardous.

Other Jewish refugees were already in southern Italy, however. A month after the landings at Salerno, the Allies had discovered a camp at Ferramonti Tarsia near Cosenza in Calabria whose inmates were all European Jews. This was the first internment camp for Jews in Europe to be liberated by the Allies. Although it had been abandoned by the Italians shortly after the Allied landings, the inmates feared leaving because it was rumoured that there were still German troops in the vicinity. So when the Allies arrived in early October they found some 1,400 men, women and children. All were non-Italian Jews, the largest contingent consisting of 500 Austrians and Czechs who had been shipwrecked off Rhodes while attempting to make their way to Palestine by sea.

Ferramonti was not a death camp or even a concentration camp on Nazi lines. In comparison, the detainees at Ferramonti were relatively well treated. During the war the camp had been visited regularly by Italian Jewish leaders and by agents of DELASEM, the charity that had been created to assist Jewish refugees in which Raffaele Cantoni had been active. DELASEM agents had been given free access to the camp where they provided assistance for the detainees, who were also visited by Italian rabbis and representatives of other Jewish charities.[15] However, the fall of Mussolini's regime placed these people in great danger because of the proximity of German units and they were fortunate to have been discovered first by the Allies. But although the Allied military authorities were prepared to provide assistance and humanitarian support, they were unsure what to do with the inmates. On the other hand, the Zionist organizations had plans, and they mobilized much the same networks that had functioned in North Africa.

From Palestine, Moshe Shertok acted as co-ordinator of the operations, which in Italy were overseen by the same Captain Urbach who a few months later visited San Nicandro. In August 1943 he had been transferred from North Africa to Sicily and after the discovery of the Ferramonti Tarsia camp he took charge of the welfare of the inmates. Urbach was also responsible for looking after the growing numbers of Jewish refugees who were turning up in Bari in desperate need of shelter, food and clothes. New camps were established on the outskirts of Bari and further down the coast at Santa Maria di Leuce but still close to Bari, the point of arrival for most of the refugees. The expectation was that the majority of the refugees would make their way to Palestine from the same port. When Wellesley Aron's Company arrived from Egypt in December 1943, he and his men threw themselves enthusiastically into the task of providing for the refugees, finding food and clothing and building camps to accommodate them. The volunteers cheerfully contributed most of their pay to help feed and provide for the refugees, and many put their experience as settlers to work, helping build and organize the camps along the lines of the kibbutzim.

As a result of these activities Urbach and Aron played important roles in establishing what was known as the Net (*Reshet*) in southern Italy in the winter of 1943–4. The Net was simply a network of organizations that worked to assist Jewish refugees in post-war Europe, providing accommodation, supplies and provisions for them in the refugee camps before the official agencies like UNRRA (the United Nations Relief and Rehabilitation Administration), the Joint and the Red Cross took over. But the Net was also active in helping those who wanted to emigrate to Palestine either by legal or by clandestine means. Its operations were initially overseen by Moshe Shertok and then by Mossad *le-Aliyah Bet* agents. Mossad's operations were later extended to the Balkans, Austria and Germany, where it played a critical role in organizing the clandestine Escape (*Bricha*) of European Jews to Palestine. But the original structure was established in southern Italy in the early months of 1944. Without knowing it Manduzio and his followers would find their way into the Net.[16]

These operations carried all kinds of risks, however, not least because the humanitarian initiatives involved the illegal use of military vehicles and supplies. Aron's men became experts in making clothes for the refugees, using 'borrowed' British military uniforms which were dyed blue to disguise their origins and then turned into blankets or coats. Flour and other foodstuffs were also taken liberally from military depots to feed the refugees. Given the scale and visibility of these operations, it was only a matter of time before they attracted the attention of the Field Security Police. Indeed, in July 1944 Aron risked facing a court martial for authorizing the misuse of military equipment and supplies. The charges were not pressed, but as Aron himself later admitted they were substantially true.

The authorities might turn a blind eye on humanitarian grounds to the misuse of military supplies and equipment for the refugees, but when it came to the question of emigration there was less room for manoeuvre. Before the war the British government had imposed strict quotas and planned to stop all Jewish emigration to Palestine. When the liberation of southern Italy began the Allies were again confronted by the scale of the Jewish refugee problem. This came as no surprise to Moshe Shertok and the Zionist leaders who knew well what to expect once the Third Reich began to collapse. But the Allies, and especially the British, although not unprepared had no clear or agreed plans. Despite the steadily growing numbers of Jewish refugees trying to reach the liberated zones in Italy in 1944, the British authorities were prepared to make only minor concessions and refused to relax controls on emigration to Palestine.

This posed major problems for those trying to care for the refugees. Unless some way could be found to resettle at least some in Palestine, the means to shelter and accommodate them would soon be exhausted.

In desperation at what he considered to be an absurd situation, Wellesley Aron went to Rome in June 1944, shortly after the city was liberated, to meet with Sir Clifford Heathcote-Smith at the Allied Control Commission HQ, which was responsible for civil administration in the liberated territories. Heathcote-Smith was in charge of refugee issues and Aron tried to persuade him of the urgent need to make plans for the refugees to emigrate to Palestine. To his dismay, the British bureaucrat brushed his arguments aside and flatly refused to accept that there was a specifically Jewish refugee problem. The European Jews, he told Aron, were no different from any other 'Displaced Persons' and once the war was over they should be given every assistance to return to their places of origin, something that Aron knew was now totally unacceptable to most of the Jewish refugees.[17]

Despite this bureaucratic intransigence, Aron and his associates nonetheless succeeded in getting many of the inmates of the Ferramonti Tarsia camp to Palestine by boat from Bari. But this became increasingly difficult, and as the voyages to Palestine became clandestine, an ever more important role was played by the Zionist organizations that had been established among the foreign Jewish refugees and by agents of the Mossad, the Haganah and of the Jewish Agency in Palestine.[18]

British military intelligence knew about these developments, but was also following contradictory objectives. It wanted to block clandestine emigration to Palestine, so British agents kept a tight rein on the activities of the Zionist organizations in Italy; for example, closing down in March 1944 a Zionist newspaper that was being printed and distributed by the refugees at Ferramonti Tarsia. At the same time, the British were now interested in recruiting Jewish refugees and young Italian Jews for the Jewish Brigade Group that the government was planning to establish in Italy.

The recruitment of Jewish refugees and Italian Jews to fight the Germans had already been the subject of discussions between sections of British military intelligence and the Zionist organizations in Palestine, including leading figures in the Haganah. In March 1944 the British government sought the advice of Moshe Shertok, who was visiting Bari to get a better picture of the Jewish refugee situation there. Shertok consulted with Aron and Aronov and reported back to London that both officers were confident that the idea of volunteering to fight in a Jewish combat force would appeal to the foreign Jewish refugees and 'the younger Italian Jews, from whom it may be possible to obtain perhaps 1,000 men if the Italian government proves helpful'. Shertok added that the two companies commanded by Majors Aron and Aronov were a model for the proposed Jewish Brigade Group: 'this idea had already been inspired by the existing Palestinian Jewish units scattered and "nameless" as they are, and I have no doubt that joining the forces of the Jewish Brigade Group will be still more popular'.[19]

The government's decision finally to go ahead with the long-debated project of a Jewish combat force had opened the way for collaboration between the British and the Jewish Agency on a range of different fronts. Shertok was in Italy in March 1944 to help organize the emigration of Jewish refugees to Palestine, something that the British still opposed. At the same time he was also working with the British to seek volunteers among both the refugees and young Italian Jews for the new Jewish Brigade. But there were other projects afoot as well, including secret operations behind enemy lines that were being planned jointly by British military intelligence and agents of the Haganah in Palestine. A direct result of these operations was that a leading anti-Fascist Italian Jew, Enzo Sereni, arrived in Bari from Palestine in March 1944 and played a brief but critical part in the San Nicandro story.

# CHAPTER SEVEN

# A Hero Comes to Visit

In Bari Enzo Sereni gathered together the different threads of Shertok's Net in Italy. A secret assignment behind enemy lines had brought him to the Apulian city, but during his short time there he worked hard to promote emigration to Palestine and to encourage young Jews to volunteer for service in the Jewish combat force that was due to be established. Given his very heavy schedule, his decision to include a visit to San Nicandro cannot have been a matter of chance.

Sereni was from a prominent Jewish family in Rome, and both his brothers had played distinguished roles in the Resistance. Since his youth, Enzo had been one of the leading advocates of the Zionist programme in Italy. Both he and his wife Ada Ascarelli were opposed to the assimilationist principles shared by the majority of Italian Jews, and like Dante Lattes and Davide Prato believed that Italian Jews should return to a fuller observance of religious law. After moving to Palestine, Sereni and his wife followed the changing situation of the European Jews closely. Enzo travelled to Germany in 1931 and again in 1934, and then to New York in 1937. In 1939 and 1940 he visited France, Belgium, Holland, Denmark, Sweden and Italy, before returning to Palestine. When the British authorities in Egypt asked Moshe Shertok in 1941 to recommend an Italian Jew who could engage in the political re-education of the thousands of

Italian prisoners of war who had been captured and were being held in camps in Egypt, he named Sereni.

Sereni was given the job of establishing a daily newspaper for the Italian prisoners and he made regular broadcasts on the British-funded Radio Italia Libera (Radio Free Italy). However, the British began to suspect that he was spreading Zionist propaganda, and he was arrested on the mistaken charge of being an illegal immigrant. Shertok negotiated his release, later claiming that the reason for his arrest was that in 1941 the British authorities in the Middle East still believed for the most part that Mussolini could be detached from Hitler. For that reason they opposed any open attacks on Fascism as a political regime, because the price of bringing the Duce into the Allied camp would be to keep Italian Fascism in place after the defeat of Germany.[1]

After his release, Sereni returned to Palestine before going to Iraq, ostensibly to report on the situation of the Jewish community, but actually in connection with a plan for the clandestine immigration of Syrian, Iraqi and Lebanese Jews to Palestine that Shertok and other Haganah officers were trying to organize. Sereni was involved in preparations for Jewish resistance in Palestine in the event of a Nazi invasion, and it was these activities that brought him into contact again with sections of British military intelligence. This was why he and a number of Haganah volunteers went to Bari in March 1944 for parachute training before being dropped behind German lines, where they were to make contact with Jews and organize resistance. Most of the agents were to be dropped in the Balkans and eastern Europe, but Sereni was given the task of establishing contact with the Jewish inmates of the Fascist and Nazi camps in northern Italy.

Shertok was involved in these plans. He knew that Sereni was an eloquent and impassioned communicator, and so before he went on his mission he also wanted him to help promote the cause of Eretz Israel and the *aliyah* among the Jewish refugees

**2** Enzo Sereni in San Nicandro, April 1944. In what is believed to be the last photograph taken before the mission to northern Italy that would lead to his capture and execution by the Nazis, Enzo Sereni (in spectacles behind the flag) stands next to Lucia Giordano (the young girl in a white dress). The boy in the black cap standing behind Sereni and next to Major Aronov is Francesco Cerrone's son Pasquale (Pesach).

and young Italian Jews. When Sereni arrived in Bari and started on his intensive ten-day parachute-training course, he agreed to meet with the refugees in the camp at Ferramonti Tarsia and to visit San Nicandro.[2]

In his later memoir, Eliezer Tritto recalled the dramatic impact of Sereni's visit and the affection he aroused among Manduzio's community:

Our dear Enzo Sereni came to visit us, and when I think of it
I can see his image before my eyes as though it were yesterday.

I was just thirteen years old at the time and Sereni came with three officers and immediately asked to be introduced to Manduzio who of course never left his house: his legs were paralysed as the result of a war wound. For many hours Manduzio explained to Enzo Sereni 'our little story', which he clearly enjoyed, and when it was finished he said: 'Manduzio, you are a true prophet inspired by God and your views are more just and more correct than those of any Jewish-born Jew.'

Eliezer went on to recall how they all listened enthralled while Sereni described to them his life in the Promised Land, the Land of Our Fathers, how he had travelled across Europe and America imploring Jews to return to Palestine to build and create their national homeland. 'He then begged us all to leave for the Promised Land since very soon, he said, God will give us a new state. Before he departed Manduzio sang a hymn, after which all joined in singing the *Hatikvah* [the national anthem of Israel].'[3]

Lucia Giordano was eighteen years old in 1944 and like Eliezer she later emigrated to Israel. She too vividly recalled the visit. Her father had died long before and her family 'lived in the deepest poverty, without food or any hope for the future'. When she decided to convert and join Manduzio's community 'my mother and my elder brother constantly chided me . . . only the strength of the Eternal kept me going'. Sereni had taken pity on her and had offered her financial assistance, which she refused. But he gave the community something far more important than money: 'he talked to us of freedom, he reorganized our little meeting house, and above all he kindled in our hearts the hope of peace for which we all so desperately longed'.

Lucia recalled that Sereni had also said that he wanted to take a souvenir of the meeting back to Palestine with him, and so one of the officers took a photograph. She later received a copy of the photograph and recognized herself standing to Sereni's left, dressed in a white frock (see the photograph on p. 130). After Sereni had left, she remembered, the other Palestinian soldiers were constantly talking about him and his heroism, and she recalled the shock when a little later they heard the news of his death. Early in May he had been parachuted into occupied Tuscany, but the drop went badly and he was immediately captured by the Germans: he was executed in Dachau on 18 November 1944.

Sereni's visit had a unique impact on Manduzio's followers. They had been excited and enthused by the interest that Major Aron's men had shown in them, but they had been able to communicate with these foreign Jews only with the greatest of difficulty through the somewhat questionable linguistic skills of Corporal Spitzer. Sereni was quite different. He was a Jew and an Italian, as well as being an officer in the Allied forces who was about to leave on a dangerous military mission. Like Jacques Faitlovich and Raffaele Cantoni, he greeted them not as would-be converts but as true Jews. He welcomed them to the Jewish community, and above all he inspired them with the idea of emigrating to Eretz Israel.

The idea of emigration was not new to the community. Faitlovich had been the first to raise the possibility when he visited in 1935. Francesco Cerrone had been determined to emigrate from that point, and had explored every avenue before the war, but at that time it was not feasible. Now the war, it seemed, had changed everything. They were not yet aware, of course, that for so many Jews the war had been fatal; for this small community it seemed that the war had finally made possible what had previously been impossible. From that moment the project of conversion and the prospect of emigration became thoroughly intertwined. Sereni's visit had itself brought about a fervent transformation, especially for the younger ones. Manduzio had converted them to the Jewish faith, but Enzo Sereni converted them to Zionism.

Wellesley Aron was a witness to this second conversion. Later he recalled that before his Company moved north 'The elders of the village called on me at my H.Q. and had tea with me at the Officers' Mess. It was then that they asked whether there was a chance of their "returning" as they called it "to the Holy Land". Obviously nothing could be discussed with them on this point, but we said we would not forget them when the time came.' Manduzio and his followers could not have found themselves in better or more capable hands. Quite inadvertently the encounter with the Jewish soldiers had brought them into contact with the organizers of the Net, whose networks, 'underground railways' and agents would assist thousands of European Jews to emigrate clandestinely to Palestine.

They had fallen into the Net quite by chance. But there was something special about this new relationship. Manduzio and his followers again fascinated many of the Jews who came into contact with them. Enzo Sereni told one of his friends, Lia Cases, with whom he spent many evenings at the Palestinian Club in Bari during these weeks, how deeply he had been moved by his visit to San Nicandro. Cases believed that 'it was above all that in the fresh and pure faith of this community he found a sort of serenity and strength. The last photograph that we have of him was taken with these "new Jews" who in turn found in Sereni's deep affection and understanding a vital support in the difficult spiritual journey that would finally lead them to become citizens of Eretz Israel.'[4]

What drew Sereni to Manduzio and his followers was similar in many respects to what had drawn Raffaele Cantoni to them before the war. The simplicity and apparent genuineness of their faith and the lack of any apparent material reasons for wanting to convert, together with their stoic willingness to put up with repeated disappointment and hardship, struck many of those who met them as an inspirational example and even as a model of what Jews should be. That idea had already been suggested in one of the first references to the San Nicandro converts to appear in print. Guido Lodovico Luzzatto wrote an article that was published in 1939 in the Zionist periodical *Nuovo Avanti!* in which he held up Manduzio and his followers as an example that all Jews should seek to follow.

Luzzato's main purpose was to denounce those Italian Jews who, in order to evade the consequences of the Fascist Racial Laws, had rushed to enter into mixed marriages or had converted to Catholicism. He was especially outraged that even among Italian Jews who succeeded in emigrating to the USA many had chosen first to convert to Catholicism, in the belief that this would 'make things easier when they reached their destination'. In deploring these actions, Luzzatto pointed instead to the contrast offered by 'the curious case of a true and sincere conversion to Judaism' in San Nicandro Garganico. Despite persecution by the Bishop and the authorities, this 'small but fearless group of families continues to refuse to have their children baptized, follows the prescriptions of Mosaic law and asks to be recognized by the Jewish community'. Luzzatto went on to state that the group was led by 'a war invalid immobilized by a fractured pelvis and who, when confronted by such a barbarous and infamous world, became persuaded that the Messiah has not yet come and that we must return to the teaching of the Old Testament'. In the actions of Donato Manduzio and his followers, Luzzatto argued, 'fifty Apulian peasants have given a lesson in courage that should be heeded by all those Italian Jews who until yesterday were observant and proud of their freedom of thought, but who today have disgracefully opted to fake the enthusiasm of observant Catholics'.[5]

Luzzatto's account of the San Nicandro community indicates why the 'curious case' of these converts exercised a strong fascination on many Italian Jews. It shows that even before the war their case was already quite widely known in Italian Zionist circles, and that many Italian Jews found something deeply symbolic in the story of the Apulian peasants who had discovered the Jewish faith and, despite obstacles and adversity, had refused to be dissuaded even though their dearest wish had not been met. As Alberto Cavaglion has noted, there was also a willingness to read into the story of Manduzio and his followers an example of a simple but nonetheless brave refusal to accept Fascism, even though in reality there is nothing to indicate that this was ever a consideration for the would-be converts. But impressions have their own force, and both Guido Lodovico Luzzatto and Enzo Sereni illustrate the different ways in which imagined accounts and symbolic representations of the San Nicandro converts were already competing with the more complicated realities of the small community.

# CHAPTER EIGHT

# A Difficult Conversion

After their encounters with the Jewish soldiers and with Enzo Sereni, the would-be converts believed that their conversion would soon be recognized. But in fact they were in for more long delays and, once the Jewish soldiers left to follow the war as it moved northwards up the Italian peninsula, Manduzio and his community found themselves alone again. Although they would have a long wait before they were able to re-establish contacts with the outside world, a number of important changes had already taken place. As we have seen, the meeting with Enzo Sereni had turned them into enthusiastic and committed supporters of the Zionist cause, and their commitment to the Zionist project meant that emigration was now inseparable from their desire to convert.

A second development that would play an even more direct part in the story was the place that the would-be converts now found within the broader organization of the Net. Before Rabbi Urbach and Major Aron left the province of Foggia in April 1944, the network of camps for refugees awaiting an opportunity to set off for Palestine had been established. The day-to-day running of the camps and the care of the inmates were now the responsibility of the official refugee agencies, the Joint and UNRRA. In these camps the San Nicandresi would meet other Italian and foreign Jews. As well as these wider Jewish encounters, it was in the camps that many of them began to learn Hebrew and to have direct contacts with established Jewish life, religion and rituals, which often differed significantly from their own self-taught and improvised variants. In the camps they also encountered the Zionist agencies that were organizing clandestine emigration to Palestine and recruits for the coming war against the Arabs.

In the meantime, many of the Jewish volunteers who had been in San Nicandro earlier in the year joined the Jewish Brigade Group when it was formed in September 1944. It went into action against heavily defended German positions near Ravenna in March 1945 and remained in the line for six weeks, losing twenty-seven men, with seven officers and fourteen other ranks wounded. Once out of the line, the men of the Brigade played a critical role in helping the Jewish communities in Bologna, Modena, Ferrara and Venice, where the conditions of the Jewish survivors were appalling.[1]

After the Germans had been defeated, these initiatives took on even broader dimensions and again the Jewish Brigade played a key role. Its final posting in Italy was at Tarvisio, a little border town far to the north of Venice on the frontiers with Austria and Yugoslavia. Its proximity to Marshal Tito's partisan forces and the Red Army meant that this was still an area of great military and political sensitivity. But Tarvisio also lay directly in the path of the thousands of Jewish refugees who were trying to escape from Austria, eastern Europe and the Balkans to reach the safety of the Allied lines in northern Italy.

Between May and early July, it was estimated that some 15,000 Jewish refugees made their way into northern Italy, many through Tarvisio where the men of the Jewish Brigade had constructed a transit camp, Merkaz Lagola (Centre for the Diaspora), at Pontebba near the border. Using captured German stores and medical supplies, they fed, clothed and housed the refugees, working closely with the Joint and with UNRRA, which were responsible for the numerous camps for refugees and Displaced

Persons that had been organized in central and northern Italy. The men of the JBG were again working closely with Shertok's Jewish Agency and with agents of the Haganah and the Mossad, the clandestine Zionist organization founded in 1938 to help Jews emigrate to Palestine.

The operations involved openly flouting the efforts made by the British authorities to prevent the refugees entering Italy, and were co-ordinated by the senior Mossad officer in Italy, Yehuda Arazi, who had secretly arrived in Rome shortly after the liberation. Among Zionist activists Arazi was known as the 'Palestinian Pimpernel' because although the British considered him a terrorist and had put a large price on his head he was never caught.[2] With typical bravado, when he moved to Milan in July 1945 Arazi set up his command post in the same building as the GHQ of the British military command in Italy. He was joined by Enzo Sereni's widow, Ada, and together for the next two years they co-ordinated the clandestine emigration of Jewish refugees from Italy to Palestine. They also engaged in a multitude of other undercover operations that included smuggling weapons to Palestine and tracking down SS men and others guilty of Nazi crimes.

The main role of the JBG, however, was transporting and caring for the refugees, and in this their contribution was critical. As a combat unit in the British army they wore British uniforms and could take their transports and equipment wherever they chose. Just as Major Aron's men had done in the South, they used British military supplies to feed, clothe and house the refugees, while every night for many weeks covert convoys of Jewish Brigade transports brought more refugees from the Austrian border down to Tarvisio and sometimes onwards to other camps near Milan. The operations were soon detected by British military intelligence in Vienna, with the result that the Jewish Brigade was transferred to Belgium in July. But its departure did not disrupt the expansion of the networks that helped the Jewish refugees make their way into Italy, nor the operations that subsequently enabled them to emigrate to Palestine. These were the same networks that would eventually sweep up the converts of San Nicandro in the great post-war Jewish Escape from Europe.[3]

By now Raffaele Cantoni was among the key figures working for the Jewish refugees in Milan after the liberation, and he was directly involved with both the men of the JBG and with Yehuda Arazi. Cantoni's reappearance in Milan within days of the liberation was little short of miraculous. After his arrest in 1940 he had been held by the Fascists until 1942, when he was released on medical grounds and allowed to return to live in his mother's house in Fiesole, outside Florence. He was still a political prisoner under house arrest and subject to strict police surveillance. But with Eugenio Artom, Rabbi Nathan Cassuto, his cousin Mathilde Cassin and others he had immediately begun to organize assistance for Jewish refugees in Florence.

From September 1943 the Nazis occupied the city. Despite the now very present danger, Cantoni and his associates continued to work under the eyes of the Germans. The Archbishop of Florence, Cardinal Elia Dalla Costa, gave his full support and arranged for the Jewish refugees to be taken into the convents of the Dominican order. Don Leto Casini, the parish priest of Varlungo, risked his life to bring the refugees into the convents, while Cantoni once again succeeded, although no one knew how, in raising large sums of money.[4] These operations ended tragically on 6 November when SS units began to raid the convents and seize the refugees. On 26 November they arrested Rabbi Cassuto, along with Don Leto and Cantoni, both the latter having been betrayed by informers. Cantoni was put straight on a train that was to take him to the death camps in Germany, but remarkably he managed to jump off as the train was passing through his home town, Padua. From there he made his way to Turin, then to Genoa and finally in December to Switzerland. Mathilde Cassin had also been arrested, but by one of the Florentine Fascist militia groups and not by the SS. She too managed to escape and reached Switzerland, where she met Cantoni in July 1944.[5]

Immediately after the liberation, Cantoni and Mathilde Cassin returned to Milan where he at once took a lead in assisting both the survivors of the Milanese Jewish community and the growing numbers of the foreign Jewish refugees who were arriving in the city. No longer a persecuted political subversive, Cantoni was now a man of considerable influence with an impressive network of contacts. When Bernard Casper, the chaplain with the Jewish Brigade, met him he was in no doubt that Cantoni was 'the driving force' in Milan. He described him as 'an idealist, a Zionist, a Jew to the core and a premier citizen in Milan who had played a leading role in the underground resistance movement which helped in the final ousting of the Germans from North Italy'.

Cantoni had close contacts with the leading figures in post-war Italian politics, with senior officials of the Joint and UNRRA, and with the Allied administration that appointed him President of the Union of Italian Jewish Communities. He threw himself into work for the refugees with all the impetuosity and frenetic energy that his friend Augusto Segre so admired, and his main priority, as Bernard Casper also noted, was the young people, the children and orphans among the refugees.[6] He frequently visited the camps. He spoke German and Yiddish, and he loved to mix and talk with the refugees, especially the children. Once again, he also showed remarkable skill in raising funds. Most of the money, and there was a great deal of it, came via Switzerland, but now increasingly from sources in the USA. In Milan, Cantoni's office at the Union of Jewish Communities was next to the one from which Arazi directed the operations of the Mossad, and Cantoni's brother, Marcello, was one of Arazi's closest collaborators. For the next two years Cantoni worked to raise funds to finance the clandestine sailings of refugee ships to Palestine from La Spezia, Ancona and Bari, and for the purchase and transport of arms that were being smuggled to Palestine.[7]

Thus, by the early summer of 1945 the principal friend and protector of Manduzio and his followers was not only back in Italy and fully active, but was now one of the most influential members of the newly reconstituted Italian Jewish community. Cantoni was so heavily engaged with his work for the refugees in the North, however, that he had little time to devote to Manduzio and his followers. According to his friend Augusto Segre, the only time Cantoni ever seemed to sleep when he was on a train between one assignment and the next. That may explain why when he travelled to Bari in February 1946 to attend a meeting of the Anglo-American Commission of Inquiry on the condition of the Jewish refugees in Europe, he did not take the opportunity make the short detour to San Nicandro before he returned to Rome. But he had not forgotten Manduzio and he knew that others had already taken up their case.

After the departure of Major Aron and his men, contacts with San Nicandro once again became sporadic. Before he left, Captain Urbach had arranged for the young Eliezer Tritto to go to one of the camps for Jewish children that had been opened near Bari. This proved to be very important since it ensured that the San Nicandresi would be able to maintain contact with the Nee through the camps after Urbach's departure. But much to the frustration of the would-be converts, there was to be no further word from outside until the spring of 1945. The main reason for the delay was the series of horrific events that had overtaken the Jews of Rome. After the mass deportations of October 1943, the community had suffered numerous subsequent arrests and hardships. It was the target for a particularly vicious attack on 24 March 1944. In reprisal for an attack on German troops in the Via Rasella by the Resistance on the previous day, the Nazis seized 355 hostages, of whom seventy-five were Jews, and massacred them in the caves of the Fosse Ardeatine close to the city.

Wellesley Aron and Rabbi Urbach visited Rome within weeks of the liberation and saw with their own eyes the desperate condition of the Jewish survivors. The community's recovery was further complicated by the controversies that surrounded the Chief Rabbi of Rome, Israel Zolli. After the liberation, Zolli came under heavy criticism – Urbach being one of the more outspoken voices – for his close relations with the Fascist regime. Not only had he and his family escaped the Nazi round-ups because they had been given refuge in the Vatican by Pope Pius XII, but he was deemed to have abandoned his community and had failed to warn them of what was impending.

Those demanding Zolli's resignation were infuriated when the American authorities confirmed his position as Chief Rabbi. Zolli held out until February of the following year, when he finally resigned. He converted to Catholicism and took the Christian names of Pope Pius XII (Eugenio Maria) in recognition of what he claimed the Pope had done for the Jews of Italy and Europe. In the eyes of many Jews this only served to compound his sins.[8]

After Zolli's resignation, many of the Jews who had been forced to leave Italy after the Racial Laws began to return. In May 1946 Davide Prato came back from Tel Aviv to take up his old position as Chief Rabbi of Rome. The leading Florentine Zionist, Dante Lattes, also returned, and was nominated to the chair of Rabbinical Studies of the Jewish Community of Rome and became president of the Union of the Italian Jewish Communities. The Italian Zionist Federation was reconstituted, and Umberto Nahon arrived in Rome as the representative of the Jewish Agency with special responsibility for organizing assistance for foreign Jews in Italy and overseeing distribution of the small quota of permits for immigration to Palestine released each month by the British authorities.

In April 1945, Francesco Cerrone and Angelo Marrochella arrived unannounced in Rome and asked to meet Giuseppe Nathan, the Commissioner for Jewish Affairs, and Umberto Nahon, who was now the President of the Italian Zionist Organization. Both men were close friends of Raffaele Cantoni and the visitors from San Nicandro were warmly welcomed. After the meeting, Nahon wrote to the President of the Union of the Italian Jewish Communities to say that the Zionist Organisation (ZO) had received 'from San Nicandro Garganico impassioned letters declaring their attachment to the Jewish faith', and he asked the Union to give some moral assistance 'to this Jewish Community'. The letter set out the background to the story, stating that 'you will almost certainly be aware of the existence of this group of some 200 [sic] individuals who converted to the Jewish faith in 1932. We believe it to be our undeniable duty to give some tangible proof of our interest in and brotherhood with these Jews who have shown themselves capable of resisting the terrible challenges of the tragic period that has just passed.'

The numbers were a wild exaggeration and the summary of the story given in an attached memo was also full of inaccuracies. But Manduzio's religious views, the memorandum concluded, could be summed up as follows: 'the Messiah anointed by the prophet Elijah was not Christ. The Credo which he chose to follow was the original one from which Christianity first arose and from which he derived the mission from that time onwards to preach the religion of the Jews among his brothers'. Nahon informed the President that Manduzio had originally gathered around him some ninety disciples, but the local priest had acted quickly to put a stop to his teaching and Manduzio and his followers were banned from holding religious meetings. However, they refused to give up the faith to which they had remained loyal for nearly twenty years. 'It is time that they were given the opportunity to enter into the Jewish family.'

These were the words that Manduzio and his followers had been waiting to hear for over a decade and the President of the Zionist Organization recommended that some 'suitably qualified person or persons should visit San Nicandro to find out more about it, organize the community and lay the basis for a more organic and complete form of religious teaching than has hitherto been available'. He suggested that Rabbi Alfredo Ravenna would be an appropriate person for this mission. The community was small and poor, but it was believed that it could support the cost of Dr Ravenna's journey and visit, although the ZO subsequently agreed to make a contribution from its funds. The Union fully supported the proposal and the Commissioner for Jewish Affairs, Giuseppe Nathan, asked Rabbi Ravenna to visit San Nicandro and 'to take our greetings to the community of Jews in that town and give them what assistance they may need'.[9]

Rabbi Ravenna duly made the journey via Bari and Foggia, and arrived in San Nicandro on 29 May 1945. Little did he expect what awaited him when he finally arrived. He found the community deeply divided, the principal reason being that Manduzio was now vehemently opposed to emigration. Although he had supported Cerrone's attempts to emigrate before the war, his opinion had now changed. Despite the appeals of Enzo Sereni and the Jewish soldiers, Manduzio was now adamant that his mission and that of the community was to 'bring Light to this Dark Corner of Apulia'. The greater the enthusiasm among his followers for the idea of emigrating to the Promised Land, the more inflexible his opposition became. As always, Francesco Cerrone, Costantino Tritto and Angelo Marrochella were his main opponents. It was Manduzio's refusal to give way that had led Cerrone and Marrochella to decide to go directly to Rome in April.

There was no reference to any of this in the first letter that Manduzio wrote to Rome in April just before the war ended, in which he introduced himself to the members of the newly reconstituted Union and was careful to stress that he was and always had been the leader of the community. Describing himself as 'Donato Manduzio, also known as Levi', he informed the 'Gentlemen of the Union' that the San Nicandro community had celebrated Passover 'as the Creator has instructed us, that is to say with a roast kid, unleavened bread and bitter herbs'. He went on to express the grief that everyone at San Nicandro felt for the suffering that had befallen the Jewish people, reminding the 'Gentlemen of the Union' that it was the consequence of a failure to observe the Laws, which was why the Creator had 'allowed the jackals to lord it over the Jews. But the Creator has ordered that if Israel observes its own Laws it will become the Lord of the whole earth.'

'Now you have heard what Israel must do,' he continued, 'but you must know too that I do not speak as someone who is above you: indeed, I am not a Rabbi nor am I a Teacher [*Maestro*], but I am a simply a Link [*Legame*] and I was created by the Law of SINAI and through that Law I became the Son of the Creator because all those who observe His Law are His Sons.' He went on to say that the Creator had confided in him a 'little prayer' that he would share with them if they wrote to him: but if they did not, he would deem them unworthy of him. 'Look at me,' he told them, 'and you will see that I am not a student, but that I have been called by a miracle. As he called Abraham, our Father, and as Dr Faitlovich, who came from Jerusalem to hear our story said, the Creator had caused a Light to be lit because he had never heard the word of Israel in a desert like this, as Rabbi Davide Prato also agreed when he heard our Story.'[10]

The letter was written in Manduzio's unmistakable sprawling hand with its approximate Italian and extensive biblical quotations. It was clearly intended to reassert his leadership, and was accompanied by some brief notes outlining the history of the community since it had last been in contact with Rome. He also inquired about the three young Florentine Jews who had come to his house in September 1943, saying that Raffaele Cantoni had given them his address in the hope that the San Nicandro community would shelter them until the Germans had withdrawn.

The tone of the letter that followed Rabbi Ravenna's visit in May was quite different, however. On 4 June Manduzio wrote to Rome to express his sense of outrage and betrayal. In response to the greetings that the gentlemen of the Union had sent through Rabbo (sic) Alfredo Ravenna, Manduzio angrily set out once again 'our story'. Exhorting them to 'Listen carefully', he informed them that for more than a year 'il Signor Francesco Cerrone and il Signor Marrocchella have set themselves apart from this community and we shall shortly explain why. The two Rebels have done what Korah, Abiram and Dathan did (Numbers Ch 16).' They had written to the Union 'without informing him and without paying heed to the Community . . . And so, at the suggestion of Cerrone and his friend *you* have sent us a *maestro*, that is to say the Rabbo Alfredo R.' This 'rabbo' had apparently informed only Cerrone of the time of his arrival, so that he alone had met him at the station of San Nicandro on 29 May at 6.30 p.m. The rest of the community knew nothing about this, and it was not until the following day that Ravenna came to Manduzio's house and brought the letter bearing greetings and *shalom* from the Union. After that he went to see Manduzio every day, but for little more than half an hour at a time.

When it came to Friday 1 June, Manduzio invited him to come to pray in his house where the community met, 'but the Rabbo said that he was going that evening to the house of Marrocchella'. However, he promised that he would come instead on the Saturday and would say the sabbath prayers with Manduzio and the others. On the Saturday they waited for him, but he did not come in the morning, nor in the afternoon, and turned up eventually around nine in the evening. At that point Manduzio upbraided him, saying that he could not believe that a rabbi could tell a lie. He explained how the quarrel with Cerrone had started and how Cerrone had 'armed himself with daggers and Bombs to kill me and how to discredit me he had gone around saying that I had put demons in his house and that I had stained the Holy Spirit of the Creator.' Manduzio said he understood then that 'the Rabbo did not believe what I told him, so I told him to call Marrochella who knows all about this and he called Marrochella and asked him if it was true that he had stopped Cerrone from trying to kill me? And Marrochella replied to the Rabbo saying: yes, it is true that Cerrone had seen the Devil and Marrochella said yes, Rabbo, all this is true.'[11]

Five days later Marrochella wrote to Rome to tell his side of the story. With a much more secure command of Italian, he thanked the 'Dear Brothers of the Union for their benevolent interest and for organizing the visit of rabbi Dr Ravenna who brought us both teaching and doctrine'. The good rabbi had attended to one of their dearest wishes, 'that is to say the opening of our new Oratory'. But Marochella then went on to express his 'immense grief' for what had then occurred and which 'Dr Ravenna will have himself explained in person'. Everything had happened because of the:

stupid and capricious behaviour of our superior Signor Manduzio, who pretends to be a Prophet and a Messiah among us – something that is utterly impossible. Dr Ravenna had patiently listened to what Manduzio had to say when he had called us liars.

Yet it is well known that this same Manduzio, with his false and invented visions has always claimed to be acknowledged and acclaimed by the whole world as a Hebrew Prophet, the Leader and Guide of Israel. It is pointless to embark on polemics with him since the Palestinian army rabbi Captain Urbach has already expressed his opinions in this respect on the basis of what he saw with his own eyes and heard with his own ears, as has Major Aronov. Both had understood that Manduzio thinks that he is inspired by God, that he believes that his interpretation of the Torah is the only one that is valid, that he does not need to study and that he has no need either of those who have studied the Judaic religion, that he does not acknowledge either Jewish Ritual or the Judaic Psalmody.

What Manduzio really needed, in Marrochella's view, was a doctor and preferably one 'who could examine his brain'. It was clear, he concluded, that 'Manduzio's ideal and his understanding of the faith have all been dreamed up for his own personal reasons, and have nothing whatsoever to do with the faith and values of the Jews'.[12]

Strangely, these alarming revelations about what was going on in San Nicandro do not seem to have raised doubts among the members of the Union. But the warring factions in San Nicandro had now found alternative external supporters. Rabbi Ravenna had clearly been irritated by Manduzio and on another occasion referred acidly to his dismissal of the Talmud, commenting that 'Manduzio thought of God as a shepherd (the theme of sheep constantly recurs in his visions) or as the owner of a large estate of which he himself was the bailiff'.[13] Ravenna had formed a more positive view of Cerrone and Marrochella, however, and he must also have spoken well of the community in general on his return because the Union responded by inviting the warring parties in San Nicandro to sign a formal 'deed of pacification'. The pact was drawn up and signed by Marrochella, Cerrone and Tritto on one hand, and by Manduzio on the other, and a copy was sent back to Rome. But the disputes worsened and in August Manduzio addressed a long letter to 'Dearly Beloved Signor Giuseppe Nathan' in which he said that he must 'talk to you as to a brother, because it is with a brother that I speak'.

More clearly than any other, this letter sets out Manduzio's understanding of his religion and his place in it. He told Nathan: 'my spirit moves me to talk to you about our birth and about how the Eternal One called me in the same way that he called our father Abraham, that is through visions and the Law of Sinai. Our story is full of visions, all of them full of truth and clear in their meaning because they come from the Creator who is also the Lord of Battles.' There was one vision in particular that Manduzio considered to be crucially important, but typically he warned

Nathan that 'if you do not believe in this vision then you do not believe in the Creator'. The vision had come to him on 27 July 1939 when he dreamed that the Creator had placed him in a field six or seven kilometres from the town, where he heard a voice that told him that 'the Great Empire is coming to vanquish Italy'.

In the vision Manduzio saw an army of men and officers whose uniforms he did not know or recognize, but then he understood that they were foreign and in his vision he ran to the commander and said to him: 'Oh mighty Commander either you must save me or I will save you.' At Manduzio's words, the commander smiled, whereupon the vision ended. But as Manduzio meditated on its meaning he came to understand that it was also a part of 'our story which was now awaiting the coming of the Great Empire'. On 28 September 1943 the meaning of the vision became apparent when 'the Great Empire, the Americans and all the United States arrived in the Gargano'. He went on to tell the story of how the Palestinian soldiers came to his house one morning in January 1944, how the officers and men greeted them with a warm *shalom* to which they replied with their own, how the commanders of the Palestinian camps in Foggia and Lucera came to visit him, along with the Jewish military chaplains. 'Here is the proof', he concluded, 'of the truth of his vision in 1939 which showed me that the Great Empire would take Italy and that the conquering Armies would be our friends.'[14]

The letter was intended as another demonstration of Manduzio's privileged role as a prophet and mediator with the Creator, and it closed with a request: 'now I want to hear what your spirit tells you of this vision which in fact came true'. But in December he wrote again to Nathan to say that 'the news from here is not good'. Manduzio complained that in the pact that had been signed by the three rebels, a copy of which had been sent to Rome, it had been clearly agreed that 'you [the members of the Union] should write to no one except to me and that all correspondence should be sent to my address'. But contrary to that agreement the rebels were now writing to whomsoever they pleased and even worse they were also receiving letters from 'all sorts of people'. They had become more corrupt than before and had again 'gone to Rome, without my knowledge, where they repeated to the Chief Rabbo so many lies about me, their father in the Law and the Jewish name'. But the good 'rabbo' 'had not understood their false Eden'. He begged Nathan to intervene because the quarrels had become public knowledge in San Nicandro, where it was now being openly said that the two rebels had challenged Manduzio because the leaders in Rome had supported them:

> if you do not force them to submit to my Will, the Gentiles will write about us in their newspapers and then we will hear the old story that was told in Jerusalem that you have killed and are killing the Prophets. You must do Justice or else Justice will be done to You . . . I will say no more, but I wish only to be recognized as the Father, the role which the Creator has given to me and I do not desire to see the work that I have done be wasted.[15]

Nathan replied to assure Manduzio that the Chief Rabbi, Professor Davide Prato, 'is very well disposed towards your community in San Nicandro'. He had been pleased to have the opportunity to greet the two members of the community who had come to Rome, but he told Manduzio that it was inconceivable they could have spoken badly of him since 'Rabbi Prato holds you in the highest regard'. Tongue-in-cheek perhaps, he added: 'Please try to stay calm and be assured that the two errant sheep who may perhaps have had a momentary aberration, will soon return to the flock'.

Manduzio did not persist, but in a letter to Nathan dated 7 March 1946 he raised another important question. When Rabbi Ravenna had visited San Nicandro in May 1945, he had 'promised that the circumcisions would be performed in the spring' and that a bath of purification would be organized for the women. Manduzio asked the Commissioner to let him know exactly when this event, which would bring 'our story to its ardently desired conclusion', could be expected.

It was for this purpose that Rabbi Ravenna returned to San Nicandro, accompanied by the surgeon Dr Arnaldo Ascarelli. Ravenna's task was to oversee the long-awaited rituals that would usher the whole community into the Jewish faith. He arrived on 30 July after a journey that he described in his subsequent report as *disastrosissimo*. Straightaway he met with those who had decided 'to undergo the operation that would enable them to enter definitively into the community of Israel' and he explained to them the procedures. Ravenna found Manduzio once again to be unco-operative: 'unfortunately Signor Manduzio showed his usual obstructionism. It became clear to me that the peace that had been made here is only superficial . . . and it was only at the very last moment that some of his followers agreed to take part in the *brit mila*'. But not Manduzio himself.

Dr Ascarelli performed the operations in two sessions on 5 and 8 August on thirteen men and boys from five families, as well as on 'five small infants'. Everything went well and after two or three days all were able to return to work. However, the event attracted much curiosity among other people in the town which annoyed the converts. So Ravenna decided that the ritual bath of purification for the women would be held in the waters of the sea off the beach at Torre Mileto, around eleven kilometres away, and the ceremony was attended by a group of twenty-five people. Ravenna concluded his report by stating that there were two more young men waiting to be circumcised who had not been present, one who was away on military service and another who was 'in a poor state of health'.[16]

At this extraordinarily crucial and understandably triumphant moment in the community's path to the Jewish faith, what Rabbi Ravenna has to say about Manduzio is significant. Both Corporal

Spitzer (later writing as Phinn Lapide) and Elena Cassin attribute the fact that Manduzio did not undergo circumcision to his age. Ravenna's own account makes it quite clear that Manduzio refused to participate because of his 'obstructionism'. The fact that Ravenna makes no mention of Lapide, who later claimed to have played an important part in the ceremonies, nor notes the presence of Raffaele Cantoni, who Lapide claimed had come to San Nicandro specifically for the occasion, throws doubt on the authenticity of Lapide's account of the episode.

Apart from Ravenna's comment about his obstructionism, we have no way of knowing why Manduzio refused to be circumcised. It may have been because of his age and health, or it may have been because he was unwilling to submit to Ravenna's authority as the two men clearly did not get on. But subsequently this became a subject for much gossip, and Manduzio's loyal supporters were quick to insist on the sincerity of his faith and his 'spiritual circumcision'.

Although Cantoni was not present, he was almost certainly responsible for all the arrangements. Indeed Rabbi Ravenna wrote as soon as he got back to Rome to inform him that he and Ascarelli had performed the circumcisions. 'Morale is very high,' he said, 'and the enthusiasm is great, but I will leave to them to write to tell you about it in more detail.'[17]

# CHAPTER NINE

# What Next?

The long-awaited entry into the Jewish community had in many ways increased the problems facing the converts. How were they now to live as Jews? They had no rabbi, no synagogue, no schools, no means of following the Jewish religious calendar or even of observing Jewish dietary laws. All of these problems might have been foreseen, but they were not, and once they became evident there was little agreement about how they were to be resolved.

Emigration was, of course, one obvious solution, but it was not yet feasible. The British restrictions on Jewish emigration to Palestine were being enforced with redoubled energy, while the transit camps in Italy were already crammed with foreign Jewish refugees whose reasons for emigrating would give them much higher priority. In any case, both Manduzio and Raffaele Cantoni were firmly opposed to emigration.

So the small community once again found itself in the throes of disputes that in one form or another came to focus on Manduzio's leadership. In his first letter to his 'Dear Friend Cantoni' after Rabbi Ravenna's visit, dated 2 September 1946, Manduzio complained that he had received no reply to his previous letters and then without going into further detail mentioned almost in passing that 'here in our midst the circumcisions have been performed'. But he went on to express his displeasure that the

Chief Rabbi had not informed him that they would be expected to pay 'the expenses of the surgeon as well as the cost of travel expenses for him and Signor Ravenna'. There had been a letter from Rome with mention of expenses, but to Manduzio's intense irritation this had been sent not to him but to Marrochella. The result was that they had been unable to pay Dr Ascarelli the 30,000 lire he had asked for: 'a sum that really shocks me, since this is a mountain village where there is no work to be found to enable us to meet such a cost'. Manduzio appealed to Cantoni as the 'father of this group of orphans' to help them pay the bill, reminding him to be sure to write to the correct address and not to Marrochella's house.[1]

On the same day Manduzio wrote to ask the Union for a reduction in the fee due to Dr Ascarelli. While 30,000 lire would be 'no more than a piece of powder in Rome', in a remote mountain village like San Nicandro it took at least a month to earn 1,000 lire. He asked them to send their greetings to Signor Cantoni and to tell him that they would always remember him but feared that he had forgotten them: 'we know that he is very busy, but he must surely have a little time to spare for us?'

Shortly afterwards Cantoni received a letter from Francesco Cerrone, who referred to his recent circumcision: 'we have paid a heavy price, but as you know what we most desired has now taken place and it is now no longer a matter of shame for us to call ourselves your Brothers . . . we feel that we are now in every respect your brothers . . . in the Holy Assembly of the House of Israel'. He thanked the Almighty that everything had taken place 'in perfect order, both with regard to the *brit mila* and also the *mikveh*', thanks to the good offices of Dr Alfredo Ravenna, to whom they were deeply grateful. He was also pleased to note that Manduzio 'has taken a step towards making peace with us'. As always with Cerrone, there was a supplementary request. His son had been unable to come to San Nicandro for the circumcision because he was on military service in the navy, even though as the son of a father of a numerous family he should have been exempted. He asked Cantoni to intervene with the Ministry of the Navy to have his son released from duty, thanking him and Rabbi Davide Prato 'for the part that they had played in bringing the hopes of the little group of converts to their conclusion'.[2]

Costantino Tritto, who had now adopted the Hebrew name Chaim, meanwhile wrote to his 'Dearest brother Raffaele' to tell him that the community was well, that in San Nicandro peace had been reached with Manduzio and that the hour of their circumcision had finally arrived. Angelo Marrochella sent a letter to Cantoni as well, although unlike the others he still addressed him formally, to inform him that 'After our long wait and with the help of the blessed Almighty, we have finally completed our journey both with regard to the pacification with Signor Manduzio and our circumcision. We now hope that after what has happened here you will very shortly be able to visit us.' He then asked for a loan to pay the expenses of Rabbi Ravenna and Dr Ascarelli, which he and his fellow converts would repay in instalments.[3]

Ravenna's suspicions that the reconciliation with Manduzio was superficial were well founded. On 8 September, Marrochella wrote to Rome in a rage, having discovered that Manduzio had written to ask that the amount requested by Ascarelli be reduced. Marrochella angrily repeated that the whole group had agreed in advance to pay the price asked by Ascarelli, and that it was typical of Manduzio that he should have acted alone without consulting the others. He went on to say that Manduzio's behaviour was a constant cause of dissent and discontent. Manduzio still refused to allow his followers to sing hymns in Hebrew or to read the rabbinical texts that had been given to them, something that Rabbi Ravenna could easily confirm. He begged the Gentlemen of the Union and Rabbi Prato to write to instruct Manduzio on how to behave for the good of the whole community.

In response, Marrochella and Cerrone received rather sharp letters from the Union, warning them that it was essential that the disputes in San Nicandro should come to an end. Marrochella responded: 'To meet your request, I have spoken with my friends and have persuaded them to reach an agreement with Manduzio.' But he warned that the agreement would not last unless Manduzio kept his word and allowed hymns in Hebrew to be sung and permitted readings from the rabbinical texts during the prayer meetings. He promised that he and his colleagues would do their best, but he asked that one of the members of the Jewish Union should come to San Nicandro to see for himself how things stood and how Manduzio was behaving.[4]

Finally, Cantoni intervened personally and in a much more conciliatory letter dated 30 September he expressed his 'great joy' at the news that peace had been restored within the community at the start of the Jewish New Year, adding: 'I am always thinking affectionately of you all and you should not take my silence or lack of letters to imply that I have forgotten you because you are particularly dear to my heart and you can always count on my support.'[5]

Despite the hopes of Cantoni and Rabbi Prato that matters would settle down in San Nicandro, the difficulties facing the new converts increased. The problems were set out coherently by Angelo Marrochella, who told Cantoni that 'we have already informed rabbi Prato that our greatest desire is to move to a Jewish centre where we can scrupulously observe the Laws and give our children a completely Jewish education'. Another reason for wanting to move to 'a Jewish environment' was the growing problem to which a *Time* magazine article in September 1947 would refer: finding Jewish marriage partners for the many younger members of the community who were growing up rapidly.

The issue had been raised by Francesco Cerrone when he wrote to Cantoni about his son Pasquale doing his military service in the navy. The boy showed 'incontrovertible proof of his devotion to our Sacred Torah', but like the other children in Cerrone's 'exceedingly numerous family' Pasquale was now of an age when he needed to establish a household and a family. For that reason Cerrone asked Cantoni and the Union to help him and his family move ('not necessarily immediately') to a Jewish centre where they would have access to teaching and moral guidance with respect to Jewish ritual and tradition, but 'above all for our children who here are lost in the midst of the darkest ignorance'. Cerrone took the opportunity again to ask Cantoni to help find a job for his son, attaching a photograph to the letter – 'you can recognize my boy from the last photograph of our dear Enzo Sereni that was published in the journal *Hè Holuz* [*Hehalutz*]. He is the one wearing the black cap and standing behind Enzo and by Major Aronov.'[6] (See the photograph on p. 130.)

Cantoni received a similar letter on behalf of another young member of the group, 'Nazario di Salvia, born in 1925', stating that he needed to find a wife:

> but in our small community there is no one, and so I am turning to you who are the President of little orphans and refugees everywhere, with the request that you help us find for him a young woman who would be willing to be his wife and come to San Nicandro. If you think this will be possible, we will write to you again to settle on a date and time when we could meet with you and get to know the girl so that our young man need not take a wife from the other People which the Creator has forbidden, and if you cannot assist us with this, then the young man will have to take a gentile wife which will greatly displease the Almighty but it will not be our fault since we do not have any means of making contact with orphans or refugees . . .[7]

Cantoni acknowledged that these difficulties were real, but admitted that he had no solutions. He gently pointed out that there were indeed many Jewish refugees in Italy at that moment, but they were all in transit and waiting to go to Palestine. Virtually none spoke Italian, so it was very unlikely that they would want to marry an Italian. As for Italian Jews, the problem would be to find a girl who, as he put it delicately, 'would be willing to move to a place like San Nicandro'. In any case, everything would depend on what happened when the girl met the young man and whether or nor they fell in love. The best solution for young Di Salvia, he suggested, would be to find a job or something else that would bring him to Rome where he could meet some Jewish girls: 'who knows whether a marriage might come out of it. However, there is nothing else that I can do and I certainly do not feel that I could make recommendations about someone I do not know in person and I can't see how the young man would be introduced to a young woman if they had not met and got to know one another beforehand.'[8]

When Manduzio came to hear of all this correspondence about finding Jewish wives and moving to a 'Jewish centre', he wrote to tell Cantoni that none of it had anything to do with religion. He said that the reason why Cerrone and all the others wanted to move away from San Nicandro was to do with matrimony, not faith. It appears that over the past years numerous suitors had made plays for Francesco Cerrone's daughters and had all been rebuffed, some quite rudely. Cerrone's wife had told Manduzio that Nazario di Salvia was much too poor. Cerrone himself had told Antonio Bonfitto and Leonardo di Salvia, who had their eyes on two of his daughters, that anyone thinking of marrying them needed to have 'a big fat wallet'. The next suitor had been Eliezer Tritto, who Cerrone said was too poor 'and in any case is a halfwit'. Pasquale Cerrone then decided that he wanted to marry the daughter of Lucia Gravina. Lucia consented, but only on condition that Cerrone made peace with Manduzio. Cerrone refused, so Lucia allowed her daughter to marry 'a young Pagan'. When he heard of this, Cerrone came to Manduzio's house shouting and accusing him of being responsible.[9]

Marriage-making was an important business in all peasant communities, one that was as liable to give rise to quarrels and feuds between families as to create alliances and solidarity. In this respect the San Nicandro community was no exception, but their decision to cut themselves off by choosing a religion that no one else in the vicinity followed compounded their difficulties. They were disappointed when this became clear to them, but it only increased their desire to meet other Jews.

Raffaele Cantoni tried to persuade them that the idea of moving from San Nicandro was utterly impractical. In one of the few long letters he wrote to Manduzio, he explained that the idea of settling somewhere else in Italy, never mind emigrating to Palestine, was out of the question. He mentioned that Cerrone's son Pasquale, 'whom I hardly recognized since he is now a grown man', had come to see him in Rome and had explained how some members of the San Nicandro community had told both Rabbi Ravenna and Dr Ascarelli that they wanted to move from San Nicandro. They had raised the same issue with Rabbi Prato, who had apparently supported the idea, leading Cantoni to explain why he could not agree:

First, because in my view San Nicandro is a community, a small one admittedly, but one that exists and has a very special significance and should not be allowed to disappear, but on the contrary should be allowed to grow and yield fecund fruit and increase the number of its members. There is, of course, nothing to prevent some of the young men and women going elsewhere to look for work and to create new lives for themselves, but a policy for making marriages must also be developed locally since it is very unlikely that people from other towns would otherwise think of moving to San Nicandro. In this way, through the marriages they make the young men and women of the community can bring new members and new recruits to the Jewish population of San Nicandro.

Cantoni insisted that to move the whole community to some other place in Italy would in the present circumstances be impossible. At that moment no housing or accommodation for whole families could be found in any city in Italy since there were still thousands of people without homes or work.

So what should be done? The first task, Cantoni suggested, would be to improve the situation in San Nicandro. He had been horrified to learn that Cerrone's eleven-year-old brother had still not finished the fifth elementary class. 'How can this be?' If the community could ensure that the boy completed his elementary schooling, the Union would be willing to find him a place in a rabbinical school so that after a certain period of time he would be able to return to San Nicandro and act as the rabbi for the whole community. What about the girls? Cantoni said that there were some opportunities that could be explored, and in particular he suggested that temporary places could be found for them in the various summer camps for Jewish girls either at the sea or in the mountains, where they would have the chance 'to come into contact with our way of life, but also to discover the sense of fraternity that we all feel for our dear San Nicandro'.

Cantoni asked Manduzio to send him a full list of all the boys and girls in the community, with their exact ages and details of the work skills that they 'really do possess' and the type of work they would be willing to undertake. He volunteered to introduce the young Cerrone to some of his friends to see whether they could find work for him as an apprentice shoemaker. There was a possibility of sending him to the Jewish community in Pitigliano in southern Tuscany 'where we have friends and he might be able to work out some project with one of the people there who has experience of working on their own account'. In closing, Cantoni noted that when they met in Rome young Pasquale Cerrone had rightly complained that he had never returned to San Nicandro. The reason, Cantoni explained to Manduzio, was that:

as you may have seen from the newspapers, my time is so heavily taken up that I have not had an opportunity to come back and see you all. But please believe and be assured that I nonetheless follow your affairs very closely and that everything that can be done for you I will do my best to achieve. But that does not mean following false trails or failing to finish what you have started. With my most fraternal affection, I send you my warmest *shalom*.[10]

Despite its warmth and affection, the letter revealed a growing frustration on Cantoni's part. He had made it clear that everything that could be done to assist the San Nicandro community had been done, and that it was now up to them to organize their own lives. He also believed that the essential next step was to provide the converts with a rabbi, hence his offer to have one of the younger boys trained at a rabbinical college.

The situation now took a more ugly turn when Cantoni received an outraged letter from Francesco Cerrone denouncing Manduzio. Addressing Cantoni no longer as his dear brother but more formally as 'Most Illustrious Signor Cantoni', he warned that his letter would be long and began by expressing his 'surprise and hurt' that despite all the letters he had written about his son's 'exceptional qualities' Cantoni had done nothing to find the boy a job, for which reason he had been forced to return to San Nicandro. Since Cantoni was familiar with the plight of his large family, Cerrone could only conclude that Cantoni was under Manduzio's sway. 'Do you not understand that for over a decade your protégé Manduzio has persecuted us?' That persecution began, Cerrone claimed, from the time of Cantoni's 'short visits to us' [in 1937] when he had instructed Manduzio how to hold prayer meetings and insisted that he must use the prayer book written by Davide Prato and the other texts that had been given to the community by Rabbi Angelo Sacerdoti 'of sacred memory'. But Manduzio had taken no notice and as soon as Cantoni had left he ensured that all those texts would become 'something for the mice to feed on'.

Cerrone protested that his only crime was his desire to 'follow Jewish ritual as it has been handed down and follow the teaching of rabbis from all over the world'. But Manduzio had opposed that because he did not 'live by the Torah'. Cerrone then claimed that Manduzio had allowed 'his only daughter to marry a Christian, simply because the man was prosperous', – a strange accusation given that all the records insist that Manduzio had no children. However, Cerrone's second accusation went back to the issue that had divided the community since Cantoni's first visit: Manduzio's opposition to the attempts to establish an independent public oratory where the group could meet freely and discuss religious matters. Cerrone said that Manduzio had made him and his family targets of remorseless persecution, and had accused him of trying to usurp his throne. 'It is like Saul and David,' he wrote, yet Cantoni continued to support Manduzio and urged the others to do the same: why?[11]

With the situation in San Nicandro again close to breaking point, Manduzio accused Cantoni of deserting him in his hour of need. He said that he had 'waited in vain for your reply, yet I now feel that you have forgotten me and I see that you have become more cold towards me, but why? Was not I the instrument of God, who instructed me to preach the Law in this barren rock? And was it not I who had the first Vision? And was it not I who wrote to you when you were imprisoned? And did you not ask me to pray for you?' Manduzio protested that those who had been denigrating him refused to acknowledge the divine nature of his visions and that only Dr Faitlovich had recognized him as a leader. For the little community of five men to grow, it could not have ten leaders, and they must recognize his authority. But his authority was being undermined by 'the Serpent' (Cerrone). 'So, dear Cantoni, please do not think that I am asking for something. On the contrary, as you well know. All I want is that the Truth should be recognized and the Truth is that through my Visions I have passed from Death to Life.'[12]

There were signs that the small community was already beginning to disperse. Some now made the choice to leave San Nicandro and settle in one of the camps for Jewish refugees and displaced persons. But the family rivalries and disputes continued. For example, Chaim (formerly Costantino) Tritto wrote to tell Cantoni that when Francesco Cerrone and his son Pasquale had left San Nicandro to move to one of the camps for Jewish refugees, they had taken his youngest son, Samuele, with them. Now Tritto had heard that they planned to emigrate to Africa and to take the boy with them, and he implored Cantoni to intervene to prevent this happening: 'I agreed to let him go to the camp to study, but I beg you to have him return home as soon as possible.'[13]

Cantoni was clearly exasperated by all this. He told Tritto that he had just written to Manduzio 'with great sadness because I see San Nicandro in the grip of total discord and with none of the harmony that one might have expected after you all became part of our family'. He knew that Tritto's son Samuele (the boy Cantoni had chosen to be trained as a rabbi) was at the Agricultural School run by his friend Racah at Cevoli, near Pisa, 'where I understand that he is very happy, and there is no question of him leaving for Africa or Palestine as you suggest'. The young Samuele had not gone to the school against his will, but had been accompanied by another of Tritto's sons who was in service as a policeman in Rome, and who would write to reassure his father. But Cantoni urged Tritto not to worry about the boy: 'You want him to complete his training, and it will not be long before he will be ready to return to San Nicandro.'[14]

At the end of June 1947, Francesco Cerrone, together with his family, was at the San Marco camp at Cevoli near Pisa. His son Pasquale, who had now taken the Hebrew name Pesach, wrote to tell Cantoni that Manduzio and Tritto were organizing a campaign against his family with the aim of forcing them to leave the camp. 'They want to drive us away from here, but who do they think they are? They seem to think that they are Gods. How can they indulge in such a persecution? They are hoping to force us to compromise ourselves through some ill-judged action, from which may the Almighty protect us!'

Pasquale Cerrone did not say what Manduzio's motives might have been, other than enmity towards his family. But he claimed that, although he had written to Manduzio and Tritto asking them to bring the dispute to an end once and for all, they had not replied. He also reminded Cantoni that when they had last met in Rome Cantoni had asked whether there were any others who wanted to leave San Nicandro and settle in one of the Jewish camps. He warned Cantoni that Manduzio was now planning to send the son of Antonio Bonfitto to the camp. He went on say, somewhat mysteriously, that 'everyone knows what Michele Bonfitto did and how he behaved when he was at the camp at Kadima. You can easily discover for yourself whether or not I have behaved badly – here there are some people who are truly religious, while the others just eat the bread they are given and take no notice of what is written in the Torah.' Of those he had met at the camp, he claimed that except for the son of the late Rabbi Ricardo Pacifici none knew anything about Judaism or anything else. Cerrone closed by asking Cantoni to write to Manduzio and Tritto to tell them to leave him alone and to stop persecuting his family.

Cantoni was angered by Cerrone's allegations about the camps, and his reply was curt. He could not begin to understand how Manduzio could possibly interfere with Cerrone and his family now that they had settled far away from San Nicandro in the camp at San Marco: 'a place', he warned, 'where you yourselves will be judged by how you behave and what you do'. He pointed out that if there was any attempt at interference from outside or other misconduct, that was a matter for the management of the *hakhsharà* (the general Hebrew term for agricultural training camps). He said that he was aware that Michele Bonfitto had behaved badly at the Kadima camp, and for that reason it was very unlikely that he would be admitted to the camp at San Marco. He concluded wearily but not unreasonably that he was 'deeply saddened by what is going on at San Nicandro and now between your family and the San Nicandresi, and I must tell you that I can no longer intervene on your behalf since you all seem determined to act according only to your own particular interests and ends'.[15]

Shortly afterwards Pesach Cerrone and his family moved to the Tedl Broscim camp near Livorno, and Pesach wrote again to Cantoni saying that 'you have always had estimable faith in Manduzio, and I can assure you that I have no evil intentions towards him, were it not for the fact that I know he has acted against my family in a hostile manner'. Manduzio's animosity was directed not only against Cerrone's family but against many others too, 'as you would immediately see, were you to visit San Nicandro'. He had no further information about Michele Bonfitto, but if Cantoni was grieved by what was taking place at San Nicandro he must surely understand how Cerrone felt: 'Imagine how it is for me: I grew up and passed my childhood there, but what was once there no longer exists: don't call me a pessimist for saying this, but let me say one more time that given your long absence you cannot possibly know what San Nicandro is like now'.[16]

In August, Manduzio complained to Cantoni that:

Your long silence leaves me thinking all the time of the dear brother who in 1937 promised us your constant protection, but now it is three months since you last wrote and in the meantime I have written you two letters and I cannot understand why my

Brother has not replied to me. I believe that it is probably your great work that has caused you to neglect your oath to us, but if you think that I have committed some sin it is your Duty to tell me how I have sinned so that by your Light I too may come to the Light.

Cantoni now sent Manduzio his longest and most personal letter. He admitted that Manduzio had good reason to complain that 'notwithstanding my best intentions and the affectionate memories I have of you and all my friends in San Nicandro, the days fly by and the months pass and I never manage to do all the things that I would like to do'. Another Jewish year was nearly at an end, he said, and the time had come once more to compose his New Year message for the members of the Jewish community in Italy, a task that it seemed he had last done barely yesterday: 'This is how I live, and this is why I have to give up so many things that would give me great pleasure and satisfaction, not least because the number of those working with us diminishes by the day.'

Turning to Manduzio's concerns, Cantoni said that he could never forget what had happened and that the bond between them was 'indissoluble'. He went on:

You talk of sin and of merit, but I am convinced that your life down there [in San Nicandro] has been dedicated in the broadest and most affectionate understanding possible to the idea that you have embraced. If in disseminating this faith you have encountered difficulties and have met with the aversion of certain people, this is simply natural and part of the logic of things in which every good and constructive deed will be met with others that are opposed and ... evil. But you must go forward and not stop, seeking new life and new blood for the body that has already been created and which when strengthened and made more robust will yield new fruits.

Cantoni reflected finally on the conflicts in the Middle East and the situation of the people of Israel who were still awaiting the possibility of living in peace. 'In Palestine there is no peace, only war, and war in the worst sense of the word and in forms that leave us in a constant state of anxiety that with each new piece of news leaves us more distressed.' Invoking God's help, Cantoni closed with the wish that Israel might once again lead the world towards justice and fraternity, and with a final *shalom* to Manduzio and 'all my brothers down there'.[17]

In September, Manduzio thanked Cantoni for some photographs he had sent them: 'You know that this Virgin family loves you like an Angel of the Creator and that you must never forget that we came to the Light through visions just as was the case of Moses and all the prophets and that anyone who refuses to believe or says that the visions mean nothing denies the God of the visions and Moses of the Sacred Book of Laws'. Cantoni's letter and photographs had arrived while they were celebrating Sukkot and he said that they all wished that Cantoni had been there with them: '29 souls both adults and children took part in the celebration, as well as two others who were Jews in name only since they had not yet received the *opera della Legge* [circumcision]'.[18]

In reality, the divisions within the community had not healed. Indeed, things seemed to be getting worse and in another letter to Cantoni Manduzio claimed that Rabbi Ravenna had openly sided with his opponents. 'Tell Rabbi Alfredo Ravenna to stop writing to us and upsetting our peace of mind.' Ravenna had questioned the reasons for Manduzio's conversion, causing Manduzio to claim that he must have been drunk when he wrote the letter. He begged Cantoni to warn Ravenna against the evils of drink and to stop writing defamatory letters. He also firmly denied Ravenna's insinuations that he and his followers had become Jews 'for their own reasons' ('per scopo') and not because they had followed the orders of the Creator'.[19]

A year after the community's conversion had been formally recognized, their situation was dire. Cerrone and Marrochella had now established themselves and their families in the camps, and many of the young San Nicandresi were eager to follow. But although they had found food, shelter and accommodation in the camps, emigration was still not feasible. For those who remained loyal to Manduzio in San Nicandro, however, the position was becoming intolerable. There was little work and they had no means of supporting themselves. They could not move because of Manduzio's opposition, but nor could they stay where they were. They could not find marriage partners, they could not practise their religion and those who had children could not raise them as Jews. Their story seemed poised to end in disaster.

# CHAPTER TEN

# After Manduzio

Just as the community seemed to be on the point of breaking up, two events occurred in the early part of 1948 that would decisively affect it's destiny. The first was the death of Donato Manduzio, followed two months later by the second event, the founding of the State of Israel on 14 May.

Early in January, Manduzio had written to the Union in Rome to tell them of the community's excitement on reading in the December 1947 issue of the monthly journal *Rassegna Mensile di Israel* the news that the United Nations General Assembly had decided in favour of the partition of Palestine and the creation of a Jewish state. They were in a state of exaltation 'for the Holy Land and the knowledge that after 1877 years the Jewish State is once again arising. May the Almighty keep it for them in perpetuity as he had promised to our fathers, and may the Children of Israel keep faith with the Sacred Torah that Moses received from the Creator.' He expressed his hope that 'when the Children of Israel come into the Promised Land they will destroy the peoples who had occupied it and their idols', and went on to say that the little group of men, women and children in San Nicandro had all been moved to tears by the news. He and his followers had prayed to God to spare the innocent, and sister Di Leo had written a special lament. When they had finished praying, the Lord sent Manduzio a vision and from the vision he knew that the tempest would pass.

Having recounted the vision, Manduzio asked 'the Gentlemen of the Union' to forgive him for the length of his message and sent them all his best wishes. There was a special note for Raffaelle Cantoni, reminding him of when he wrote to Manduzio from Macerata asking Manduzio to pray for him, 'because I know that your prayers are heard in the highest places'.[1]

In Rome, excitement about the news was even more intense. Augusto Segre had been elected secretary of the Zionist Federation shortly before, and he later described how when the news of the UN resolution of 29 November 1947 arrived the offices of the Federation were already crammed with people waiting for information. Raffaele Cantoni was the most excited of all, and it was he who drafted a statement on behalf of Italian Jews to the provisional President of the Italian Republic, Enrico De Nicola.[2]

Manduzio wrote what was to be his last letter to Rome on 19 January 1948. He expressed the concern and grief of the San Nicandro community at the situation in the Middle East, the conflicts between the Jews and the Arabs and the events taking place 'in the bosom of our Mother'. He then launched one of his homilies. 'Woe unto those who go down into Egypt without first seeking my authority,' and he reminded the Gentlemen of the Union that Moses had sent the cloud to show the Jews the way. He warned that while others put their trust in arms, they must trust only in the name of the Lord. 'By virtue of the Torah we alone can become the Queen of the World.' Complaining that the Union had not replied to his previous letter, he ended by saying: 'now you must send me your reply, just as a King must reply to the humblest of his servants. Yours, Manduzio.'[3] Cantoni had time to write only a quick note of reply on behalf of the Union to say: 'We are living in an exceptional and decisive moment of history and I fervently hope that very soon the day of peace in the world will dawn for Israel too, so that in peace and tranquillity we can discuss all those spiritual matters with which you are so deeply engaged.'

On 15 March the Union received a telegram that simply stated: 'With profound grief, the Community of San Nicandro wishes to inform you of the death of Manduzio. Signed, Cirò di Salvio.'[4] The death of the leader and founder of the San Nicandro community was unexpected, and in many respects so too were its consequences. Given the strength of the internal disputes that had gripped the community since their conversion, Manduzio's death might easily have caused it to disintegrate. In fact the result was quite the reverse. The death of their leader seems to have given his followers a new sense of cohesion, determination and direction.

One reason was that Manduzio's most vocal critics, Francesco Cerrone and Angelo Marrochella, had already left the town and after the proclamation of the State of Israel in May they and their families made their way there. Those who remained in San Nicandro were the ones who had stayed loyal to Manduzio, including Chaim Tritto, who had broken his ties with the 'rebels' in the previous year. In terms of age and gender, Tritto had strong claim to be Manduzio's successor, and shortly after Manduzio's death he begged Cantoni to come to San Nicandro to give the community new direction and to collect in person the 'enormous' offering that they had raised for the defence of Israel. He also assured Cantoni that the 'Tritto family' was ready and willing to take on the role and functions formerly performed by Manduzio and could guarantee 'the proper observance of religious ceremonies and gatherings.'[5]

While Tritto remained an important voice, the person who emerged as the most powerful force within the community was Concetta di Leo. Her role in the community had been noted by visitors from the early 1930s, and while her relations with Manduzio had sometimes been stormy, she was his closest and, after his wife, most loyal follower.

It would be tempting to say that after Manduzio's death Concetta di Leo found an independent voice. But reading the copious letters that she now began to write to Rome, to Cantoni and to others, the style and tone is so close that one suspects that Concetta had already been Manduzio's scribe and principal adviser for some time. When she wrote to thank Cantoni for his condolences and to express the hope on behalf of the community that he would, as he had promised so often, come to visit them and give them guidance, she addressed him in the same style as Manduzio: 'Dearest Brother'. Using the same tone and the same language as Manduzio, she assured him that despite the loss of their leader the community knew exactly what they had to do. Manduzio had taught them that the only salvation lay in following the Law, and it was because the people of Israel had forgotten this truth that the Almighty had chased them out of Israel. They would not be able to return until they were ready to follow the prescriptions of the Law.[6]

Like Manduzio, Concetta turned to Cantoni when she needed guidance. In June, she begged him not to forget the community now that they had been left 'like orphans'. She asked for his advice on how to send to Rome the money they had collected for the defence of Israel; that they did not want to risk sending it by mail 'because everyone hereabouts hates us' gives a clear indication of their neighbours' hostility towards the new Jews. A note of uncertainty and insecurity can also be detected in Concetta's letter to Cantoni asking him to send them a lunar calendar for the New Year. They wanted to be sure that they followed all the religious festivals and rites since they could no longer count on 'the famous Hammer that constantly used to sound in our ears'. Despite all his teaching, Concetta realized, it was difficult for them to follow the Law without Manduzio's presence.

She wrote to Cantoni for further guidance after a confusing journey to Bari made by some of the members 'out of fraternal love' and the desire to make contact with other Jews. They went to the Palestinian Office in the town, and although they had made a long journey and were very tired they had been treated very discourteously. They were made to sit on the floor and were told many things that puzzled them; for example, that Jews were permitted to leave their houses on the sabbath, that they could buy goods and could keep either Saturday or Sunday as holidays as they chose. Concetta knew that all this was wrong and she begged Cantoni for his advice.[7]

By October, however, the tone of Concetta's letters had become more confident. One reason, as she explained to Cantoni, was that to her great joy her husband, Antonio Bonfitto, had decided to return to the faith. She was delighted that her house was now spiritually united again, and since her husband was eager to undergo circumcision she asked Cantoni where, when and how this could be arranged. She added that a number of people had expressed interest in joining the community, including one of the sons of Costantina Augella, whose fiancée also wanted to convert.

Cantoni congratulated Concetta on the news about the new members of the community and asked her to send details of all those waiting to join the group, and in particular how many were male so that arrangements could be made for a surgeon to come to perform the circumcisions. He was especially pleased to hear that the community was attracting new recruits, because that was precisely how he wanted it to develop. For the same reason, he reminded Concetta that the young Samuele Tritto, who had been sent to study at the rabbinical school, would soon be ready to rejoin them in San Nicandro so that he could 'do good work among your group and speak of Israel to those who do not know it'.[8]

In April 1949, Concetta asked Cantoni to send various books of hymns and prayers that were being copied and bound in Rome for them, among them a history of Manduzio's community that she had written herself. This short document spelled out why Concetta believed that she should be Manduzio's successor. She explained that she had written what followed 'for all the Jews of

Italy who might wish to study the life of our Illustrious Master, that is to say Donato Manduzio, known also as Levi'. Using almost identical words to the ones with which Manduzio had opened his own Journal, Concetta asked her readers to excuse her 'for any errors in the spelling, since I am not an educated woman but the daughter of a rough-handed peasant'. She then explained that Manduzio had taken the name of Levi because it was by that name that he had been addressed in one of his visions. 'His doctrine was clear and simple, he made difficult things easy to understand, very easy, and everyone understood him immediately'. He was generous and caring, and whenever one of his disciples was ill, he knew how to take away their pain. Like Abraham, he was blessed with visions and hence he had inspired his followers with his prophetic spirit and had created around him what she called a 'prophetic community'. None of them would have dared to move a hand or a foot without the orders of the all-powerful Almighty. Manduzio had warned them expressly that 'after his death they should not fornicate with false gods but rather follow the Law of the Creator'.

She recalled that Manduzio had been a wonderful teacher and had always been especially fond of children: 'he loved to be with them and could keep them enthralled with his stories and teachings which kept them away from temptation and corruption'. Concetta at least gave a nod to the internal disputes that had wracked the community, one of which had involved her directly. Because Manduzio had no children, he said that he would divide equally among the first two couples to be married the single hectare of land he owned. Concetta should have been the beneficiary, but 'something quite unbelievable' happened and the legacy was forgotten, for which she blamed Manduzio's brother and his sons who treated him 'as a leper and showed no interest in his sacred teachings'.

For nineteen years, she went on, Manduzio had led the group, but by 1947 his strength was failing and he wept constantly day and night as his fears grew for the community's fate after his passing. Then one night in a vision, the Eternal One had told him to instruct 'his sister Concetta di Leo to write a lament for his sufferings', which he asked her to do when she visited him the following day. Concetta's Lament was included in the typescript, followed by a prayer. Her account closed with an exhortation: 'You who read this little book please study it carefully. Donato Manduzio, known as Levi, lays before you a long and fine story that will astonish you when you read it. He wrote canticles and poems and prophetic statements that you can read for yourselves in the book of our Canticles. They are simple, but beautiful.' She concluded by saying that when they learned of the war in the Motherland in February of the previous year, Manduzio had summoned the whole community and said to them: 'Brothers and sisters, it is our duty to make every sacrifice to defend our people: we must eat polenta and make savings. And straightaway he began making a collection, but before it was completed he died.'[9]

The purpose of Concetta's document was to show that Manduzio had chosen her to be his successor. With this new confidence she began to take decisions without consulting Cantoni. In March 1949, for example, she informed him that after Passover the men and women who had not yet converted 'will come to Rome, the men to undergo circumcision, the women to perform the ritual bath'. In alarm, Cantoni immediately telegraphed back to say that on no account should the men and women come to Rome. These were matters that must first be discussed with the Chief Rabbi and they needed to give more thought 'to the question of what to do about the conversion of the others who wish to enter into and become part of those who observe the Torah'. Cantoni was alarmed because he feared that in trying to recruit new followers the converts were taking the law into their own hands. In addition, he still believed that their determination to emigrate to Israel was impractical and undesirable, even though the Jewish state was now in existence.

Following the declaration of the new state, both the Jewish bodies in Rome and the Italian government had come under pressure to organize as soon as possible the emigration of the foreign Jewish refugees who were still waiting in transit camps in Italy. By the summer of 1948 it was estimated that there were as many as 20,000 refugees in the camps, and despite the assistance provided by UNRRA their maintenance was a heavy burden for the Italian government. There were also concerns about public order, especially when major anti-British demonstrations were organized in one of the largest of the camps near Bari that housed over 3,000 refugees.

The situation was particularly tense not only because of international events but also because Italy was undergoing its first major political transition since the fall of Fascism. On 18 April the coalition led by Alcide De Gasperi's Christian Democrats had won a resounding electoral victory which resulted in the Italian Communist Party and its left-wing Socialist allies being expelled from the government. Then on 4 July a failed attempt to assassinate the Communist leader Palmiro Togliatti had raised fears that Italy might slip back into the civil war that had been waged between Fascists and anti-Fascists after Italy's defeat in 1943.

The 1948 Italian election had been played out against the backdrop of the emerging bipolar alignments of the Cold War, which also created new concerns about the Jewish refugees. Italy had not yet recognized the new State of Israel, but the USSR and Czechoslovakia had. For that reason the newly-elected Italian government was concerned about intelligence reports on the activities of Zionist organizations in the refugee camps, which suggested that there were links between pro-Communist Zionist organizations in the refugee camps, Czech espionage agencies and sections of the Italian Communist Party.[10] These speculations were almost certainly fanciful, but they gave the Italian government another reason for having the refugees emigrate to Israel as soon as possible. That in turn placed additional pressure on the bodies responsible for organizing the exodus, in Italy and also in Israel, where suitable space and accommodation had to be found for the immigrants. Since Israel was at war with the Arabs, only those who were able to fight or make some active contribution could expect priority. The others would have to wait their turn.

Hence Cantoni's telegram to Concetta di Leo telling her not to send anyone to Rome until he had discussed the matter with the Chief Rabbi. Concetta's reply must have given him pause, however. With undisguised frustration and anger she wrote: 'Dear Brother, I have received your letter which tells us what is always the same story and it is five months now that your guitar has been playing the same tune.' She scolded him for not listening to her words, and then adopted the stratagem that Manduzio had always used. Her words 'were not the words of man but of God'. She went on to tell him of a recent vision in which she had received instructions in allegorical but clear form that if the community of San Nicandro did not emigrate it would be destroyed. In any case, she told Cantoni, 'after the proclamation of the State of Israel and of that glorious and Famous Flag how could we possibly not return to our Homeland?'

Warning Cantoni again that these were not her words, but those of God revealed through the vision, she spoke of the difficulties facing the community: 'We have no temple and you know what our situation is: we are like sheep abandoned by their shepherd and although we have the protection of the Eternal One, we are still lost sheep. Now that we have once again come to the time of the harvest and the landowners demand that we sign and renew our contracts for the coming year, we do not know now where to turn for guidance.' She asked Cantoni – 'my brother' – to take her letter immediately to Rabbi Prato, to read it together with him and ask his advice.[11]

Cantoni was not impressed. His reply was courteous but firm. He said that he had given the vision that she described 'the consideration that it merits', but he went on to say that 'notwith-standing what may have been revealed to you, you absolutely must take into account what can and what cannot be done'. He then set out the arguments against emigration: 'We are talking about sending to Israel, a country where thousands of people are waiting to find some way of establishing themselves, a group whose lives, unlike those who have already arrived there, have never been in danger in their own country.'

Cantoni said that he had repeatedly been berated by the authorities in Israel for assisting Italians who had no pressing need to emigrate. To reassure Concetta, he said that if they took things gradually it might be possible for 'some of the brethren of San Nicandro' to emigrate, but not in the present conditions. He reminded her, too, of the considerable practical difficulties that would confront anyone from San Nicandro trying to immigrate to Israel, not least the language: 'the people of San Nicandro speak only Italian and would find themselves in a country where everyone speaks Hebrew, of which the only word they will recognize is *shalom*'.

The only solution, he insisted, was for as many of the youngsters from San Nicandro as possible to go to study at the *hakhsharà* at San Marco in Cevoli, where they could learn at least some Hebrew. As for Concetta's complaints about the precariousness of the community, Cantoni said that her fears were groundless. They were now officially affiliated with the Jewish community in Naples, which would provide for their spiritual needs. They were also under the protection of the Union of Italian Jewish Communities, which could vouch for the fact that 'your men are Jews, sons of the Covenant and hence in full compliance'. Cantoni closed by advising her that they should go ahead and confirm the contracts with the landowners for the coming year 'since the situation in Israel that I have already described to you means that it will not be possible in the immediate future for the people of San Nicandro to leave Italy and go to Israel'.[12]

This was more than Concetta could bear. Indeed, her reply was quite extraordinary when we bear in mind that she was a woman of no formal education addressing perhaps the most senior and influential member of the Italian Jewish community at that time. She told him that she could not hide the 'immense grief' that his letter had caused her, and she recounted another vision that had come to her the previous night. In the vision she was in a house that she did not recognize and from behind her she heard a voice that told her that she must fulfil 'the duty of circumcision'. When she turned, there was no one there, but the message was repeated clearly three times, and after the third time – in her dream – she asked God how she was at fault. At this point the narrative of the dream and the reply to Cantoni came together. 'What do I signify – she asked the Almighty – in comparison with the men who lord it over us in every respect?'

Concetta accused Cantoni of failing once more to understand that what she had written were not her words but those of the Eternal One. The people of San Nicandro had no material reason for wanting to leave, the Almighty provided for them, they had the produce of the land to eat and holy water to drink. But they must leave for Israel because that was what the Almighty had ordered, and he had ordered that they should do so immediately. She closed with a rather opaque warning: if Cantoni did not believe in her visions, he should bear in mind 'that in the last days all will become Prophets'.[13]

It was now Cantoni's turn to reveal his irritation and anger. He said that the 'misunderstanding' that Concetta persisted in was becoming a source of profound discomfort for him. She repeatedly refused to understand what needed to be done to resolve the situation. He accepted that no one could deny to any Jew who wished to return to Israel the right to do so, but there was also an obligation to ensure that this was done in the proper manner and in ways that contributed to the interests of all. 'What do I mean by "the interests of all"?' Cantoni asked.

It means, first of all, in the present situation in which Israel finds itself, not sending more people whose lives are not in danger in the countries in which they have previously lived. It means not sending large groups of people all at once, but rather having them make the transfer one at a time. It also means not making so much fuss and not attracting all the attention that has for some time now been focused on you Jews of San Nicandro, who have been the subject of numerous newspaper articles.

My dear Concetta, I must tell you that with all the respect in which I hold your visions, one has to take into account the whole situation if we are to take decisions that will prove constructive and not harmful either for individuals or for the whole group.

The situation, he said, was becoming chaotic and he found himself having to deal with numerous young men from San Nicandro who had taken it upon themselves to come to Rome and seek him out saying: 'here we are, you must find some way of supporting us, we need your help because the wife is about to have a baby, help us to get to Israel because in San Nicandro we have no work and our sack of grain has run out'. This could not continue:

The situation of the community at San Nicandro has not changed in material respects from yesterday to today. As we have said over and over again, we are ready and willing to provide whatever assistance we can both for those who plan to stay in San Nicandro and for those who may in the future decide to leave for Israel. But we cannot accept or tolerate a situation in which individuals simply leave the town without taking advice, come here to Rome and then expect that all their problems will be resolved.

Poor Manduzio would certainly be far from content were he able to see what has befallen his San Nicandro in barely a year since his death. With great affection, but also in all sincerity, I must tell you that all this putrefaction, which you yourself have created and encouraged, is to the detriment of everything that Manduzio desired and wished to achieve.

Cantoni advised her to act as a peacemaker, to restore tranquillity to the community and restrain the impetuosity of some of its members. Those who wished to immigrate to Israel must enter into formal communication with the Union of Italian Jewish Communities like all other aspiring immigrants, and the young men must all attend the Jewish School at San Marco. Those who were not young should also be prepared to wait until the younger ones had already left, so that they could establish themselves and make proper preparation for the remainder of the community. 'This is what we have been doing for decades through the activities of the Zionist Organization, and with excellent results. The other methods that you seem to have in mind would simply throw the people of San Nicandro into disarray and in Israel would do no good but simply cause confusion.'[14] Very soon, however, events would develop a momentum of their own that Cantoni was no longer able to control.

# CHAPTER ELEVEN

# The Promised Land

Cantoni's exasperation with Concetta di Leo is understandable. He was working day and night for the Jewish refugees, and in recognition of his work had been honoured with the issue of the new state's first foreign entry visa when he visited Israel in June 1948. But all the while he was now struggling to fend off the increasingly persistent demands from his dear friends in San Nicandro despite everything that he had done for them. He had assumed that once their conversion had been formally completed they would carry on as before. Yet despite his repeated advice they were still determined to emigrate and seemed to consider that he was obliged to assist them in meeting all their needs.

The demands made on him especially by some of the young men who began to make their own way to Rome were quite peremptory and showed a rather arrogant sense of entitlement. But while Cantoni was becoming increasingly irritated, these demands were indicative that even before Manduzio's death the situation in San Nicandro had changed. This was mainly because of the experience that many of the younger men had gained during the time they spent in the camps for Jewish refugees. As well as picking up a smattering of Hebrew, they had been exposed more fully to the Zionist ideas that they had first learned about from Enzo Sereni and the Palestinian soldiers. In the camps, many of the San Nicandro converts established new contacts that made them more independent of the community in San Nicandro.

Francesco Cerrone and Angelo Marrochella, who had decided to make their own way to Rome in the spring of 1945 to challenge Manduzio's authority, succeeded in establishing their own contacts, not only with Cantoni but with other members of the Jewish community as well. Many of these people held positions of influence, like Cantoni's friend Augusto Segre who later became president of the Zionist Federation. While all of these men knew about the San Nicandro story from what they had heard from others, none of them had any direct experience of it or had even been to San Nicandro. The exception was Alfredo Ravenna, who on his two visits had openly sided with Cerrone and Marrochella against Manduzio. This meant that those who did not want to follow Manduzio's leadership could look for alternative patrons and sponsors, a process accelerated when it became evident that Raffaele Cantoni was also unbending in his opposition to plans for the whole community to emigrate to Israel. As the story approached its finale, Cantoni's was no longer the determining voice. Thanks to their close contacts with Segre and with the assistance of the Zionist organizations, both Francesco Cerrone and Angelo Marrochella, together with their respective families, had been able during the summer of 1948 to move to Israel where they were settled on kibbutzim. As news of their departure spread, the families who had been loyal to Manduzio and who remained in San Nicandro began to feel a sense of betrayal, even though their determination to emigrate strengthened.

Cantoni continued to be their first hope of assistance, however. Even before Cerrone and Marrochella left for Israel, Concetta di Leo's son Michele Bonfitto wrote to him for help. Michele had originally planned to join the police force in Foggia, but his mother Concetta had asked him why he should defend De Gasperi, the Italian Prime Minister, when he could be defending the Motherland instead. Reflecting on this, Michele realized that his enemies – including the Cerrone family, who had accused him of misbehaving at the Kadima camp near Rome in the previous year, with the result that he had been forced to leave – had made it impossible for him to emigrate. 'When I was sent to the refugee camp, the three gentlemen Korah, Abiram and Dathan, as you know, plotted to get me thrown out, saying that I was a thief and that all my family were thieves when in fact I got a certificate for good conduct and in any case it was our Master Manduzio who had sent me: How could he have done that if he knew I was a thief?'[1] The reference to Korah, Abiram and Dathan was a direct quotation from Manduzio and suggests that the letter was written by Michele's mother. He went on to beg Cantoni to help him clear his name and more specifically to obtain the papers he needed to emigrate to Israel before he received his call-up papers from the police in Foggia. The prospect of doing military service in Italy was something else that made emigration to Israel a more attractive and more urgent matter for many of the young men on the cusp of reaching military age.

Although he was firmly against the emigration of the whole community, Cantoni was no longer opposed in principle to these young men leaving. He told Michele that he would do what he could to help, 'but only so far as the forms and procedures laid down by the Consulate for issuing the visa are concerned'. He was irritated by Michele's inability to produce the relevant paperwork. Michele clearly expected more and in January 1949 he wrote again, this time together with Eliezer Tritto, the son of Cantoni's long-standing friend Costantino (now Chaim) Tritto. The two young men explained that they had decided to travel to Israel together, but planned first to get married. Michele's betrothed was Adelina de Angelis, as the identifying paperwork stated, 'the daughter of the late Sabattino de Angelis and the late Concetta d'Aquila, born in San Nicandro 6.7.1932, occupation dressmaker'.

Michele added that Eliezer Tritto and his wife had agreed to wait for them 'so that we can all make our *aliyah* together'. Warning Cantoni to take care 'not to lose the certificates', Michele made a further request: 'we are poor, so when everything is ready in about two weeks' time we will send you a telegram so that you can send a lorry to take our few possessions with us to Rome where the two women can take the ritual bath and I can have the circumcision, of course, and then perhaps we would need somewhere to stay for a few days until our departure'.[2]

Eliezer Tritto wrote a separate letter that was punctuated with random phrases in the Hebrew that he had learned at the camp for Jewish refugees near Bari. In fact, his letter revealed both the obstacles that faced would-be emigrants and how much support and assistance they had received. The eighteen-year-old Eliezer informed Cantoni that he had wanted to make his *aliyah* to Eretz Israel ever since Rabbi Urbach had arranged for him to attend the camp. But this had been impossible before because of his age and his father's recurrent illnesses, which had forced him to return frequently to San Nicandro.

Eliezer believed that his opportunity had come when the State of Israel was founded, but he had been frustrated because in May 1948 he received instructions to report immediately for the medical examination in Foggia needed before he began his military service. At the time he was in the camp near Bari and the directors advised him to go to Foggia at once for the medical examination. Afterwards he made a short visit to his family in San Nicandro, where he met up with Michele Bonfitto. It was then that the two of them decided to go to Rome and seek out Augusto Segre at the Zionist Federation. While they were in Rome, Eliezer was reunited with his elder brother, Antonio, who no longer practised the Jewish faith and was serving in the police force. He told Eliezer that since he was still a minor he could not do anything without parental permission, and if he acted without their consent, it 'would cause a lot of trouble for our parents'.

He told him to go straight back to San Nicandro, which Eliezer did, and as a result and to his great disappointment he missed the chance of joining his companions from the camp in Bari, who in his absence had left for Israel.

Once Eliezer came of age and decided to emigrate there were further delays. Michele Bonfitto had been ill and was still waiting for the necessary medical tests to show that he was fully recovered so that he could obtain a visa for Israel. Eliezer told Cantoni that he and Michele both wished to have the opportunity to defend 'our Jewish Motherland', and asked him obtain the necessary passports for them from the Israeli Consulate. The two young men were still waiting to get married so they could take their new wives with them to Israel. He promised that they would send a telegram as soon as the dates for their marriages were fixed, adding that he and Bonfitto planned to come to Rome and wait there until the time for their departure. That would also give Michele Bonfitto the opportunity to be circumcised. Tritto added that he had been circumcised in Florence by Dr Elio Levi in January 1948, and that his wife Incoronata Buchs 'is of our religion and is the daughter of Luigia Iannone (the widow of Giuseppe Buchs)'.[3]

By May 1949, however, there was still no sign of Bonfitto in Rome and Cantoni wrote to express his perplexity, saying that arrangements were now being made in Rome for all those who wished to emigrate to Israel and needed first to be circumcised or perform the ritual bath. By then both young men had married and Bonfitto wrote to say that his wife would give birth early in July and asked for assistance since there was no work to be had in San Nicandro at that time of year. He also asked Cantoni's assistant, Della Seta, to arrange for 'a lorry, perhaps one from the Joint, to be sent for them'.[4] While Cantoni was prepared to help these young men find their way to Israel, the obstacles were still considerable. In addition to acquiring exit permits, entry visas and passports, the would-be emigrants also had to deal with

Italian bureaucracy, and especially with the Italian military authorities since most of them were either approaching or had reached the age when they were required to perform military service. Particularly on public transport, the police regularly and carefully checked the documents of all young men to ensure that they were not evading the call-up.

By the summer of 1949 even the young San Nicandresi had not been able to emigrate, while the situation of the community in San Nicandro was becoming increasingly uncertain and difficult. The reasons that Cantoni had given to Concetta to explain why he was discouraging any attempt by the whole community to emigrate were eminently reasonable, but he had failed to appreciate both the very difficult situation in which the converts now found themselves and the strength of their determination to leave. He had also underestimated the resolve of the women whose role at this point proved to be critically important. Like Cantoni, Manduzio had been firmly opposed to emigration, and his widow Emanuela Vocino remained loyal to his wishes. Emanuela shared her husband's belief that their mission was to 'bring Light to this Dark Corner of Apulia'. But despite her closeness to Manduzio and her proud defence of his legacy, it was Concetta who had made the decisive break when after Manduzio's death she declared herself to be in favour of emigration. Her decision may have been influenced by her desire to support her son Michele, but it also reflected her recognition that, in this at least, Angelo Marrochella had been right. The converts could not live as Jews in San Nicandro. If there was nowhere else in Italy for them to live as Jews, they must go to Eretz Israel. Since the State of Israel now existed, what reason was there for them not to go?

There was now a new concern among the remaining community that the younger men and their families might leave for Israel and consign the others to their fate in San Nicandro. For that reason in the summer of 1949 Concetta di Leo took the unprecedented step of travelling to Rome to explain their predicament to Cantoni in person. She did not travel alone (she was probably accompanied by Maria Frascaria), but she had never made a journey of this sort in her life before. The trip was tiring and frightening, but even worse it also proved to be a fool's errand. Their plan was to go to the offices of the Jewish Union in Rome and meet Cantoni and Rabbi Prato, but the women had given no prior notice of their arrival and when they finally reached the organization's offices it was late in the day and there was no one there. The two women decided to find a hotel, but soon realized that they did not have enough money. Unsure what to do next, they walked the streets of Rome until it was nearly midnight, when they found themselves near the railway station. Ashamed to be alone at night, they boarded a train that was due to leave for Foggia early in the morning, where they slept until the train left for its destination many hours later.

After she had returned to San Nicandro, Concetta wrote to Cantoni and quietly rebuked him for the fact that the Union did not have somewhere appropriate to accommodate visitors, especially women. In a more conciliatory tone, she said that she had left some photographs of the members of the San Nicandro community and of Manduzio which she asked him to share with Rabbi Davide Prato. Then she turned to her main business. The women of San Nicandro, she told him, were overcome with grief because they had heard that they were not to be permitted to emigrate to Israel with their husbands. 'You have to consider our group as though it were a single body and our Community will plant itself in Israel without leaving behind a single person.' She warned Cantoni again that this was not merely their desire, but that of the Creator, which he could ignore only at his peril.[5]

The sense of the community's solidarity evident in Concetta's letter was reinforced by a commitment to the Zionist cause that was no less fervent than that of the young men. Nor was Concetta alone. In January 1949 the widow Maria Frascaria had written to tell Cantoni of her joy on reading in the latest issue of *Rassegna Mensile di Israel* of the recent successes of 'our brave soldiers', which demonstrated that God had given victory to the Jews. She added, however, that she had been deeply shocked to read that the President of Israel had sent his greetings to Christians for the recent celebrations of Christmas. Why, she asked, should Jews send greetings to Christians who had always hated them and were the main opponents of the creation of a Jewish state? 'Those of you who are at the heads of things should write to the newspapers about what the Jewish people must do to have their redemption and forge in the hearts of man a love for the Laws that came down from Sinai . . . and you must tell the men who write in the newspapers that they should not use words of weakness.' She was no less outraged that publication of the recent issue of *Israel* had been delayed by the holiday for the feast of the Epiphany: 'but this is a festival that is celebrated by Christians and not by those of us who call ourselves the people of God.'[6]

Maria Frascaria's letters, like those of Concetta di Leo, Lucia Gravina and others, illustrate that the women in this community were well able to express themselves, even though they were part of a rural society where girls and women received little formal education. Despite the aggressive tone, Maria Frascaria's denunciations offer a clear indication of the small community's strong sense of its own identity and what made them feel different from – and better than – their neighbours. This was something that the women were willing to fight for, and in contrast to the disputes that divided the males, the strong sense of solidarity they shared ultimately ensured that the community would remain together. But this was not what brought them to Israel. Nor was Raffaele Cantoni the prime mover, since to the very end he remained opposed to their emigration. The critical intervention came from a different and quite unexpected source: Pesach Cerrone, the son of Francesco Cerrone, who had left for Israel in the summer of 1948.

Relations between Cantoni and Francesco Cerrone had never been good given that Cantoni had very much sided with his friend Manduzio. But in the camps Francesco's son Pasquale, now Pesach, had got to know many members of the Italian Jewish community, on whom he seemed to make a good impression. One of these was a young Jewish boy, Emanuele Pacifici, the son of Rabbi Riccardo Pacifici who had been deported in 1943 and died in Auschwitz. Like many other Roman Jews made homeless by the war, after the liberation Emanuele's family had been accommodated first in the Kadima camp near Grottaferrata and then at Cevoli near Pisa, where the children worked on the farms during the day and took Hebrew lessons in the evening. It was here that the young Emanuele met Pesach Cerrone, who among other things taught him how to repair shoes.[7] During a visit to the same camp, Augusto Segre also met Pesach and they too became friends. It seems very likely that Segre helped the Cerrone family leave for Israel in the summer of 1948, where they settled on a kibbutz and Pesach joined the Israeli army. The following year, however, he returned temporarily to Italy and it was then that he contacted Segre in Rome and asked him to help the converts who were still in San Nicandro.

Segre agreed and wrote to the President of the Milanese section of the Zionist Federation to say that he had been talking in Rome with a certain *chaver* (member of a kibbutz) called Pesach Cerrone from San Nicandro who had already served as a volunteer in the Israeli Defense Force (IDF) in Eretz Israel, but had returned temporarily to try to assist his fellow villagers. Segre was sure that the Milanese branch of the Zionist Federation would be well aware of the situation of the group of Jews from San Nicandro Garganico. He said that fifteen of them had already made their *aliyah*, while a further twenty-eight were waiting to do so. The latter group consisted of nine children aged from three to twelve years, three labourers, seven farmers, two cheesemakers, two gardeners, two dressmakers, one shepherd and two housewives.

Segre went on to explain that although they were Italian Jews and could claim no priority to emigrate at this time, a special case could still be made for them:

> As you will certainly be aware, this is a group of very religious *gerim* [converts] who have embraced the Jewish religion in recent years. There is no question that they face the same difficulty that we have encountered in the case of other Italian Jews and they too will certainly have to wait for a better time. But even if we do not take account of the fact that many of these people have sold their land and their houses and have prepared thoroughly for their *aliyah*, it is also true that they have individually and collectively skills and experience in farming that are far from common . . . On the other hand, it is also true that they do not know the [Hebrew] language and that in general they have a somewhat limited culture. But if we could get some confirmation from the kibbutz at Jaune [Yavneh], or of the proposal made by *chaver* Beppe Artom to set this group up (together with their compatriots who are already in Eretz Israel) in a little village not far from Jaune, making sure at the same time that the group would be under the guidance of that kibbutz, I think that the project would merit closer consideration.[8]

Anna Levi Minzi, the President of the Zionist Federation in Milan, contacted Cantoni who said that on the San Nicandro question he had nothing to add to what he had already said in discussion with his friends Segre and Prato. He made it clear that he did not share their enthusiasm for the project, but went on to say that although he no longer had any influence over the matter he hoped that those who did would get a move on and make some decisions: 'I can only hope they are better than the ones they have made so far, since they have taken upon themselves to permit "a trouble-maker like Cerrone" to go to Israel, even though he would have been much better off down there in

San Nicandro instead of out there [in Israel].' Cantoni restated his own position:

> The problem, as I see it, is not to try to solve everything at once. But since my opposition to their project became known, the San Nicandresi have been rushing around knocking on the doors of everyone, all of whom seem happy just to say "yes" whatever the demands, which has created a total mess [*pasticcci*] and now the San Nicandresi are all saying: 'You must let us go.'
>
> As far as I am concerned, I cannot see that there is anything to be gained by letting the whole group go. Once the young ones have spent some time in the *hakhsharà*, and once they have achieved a certain degree of proficiency in Hebrew, there may a case for them to go and they may be able to do something useful. But as soon as they get to Israel they should all be sent to work in the kibbutz, otherwise we will have a repetition of what happened in the case of the Cerrone parents, who with the typical Spanish-style mentality of southern Italians once they got to Israel decided that they did not want their children to be in a religious kibbutz and tried to keep hens and chickens in their house. In my opinion, people who are likely to finish up in an Arab village near Jaune should at least be able to show that they have absorbed the ideas and civilization of Israel and not behave worse than the Arabs.[9]

In July Cantoni received a letter from the Mizrachi Organization World Centre in Jerusalem informing him that they had received information about the case of the San Nicandresi who were in Rome. The head of the office, Judah Domnitz, knew Cantoni well and he too asked his advice and opinion, although he also informed him that their organization had already reserved a suitable number of places for the group in a village that had recently been 'cleared' of Arabs. The assistance of their organization would ensure that 'the San Nicandresi were not faced with the difficulties and discomforts encountered by most new *olim* [immigrants]'.[10]

So the decision had been taken, and despite Cantoni's objections special arrangements were to be made for receiving the San Nicandro converts and finding them suitable accommodation. But matters dragged on, and in September Pesach Cerrone, who was still in Rome, wrote to again to Cantoni ('Caro Raffaele') to express his concern and frustration. Referring to what had been decided with regard to the San Nicandresi, Cerrone said that he was sorry that Cantoni had become a victim of the situation, but even though he understood that Cantoni was annoyed by the turn of events he knew that he could talk frankly with him and he insisted that they must do everything they could to see the business through to the end.

> I have just returned from San Nicandro and have seen with my own eyes how things are down there. Some of them are surviving with the greatest of difficulty, some are sleeping rough and most of them are desperately poor because they have no work. They are all anxious to leave, but they are also exhausted. I am convinced that at this point the only solution is to place these people in a camp in preparation for their *aliyah* and where they can wait until the blessed passports are ready. The people in the town hall are sending them from one office to another and every time the papers seem to be ready, they tell them that all the signatures have lapsed and that they must start all over again from the beginning.

Cerrone said that it was essential to get them out of San Nicandro because 'they are being criticized from all sides, and the other people in the town are saying they are mad or using other similarly deprecating terms'.

Cerrone feared that bureaucratic snags might still cause everything to unravel. It was essential, he insisted, that Cantoni and

Prato should intervene again on their behalf and go in person to the Ministry of the Interior to ensure that the passports were issued quickly. Cerrone undertook to write to Davide Prato and to Umberto Nahon as well, so that all three of them were aware of the situation: 'I go round and round, and without your help all my peregrinations will be empty and meaningless.' Cerrone's letter closed with his best wishes for Rosh Hashanah and a personal comment:

> Raffaele, you have followed more or less every phase of the San Nicandro story and you know me well although I don't know what opinion you may have of me. So let me tell you in good faith that I have lost the holy bigotry that I learned from the priests, but I have gained a lot of experience. It seems clear to me that those who should exercise justice are failing to do so, and we are in a situation in which justice may never be done: please be aware that this is not directed at you personally. Prato started this business, and he is now acting like Pilate.[11]

In mid-October Cerrone again contacted Cantoni's office to check that representations had been made with the Interior Ministry with regard to the passports. Whatever remaining obstacles or objections there may have been were finally cleared and on 14 November Cantoni received a telegram from Cerrone in Bari announcing the imminent departure of the San Nicandresi for Israel. A second telegram on the same day simply stated: 'The San Nicandresi have left [*Sannicandresi partiti*].'

A week later, on Monday 21 November, the Italian daily *Il Paese* carried the small announcement that twenty recent converts to Judaism had landed at Haifa from the Israeli ship *Galilee*, 'the first group of emigrants from the Italian village of San Nicandro who have embraced the new religion. No sooner had they landed in Palestine than they knelt to kiss the soil of their new country. Thirteen more emigrants are expected to join them in the next week.' Two days later Cantoni's office sent the full list of names of those who had embarked on the *Galilee* in Bari to the offices of the *Irgun Olé Italia* in Tel Aviv. The San Nicandresi had finally reached the Promised Land.[12]

# CHAPTER TWELVE

# The Story's End

The emigration of the San Nicandresi proved to be a highly complicated operation. Although the main group sailed from Bari in November 1949, others had preceded them and others would follow soon after. But none of this would have been possible without the intervention and assistance of the Zionist Federation and the Jewish Agency in Rome. This was true even for the younger migrants who had tried to make their own arrangements, as the young Eliezer Tritto discovered. Although he had told Cantoni in the previous year of his plans to marry before he left, the marriage had caused additional and unexpected complications. His bride, Incoronata Buchs, came from one of the San Nicandro families and the marriage had been brokered by Manduzio before he died. But Incoronata (who now took the name Ester) was only fifteen years old, so the couple had to wait a year until she was old enough to marry.

In the meantime, Eliezer had passed his eighteenth birthday, making him liable for military service, which in turn would have forced him to put off emigrating until he came out of the army. Luckily for the couple the Zionist Federation in Rome came up with a solution, and provided them with false identity papers so that they could pass themselves off as immigrants from Libya. They made their way to Rome, picked up the false papers and boarded the train to Bari, fearing all the time that they would be exposed when the railway police checked their papers. They arrived without further adventures, however, and in time to join the other converts from San Nicandro who were waiting to leave for Israel.

Forty-five years after the event Eliezer Tritto could still vividly recall the excitement and the expectations of the emigrants as they set off in November 1949 to start their new lives. They were quite unprepared for what awaited them, but Eliezer believed that their backgrounds had accustomed them to hard work, especially farm labour, as well as hardship and how to get by on very little, in ways that made them well qualified to become successful settlers. The challenges were considerable and even though arrangements had been made to welcome and accommodate them when they arrived, the lives of the new immigrants were by no means easy and the promise that they would not experience 'difficulties and discomforts' proved to be over-optimistic.

Eliezer Tritto was the only one of the San Nicandro immigrants who later chose to record his family's experiences after their arrival in Israel. He remembered after disembarking at Haifa that they were first sent to a transit camp where they underwent more medical examinations and tests by the immigration and public health authorities. They then spent a whole year living under canvas, with as many as twelve persons in a single tent. 'No one complained,' Eliezer recalled, 'the important thing was that we were all true Zionists.' But they were sorely tested. Ester by now was pregnant, and Eliezer worked all hours picking stones from the fields and other jobs that paid little. Things looked better when they were moved to a former Arab village, Migdal Gad (near the present day Ashkelon), where for the first time they were given houses and apartments. There was more work available and they were now joined by other immigrants from San Nicandro, including Ester's mother and brother.

As a result they needed more space, so the family now moved further north where they were placed in a settlement of Jews

3 Two boys from San Nicandro reading the scripture, Meiron, Israel, 1950s.

from Tripoli at Raslel Achmer (now Kerem Ben Zimra) in Galilee near Safed, some 25 kilometres from the Lebanese border.[1] But there was little work to be found there either, and when their first son, David Chaim, was born, Eliezer and Ester moved again, this time to the nearby *moshav* Alma. But there was no work there either so Eliezer took a job with an organization that was laying water pipes in many different kibbutzim and settlements. The work was hard and he was always travelling, returning home every Friday and leaving again on the Sunday.

In the meantime, Ester had two more children, and in the hope of improving their situation they moved again in 1954 to Safed, where Eliezer tried his hand at raising sheep. When that proved unsuccessful they moved again to Biyia where they raised cattle, then opened a haberdasher's shop which soon failed. To keep the family going Eliezer continued to work as a builder, until finally in 1964 he and Ester opened a falafel shop in Biyia. The shop soon attracted customers and started to do well. In 1960 their fourth child, Batsheva, was born and in 1972 their eldest daughter Miriam got married.

Eliezer proudly concluded that he and his wife had proved to be 'true Zionist Idealists who have given everything to help build Israel'. But this had been possible only because of Donato Manduzio, 'a man who had been inspired by God and whose special powers were recognized by everyone'. Manduzio's greatest achievement was that 'it was he who had brought us all to *Eretz Israel* . . . We are all of us very proud to live in Israel'.[2]

Concetta di Leo had also kept in touch with Cantoni. Despite the bitter note on which their previous correspondence had closed, the two were now on good terms and had remained in contact through a mutual friend, Giuseppe (Beppe) Artom. In her first letter written in the summer of 1950, six months after arriving in Israel, Concetta announced that she had taken the Hebrew name Devora and she greeted Cantoni once again as her 'dear brother', thanking God and the prophets that they had achieved everything that they had hoped for. She told him of her joy that they had succeeded in following God's orders and settled in the Holy Land: 'We have an excellent rabbi, our children are already learning to speak and sing in Hebrew, and the rabbi has also taught us adults new hymns.' In April, they had visited Jerusalem and her grandchildren were both doing very well at school, while her husband Antonio Bonfitto was also happy.

Looking back on the events that had brought them to Israel, she underlined the decisive impact of the meeting with 'Enzo Sereno' (that is, Sereni) in March 1944 'during the time of the English'. She remembered how he had sung their hymns with them and set them an example of courage and heroism, and she acknowledged that this had been a second conversion. Manduzio had led them to the true God, but Sereni had shown them what they must do. Concetta ended her letter with a request that Cantoni send them a subscription for the Italian journal *Rassegna Mensile di Israel* so that they could keep up with the news from Italy, and for an Italian edition of the Jewish lunar calendar because the Hebrew version was still difficult for them to follow. She asked him to give her greetings to Rabbi Prato, and sent her warmest *shalom* on behalf of 'all our little flock'.[3]

The requests for Italian-language materials suggest that it was taking time for the immigrants to assimilate to their new surroundings and language. Leo Levi, who as an envoy of the Jewish Agency was directly involved with the San Nicandro immigrants and acted as their guide during their 'absorption in our country', commented on the difficulties they still faced a year after their arrival in Israel. By then the families were spread over some five different settlements, the one at Alma and four others. But Levi noted that despite the fact that some of them had received careful preparation for their *aliyah* from the military rabbis (as well as Urbach he mentioned Rabbis Ishkoli and Eliner) and from envoys from the Jewish Agency in Rome (including himself), 'the completion of their Hebraicization has made little progress in Israel'. He also complained that 'they continue their rituals, their psalms in an *italoid* dialect all of which, although beautiful and of biblical inspiration, are certainly not orthodox!'[4]

When Elena Cassin, who had first met some of the San Nicandro settlers in April 1952 when she started writing their story, returned to visit them in the early 1990s she also noted that like many other immigrants they had initially been treated with some hostility by Palestinian Jews and had faced many difficulties in adapting to their new surroundings.[5] But this was an experience common to all immigrants and with time the issues of 'absorption' were resolved. In this sense at least their arrival in

4 Group of families from San Nicandro stringing tobacco leaves at Alma in the 1950s.

Israel and the process of assimilation into Israeli society were a continuation of their earlier story, which from the start had been about choosing new identities and about understanding their new faith and what it meant to be a Jew. But once in Israel, and as their children and then grandchildren began to grow up, the experiences of the immigrants from San Nicandro were not essentially different from those of the thousands of other families who chose to settle and make their lives in the new Jewish state. As those new stories began, it soon became clear that their departure from Bari in November 1949 marked the final chapter in the older story that had begun two decades earlier in San Nicandro.

That older story did have a brief aftermath, however, and, as the journalist Giovanni Russo remarked, the converts' departure did not go unnoticed. Indeed, as the news spread, the story of the families from San Nicandro who had gone to Israel seemed to realize the fondest dream of many poor southerners for whom in 1949 emigration was still not a possibility.

The first to spread the story had been the converts themselves. In June 1949 Cantoni and Rabbi Prato received a letter from Giuseppe Corso and Matteo Russo, both from San Nicandro, who had written to say that three months previously they had converted to the Jewish religion and had been advised by Signora Concetta di Leo on how to follow 'the doctrines and rituals of Israel. We were gladly accepted and from that time on we have fully frequented that community.' They wanted to go to Israel like the others, but had been dismayed when they met 'an arrogant young man named Cerrone' who had recently returned from Israel and visited San Nicandro to tell everyone about his experiences in Palestine. As we have seen Pesach Cerrone had come back to Italy in an attempt to encourage others to follow his family to Israel, probably so that he could have some Italian neighbours. But he appears to have behaved most disrespectfully towards the two would-be converts, who complained that he had used terms that were 'quite inappropriate and not at all relevant to our question, as if he wished to deter us from our idea of leaving for Israel and giving the impression that he was the one that controlled these things (even though we do not attach any importance to what he said)'. The two men asked Cantoni and Prato to help them, but Cantoni told them that the Jewish Union had no responsibility for emigration to Israel and he advised them to contact the Palestinian Office and the Israeli Consulate in Rome.[6]

As well as intervening on behalf of the San Nicandresi, it seems that Cerrone was hoping to act as a broker or intermediary for other would-be converts and emigrants. Angelo Marrochella was probably on a similar mission when he too came back to Italy in

1949 to try to persuade a group of families in Apricena to convert and join him in Israel. He had relatives in the town, where he also owned a small piece of land, and the families he approached were connected to the Pentecostalists who had been in touch with Manduzio and his followers before the war. Had he succeeded this might have been a nice example of reverse proselytizing, but he was no more successful than Cerrone.

In his attempts to persuade them to become Jews and join him in Israel Marrochella recruited Chaim Tritto, Eliezer's father, to act as his intermediary. In a scrawled and almost illegible letter written in August 1949 Tritto asked Cantoni to help, saying that there were six or seven families in Apricena that he knew personally. He could vouch that they understood and followed the teachings of the Torah, and they had told him that they wanted their children – twelve boys aged from twelve to eighteen years – to be given places at a Jewish college where they could study.

Cantoni's reply was cautious. Before any further consideration could be given to the case, he said, he needed to know more about the religious sentiments of those who wanted to become observers of the Torah. More specifically, if the children were to enter a Jewish college, the men in the community had to be circumcised and the women had to take the ritual bath: 'all these things must be done first, because we would not want it to be the case that their faith was limited simply to wanting to get their boys admitted to a College and nothing else!' Tritto again insisted that all were well educated in the Torah and had carefully studied the Hebrew religion and that they were eager to undergo the necessary rituals as soon as possible. But a message from Rome written on Cantoni's behalf simply said that for the time being it was best to put off any further decision:

As you well know, Manduzio studied and reflected for a very long time before he was welcomed to join the family of Jews, and this was the case for all the other converts from San Nicandro. The Torah is a great thing, but is not easy to understand or to

5 One of the San Nicandro settlers photographed at Alma in the early 1950s.

observe. You also know that those who ask to become part of the people of Israel are turned away seven times, so you should not take it amiss if we are unable immediately to accommodate the requests of the inhabitants of Apricena.

Irritated by the lack of response, the leader of the would-be converts in Apricena, Achille di Lella, wrote to Rome in January 1950 complaining that their request had not been taken seriously. With no reply forthcoming, Di Lella wrote instead to Cantoni, saying that they had embraced the new faith over a year earlier and wanted to have the promises that God had made to Abraham: 'We yearn to become part of the people of Israel, no matter what sacrifice that might entail.' Changing tack to a possibly more persuasive argument, he added: 'We have many sons and we are all agricultural workers and we are willing to work the land wherever you may wish to send us.'[7]

Cantoni did not reply, but shortly afterwards he met Chaim Tritto in Rome and told him not to pay any attention to the people from Apricena: 'they may seem sincere to you and to speak honeyed words, but they have only poison in their hearts.'[8] Presumably Cantoni meant that they were not interested in conversion, only in emigration. In June, Di Lella received a letter from the Vice-President of the Union explaining that before their case could receive further consideration they should study, learn and obey Jewish Law and follow the example set by 'the brothers of San Nicandro who had to wait for many years, which is perhaps the best example of what it means to become a Jew'. The converts of San Nicandro had had the constancy of purpose to wait for so long and to prepare themselves fully before they became Jews: 'This is not something that can be done in a short time, but only after months and years of meditation and study. So you should continue to study the Bible and to prepare yourselves slowly in its observance.'[9]

Di Lella was outraged and he vented his anger on Tritto, who in turn complained to Cantoni that the people of Apricena were blaming him personally and also saying that the San Nicandresi converts were all liars who had converted only to have the opportunity to emigrate to Israel. But Tritto was angered even further after discovering that the people of Apricena had also written to Marrochella, now back in Israel, who had told them not to worry about the messages from Rome because he could arrange for as many of them as wanted to emigrate to join him. 'Does this mean, dear brother Cantoni,' Tritto wrote bitterly, 'that Palestine is now being run by Pasquale Cerrone and Angelo Marrochella?' He claimed that it was widely known that Cerrone had come back to Italy for personal gain and was reported to have acquired a million and a half lire. 'Now Angelo Marrochella also plans to come back to Italy, and he has written to tell the people at Apricena that he will take them all back with him, and he has written also to other people at San Nicandro with the same message.'

Tritto reminded Cantoni that when they had discussed the Apricena case in Rome, Cantoni had said that even though the San Nicandresi had been so religious, they too had done some 'really disgraceful things [*porcherie*]': 'exactly the words you used, dear brother Cantoni'. Tritto now agreed that the people from Apricena 'want to become Jews but without God, and they are pretending only so that they can go to Israel. What they are really concerned about is that there is too much hunger here in Italy, which is the only reason that they want to go to Palestine.' Without giving any further reasons he also warned Cantoni to be wary of Marrochella should he come to Rome, and to warn the 'American governor' that he was a trickster and a fraud.

Tritto's grasp of events was shaky. He still referred to Israel as Palestine and there was of course no longer any American governor in Rome. Nor do have any way of knowing whether there was any truth in his insinuations that Marrochella and Cerrone were trying to profit by acting in effect as emigration-brokers for those wishing to go to Israel. But Tritto was certainly concerned that his own role as gatekeeper of the Jewish community in San Nicandro had been threatened, and he complained to Cantoni that after the others had left he had told the Chief Rabbi that 'no one else down here should be circumcised without my permission'.[10]

Nonetheless, Rabbi Ravenna and Leo Levi[11] did eventually go to Apricena and made a favourable report. Tritto was again outraged, protesting to Cantoni that when he had spoken in favour of the people in Apricena his advice had been ignored. Since in the meantime Ravenna and Levi had visited Apricena, Tritto could only assume that the 'gentlemen in Rome' had listened to Marochella. But Marochella had been in Israel for three years and knew nothing about Apricena or San Nicandro, while he, Chaim Tritto, did. Yet his word counted for nothing, whereas they listened to the word of those who did not heed the Law: 'But no one listens to me, no one believes me, and you do what Marochella who lives in Palestine tells you to do.'

Although clearly frustrated by all these squabbles, Cantoni nonetheless wrote to reassure Tritto that Rabbi Ravenna and Leo Levi had visited Apricena simply to review the situation there and he confided: 'I can tell you definitively that after talking with Rabbi Prato we have come to the decision that we do not wish to do anything more about this matter. You have all my trust and affection, because I know you to be a man of faith and true feelings.'[12]

The Jewish Agency in Rome later decided that the group in Apricena could convert and emigrate to Palestine, but by then they had changed their minds. In the meantime others had heard the story, however, and more requests began to reach Rome.[13] Luigi di Seri, who described himself as 'an orphan in the world aged 27 with no father or mother', wrote from Potenza in August 1950 to say that he had converted to the Jewish faith and wanted to live in Palestine because he could not find peace with the 'religion of Italy'. In his own mind, he said, he was already part of the Jewish people, but because he preached the Jewish religion wherever he went he was hated by all and he needed to 'leave the houses of the worldly'. He asked that he be admitted 'to the circumcision of the Law'.[14] Francesco Giramonte from San Giovanni in Fiore near Cosenza in Calabria wrote more simply to ask for assistance in getting a job. He had been without work for a long time, and needed help in approaching the Southern Electrical Company that was engaged in various operations near his home, making the very curious claim that 'it is well known that the majority of those working there are Jews'.[15] How Giramonte had come by such obviously false information is not easy to guess, but his request offers another if rather bizarre illustration of how for a brief moment at least the path to the Promised Land was one that many people in southern Italy wanted to follow. However, very soon other and more accessible destinations would become available for those who wanted to escape the poverty and hardship of their lives in southern Italy, and with them went identities that were perhaps less difficult to acquire than the ones chosen by the followers of Donato Manduzio.

Not only at its conclusion, but at every stage the story of Donato Manduzio and the San Nicandro converts proved to be anything but uncomplicated. Even their emigration, when it came, did not quite conform to their idea (and that of some subsequent writers) of a whole community setting off together for Israel. The often bitter divisions and disputes that had preceded the emigration seem to have continued afterwards, and there was little subsequent contact between the Cerrone and Marrochella families and the others.

It is clear that most of the key stages in the story were determined by external interventions. While its origins were rooted in the desire to escape from a land of remorse and despair, it was the war that unexpectedly opened up new possibilities of escape. San Nicandro found itself within close reach of the networks of camps for Jewish refugees in Italy, hooked up in the Net that enabled many to reach Palestine. Once Bari became one of the principal points of departure for those seeking to reach the Gates of Zion, the story of Manduzio and his followers could no longer be contained within the narrow confines of San Nicandro. And the founding of the State of Israel in May 1948 ultimately made feasible what had previously been no more than a dream.

But without the interest and commitment shown by so many Italian Jews, it is unlikely that the conversion could have taken place at all. This was true both of the decision by Davide Prato and his advisers in 1946 to formalize the conversion of the whole community, and of the events leading up to their emigration. Without the direct intervention of Raffaele Cantoni in the first case, or of Giuseppe Nathan, Augusto Segre and many others in the second, it is unlikely that either would have happened as it did, if indeed at all.[16]

What was it that drew these men to Manduzio and his followers? The themes of simplicity, sincerity and absence of ulterior motivations recur time and again in the words of those who were most closely involved in the story. Angelo Sacerdoti, Alfonso Pacifici, Raffaele Cantoni, Enzo Sereni, Augusto Segre and Leo Levi all found something irresistible in the story of a group of simple peasants who had found the Jewish faith unassisted and unaided. Even those who knew the community best, like Cantoni, and could see at first hand the frequent contrasts between image and reality, nonetheless stood firmly by that judgement. Indeed, no sooner had the converts left for Israel than their case was being held up as an exemplary model that other would-be converts would have to learn to emulate. For that reason, despite its factual inaccuracies, Phinn Lapide's transformation of their story into a biblical allegory intuitively at least captures a bigger truth, even though everyone connected with the story knew that Lapide's version was a fiction and they were quick to dismiss it.[17] In fact, the determination of the San Nicandresi to become Jews caused many Italian Jews to reflect on what it really meant to be a Jew.

Those reactions again bring to mind Carlo Levi. In *Christ Stopped at Eboli* Levi made it clear that he had discovered forms of human dignity, compassion and collective solidarity in the harsh and bleak world of the southern peasants that he believed had been lost in the more cosmopolitan and more modern Italy of the North that had allowed itself to embrace Fascism. Levi was not alone in believing that the regeneration of Italian democracy after the war would have to start in the South. The land of remorse had unexpectedly now become a land of redemption too. Something very similar drew those Italian Jews who were also enemies of the Fascist regime to see in the conversion of Manduzio and his followers an inspirational revelation of the essential spiritual values of their faith.[18]

True or false, the image prevailed and all of those who were most directly involved in the story adopted their own idealized interpretations, in ways that influenced its outcome. But of those who played the most decisive roles, only Cantoni and Rabbi Ravenna had ever been to San Nicandro. Davide Prato and those who decided to formalize the conversion of the whole community in 1946 knew the story indirectly from the correspondence they had read, but not at first hand. Indeed, much of the information on which they acted was inaccurate. Raffaele Cantoni certainly had no desire to correct the image of the would-be converts as a small community united by their simple faith. That image was shared by Augusto Segre, for example, who played the decisive role in organizing the emigration of the San Nicandresi in 1949. But although Segre had met some of the converts in the refugee camps, he knew their story above all from what his friend Raffaele Cantoni had told him.[19] In short, it was the wider moral and symbolic meanings that contemporaries read into the story that made it possible for Manduzio and his followers to achieve their great ambition of becoming Jews and for many of them then also to emigrate to Israel.

It would be wrong to underestimate the importance of these external interventions, but it is also true that the converts were the agents of their own story, not just passive beneficiaries of others' actions. Despite their internal divisions and constant wrangling, their recognition, conversion and emigration came about only because of their persistence. It was their tenacity even to the point of importunity that constantly impressed outsiders.

The disputes and divisions within the community make its survival over a period from the late 1920s to the late 1940s little short of miraculous. Many things contributed to make that

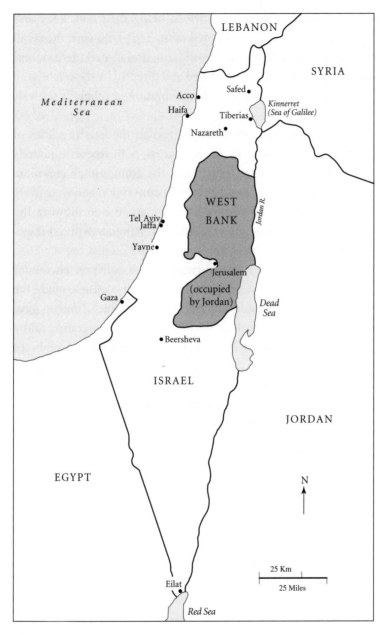

2 Israel in 1949.

miracle possible, the most obvious being their constancy and their adherence to their adopted faith. That faith gave the small community a strong sense of solidarity and shared identity, and their lives were indeed dominated and directed by the calendar of weekly prayer meetings and the celebration of religious festivals and high holy days.

The San Nicandro story vividly reveals the harsh realities of the lives of the rural poor in these years, with frequent quarrels and disputes constantly threatening the community's cohesion. These challenges continued after their conversion and were overcome by the steadfastness of the women in not allowing the community to be split up, or the men to emigrate without them, and by the group's firm commitment to the Zionist cause.

This second conversion, initiated by the converts' encounter with Enzo Sereni, was critically important because it made the ideals of conversion and emigration inseparable. Zionism gave the converts both a further set of reasons for emigrating and a commitment that went beyond their religious faith to embrace the political cause of their new country. After the death of Manduzio, the Zionist cause also gave them a new source of authority and legitimacy and once they emigrated it helped them to overcome the problems of assimilation in their new homeland, and assume new identities. This second conversion was just as fundamental as the first, but it made their story something more than a case of simple, spontaneous spirituality.

# Notes

## Abbreviations

| | |
|---|---|
| ACS | Archivio Centrale dello Stato, Rome |
| ASV | Archivio Segreto di Vaticano, Rome |
| BCUCEI | Biblioteca Centrale della Unione delle Communità Ebraiche Italiane, Rome |
| CAHJP | Central Archives for the History of the Jewish People, Jerusalem |
| JBG | Jewish Brigade Group |
| NA | National Archives, Kew, London |

## Introduction: The Prophet of San Nicandro

1. *Time*, 15 September 1947.
2. On contemporary Pentecostalism see David Martin, 'In Tongues', *Times Literary Supplement*, 19/9/2008, and Martin (1992) and (1996).
3. On the South as a 'land of remorse', see De Martino (1961/2005); on San Nicandro in the 1930s, see Cassin (1993), p. 27.
4. Levi (1947/1963).
5. Levi discusses the *americani* (ibid.) and the impact of of emigration throughout his book.
6. See the outstanding recent book by Sergio Luzzatto (2007).
7. Lapide (1953). As Lapide (Pinchas) he was also the author of *Three Popes and the Jews* (1967) and other studies defending Pope Pius XII.
8. Russo (1952).
9. Cassin (1957). Despite omissions, this remains the most important and detailed account of the conversion.
10. For a definition of 'primitive rebels', see Hobsbawm (1959), but Cassin was following Levi (1947/63).
11. Although Cassin says nothing about her background in the book, there is a large file on her in the Casellario Politico Centrale, where Mussolini's police kept records on all those the regime believed to be suspicious. Cassin's mother was a Rosselli, so she was a cousin of the brothers Carlo and Nello Rosselli, leaders of the Italian anti-Fascists in exile until they were

assassinated in France in 1937 on the orders of Mussolini's government. This was why Elena Cassin and her brother were suspected by the Fascist police and her movements were closely followed from 1936 until she left to live in Paris. Her aunt Mathilde Cassin was a close friend of Raffaele Cantoni, it is very unlikely that she was unaware of Cantoni's role in the story, or indeed of the other external events that played a major part in determining its outcome. See ACS Casellario Politico Centrale, Cassin, Elena.

## Chapter One: Manduzio's Story

1. Many copies were made of different sections of Manduzio's Journal at different times and for different people. However, a complete handwritten transcription of the text (together with a typed summary of the main points) can be found in the CAHJP in Jerusalem (Minerbi Papers: P 262/7). The copy in the BCUCEI in Rome has been misplaced. All references in the text are to the CAHJP copy.
2. See Cassin (1993) p. 31.
3. The first Italian Pentecostal Church was founded in Milan in 1910. After the Great War, almost all the new evangelical congregations were established in Sicily and southern Italy by returning emigrants. See Stretti (1988) pp. 30–1.
4. Journal p. 2.
5. Ibid., pp. 1 (the first version) and 2 (the second).
6. In the Journal the names of the first converts in 1929 were given as: Matteo Palmieri, Matteo Cataldo, Antonio Bonfitto, Francesco Cerrone, Rocco di Paolo, Costantino Tritto, Vincenzo di Salvia, Leonardo Leone, Maria Luigia Iannone, Donato Manduzio. But the list is inaccurate as Cerrone and Tritto joined later and on different occasions Manduzio subsequently claimed that there were both five and nineteen founding members.
7. The blind man Rocco di Paolo was the cousin of Concetta di Leo. The sisters Incoronata and Costantina Angello were the wives respectively of the Di Salvia brothers Cirò and Vincenzo. Giuseppa Iannone's son, Michele Soccio, was the husband of Lucia Gravina, and her daughter Luigia later married Giuseppe Buzicchio (known as Buchs): their daughter Incoronata later married Eliezer (formerly Nazario) Tritto and changed her name to Ester.
8. On the role of women and gender in the community see Trevisan Semi (2002) pp. 65–86.
9. The details are in the Journal but see also Cassin.
10. Eliezer's diary was published in the Italian edition of Cassin's book (1995); a copy can be consulted in the CAHJP (Minerbi Papers: P 262/8).
11. The date of Eliezer's birth is uncertain. He gives it as 26 July 1928 in his Diary; but later he says that he was thirteen years old in the spring of 1944, and that he came of age (eighteen) in 1948.
12. This was a Zionist charitable organization that raised funds for the purchase of land in Palestine.

## Chapter Two: Jewish Encounters

1. On the railway see Tancredi (1938/2004) published to celebrate the Fascist regime's achievements but with a wealth of detailed local information. On malaria see Snowden (2006).
2. CAHJP Pacifici papers P 172/156 contain copies of all the correspondence between Manduzio and Angelo Sacerdoti dating from September 1931.
3. BCUCEI f. 75, Pacifici's reports 6/10/1931 to 11/11/1932.
4. See, for example, Molho (1997).
5. BCUCEI f. 75 6/10/1931.
6. CAHJP Pacifici papers 28/1/1932.
7. Luzzatto's report is in BCUCEI f. 75, doc. 10119 'Breve esposto sulla communità pseudo-ebraica di San Nicandro'.
8. CAHJP Pacifici papers, doc. 502, Manduzio to Sacerdoti 22/11/1932; 4/12/1932.
9. On Jacques Faitlovich see *Encyclopaedia Judaica*. On his visit to San Nicandro see Trevisan Semi (2002) pp. 65–86. On the regime and the Falasha see Trevisan Semi (1987), Kaplan (1992) and Ullendorff (1965) and (1988).
10. The account of the visit is from Manduzio's Journal.
11. On Italian Zionism see Capuzzo (2004) and Toscano (2005).
12. CAHJP Pacifici papers, Francesco Cerrone to Pacifici 6/2/1935.
13. Ibid.
14. Ibid., Manduzio to Pacifici 4/4/1935.
15. The correspondence between Ascher and Cerrone is in BCUCEI f. 75.
16. CAHJP Pacifici papers, Pacifici to Manduzio (typed copy, no date).
17. Ibid., Manduzio's reply (no date).

## Chapter Three: The Duce and the Pope

1. On the origins of Fascism in Apulia see Colarizi (1971), Vivarelli (1967) and in English Snowden (1986).
2. See ACS Min. Interior DGPS (Affari Generali: Categoria G1), Regia Prefettura di Foggia 9/2/1925.
3. See Cerrone to Pacifici 6/2/1935: CAHJP. Pacifici Papers.
4. See Kertzer (2004).
5. For this and what follows see especially Violi (1996).
6. Ibid.
7. Ibid.
8. For the regime's policies on Protestants and religious minorities see Rochat (1980) and Stretti (1988).
9. Rochat (1980) pp. 19–23.
10. Ibid., pp. 113–14.
11. Ibid., p. 35.
12. Stretti (1988) p. 36.
13. Rochat (1980) p. 142; on racism in the Italian colonies see Ben Ghiat and Fuller (eds) (2005).
14. Cited in Stretti (1988), pp. 1–12, 43.
15. The court orders are in BCUCEI f. 75.

# Chapter Four: The Man from Milan

1. The account is from Manduzio's Journal.
2. The correspondence is in BCUCEI f. 75.
3. The account of Cantoni's visit is based on the Journal.
4. All this was recorded in the Journal.
5. Cited by Cantoni's friend and biographer Sergio Minerbi (1987) p. 69.
6. See Minerbi (1987) but also the extensive data on Cantoni held by the Fascist police: ACS Casellario Politico Centrale.
7. Segre (1978/2008) p. 225. Segre's memoir also contains part of the police file on Cantoni.
8. Della Seta and Carpi (1997) pp. 472-4.
9. See Minerbi (1987) and Franzinelli in Rossi (2000) passim; there were files on Cantoni held both by the Polizia Politica (ACS) and in the Casellario Politico (ACS).
10. Minerbi (1987) p. 63; see also ACS Min. Interno to Min. Affari Esteri 27/8/1936.
11. ACS DGPS (Div. AAGGRR) Cat. G1, busta 83, fascicolo 396, Communità Israelitiche Foggia.
12. Ibid. The same file contains all the intercepted correspondence and comments.

# Chapter Five: Persecution

1. Michaelis (1978) p. 165. There is now an extensive English-language bibliography on anti-Semitism in Fascist Italy. In addition to Michaelis, see De Felice (2001), Toscano (2005) Sarfatti (2006) Cavaglion and Romagnini (1988/2002), Collotti (2003), Stille (1992), and the essays by Sarfatti, Stille and Toscano in Zimmerman (ed.) (2005). For a recent critical review of the literature, see Vivarelli (2009).
2. Minerbi (1987) p. 74. See also Della Seta and Carpi (1997) pp. 1343-5.
3. Michaelis (1978).
4. Trevisan Semi (1987) pp. 70-2.
5. See Michaelis (1978) pp. 101, 108-9, 117.
6. See Blatt (1955). On Ovazza see Stille (1992) pp. 49-89.
7. On the Italian Zionists, see Della Seta and Carpi (1997), Bettin (2005), Stille and Toscano in Zimmerman (ed.) (2005).
8. On the Italian Jews see Collotti (2003) Stille (1992) pp. 11-16, Beltin (2005) and Siporin's introduction to Segre (1979/2008).
9. Della Seta and Carpi (1997) p. 1334.
10. See Segre (1979/2008) pp. 374-80 Dante Lattes and Alfonso Pacifici, for example, had founded the monthly journal *Mensile d'Israel*, the principal organ of the Italian Zionists, in Florence: Manduzio and his followers were not only subscribers but avid readers as well.
11. Trevisan Semi (1987).
12. Minerbi (1987) pp. 69-70.
13. See Della Seta and Carpi (1997) pp. 1345-9; Hametz (2007).
14. ACS Polizia Politica 26/11/1939; Direzione Generale Affari Generali, DGPS, busta 3, Ebrei internati 'Raffaele Cantoni'. Although Farinacci had

been prominent in the anti-Semitic campaign, he refused to sack his own secretary despite the fact that she was a Jew. Whether Farinacci did act as Cantoni's protector was never proved, but was widely suspected.

15. ACS Polizia Politica 26/11/1939; Direzione Generale Affari Generali, DGPS, busta 3, Ebrei internati 'Raffaele Cantoni'.
16. ACS Casellario Centrale Politico, 'Raffaele Cantoni' 11/6/1940.
17. Manduzio's Journal.
18. BCUCEI f. 75, Cantoni to Manduzio 3/2/1939.
19. ACS Direzione Generale Affari Generali PS, busta 83/396, Fasicolo 13, Communità israelitiche. According to the police file the members of the group were: Francesco Cerrone fu [son of the late] Pasquale, shoemaker with his wife and eight children; Donato Manduzio fu Giuseppe, cripple, and his wife; Cirò di Salvia fu Leonardo, cripple, with his wife and three children; Vincenzo di Salvia fu Leonardo, peasant with his wife and five children, Costantino Tritto fu Antonio, shoemaker with his wife and five children; Matteo del Mastro, peasant; Rocco di Paolo, blind; Antonio Bonfitto, with wife and children.
20. ACS Direzione Generale Affari Generali, PS, busta 83/396, fascicolo 17 Foggia, Propaganda evangelica 1936–9, 29/3/1938, 26/6/1938.
21. ASV Segreteria di stato 1938 No. 171283: 'Proselitismo ebraico nel Comune di San Nicandro Garganico. R. Ambasciata d'Italia presso la S. Sede. Riservato No. 2355, Roma 2/9/1938 – anno XVI'.
22. Rochat (1980) pp. 261–76; Stretti (1988).
23. ACS Min. Interno Dir. Gen. PS. & 83/396; fascicolo 17.
24. Carlo Levi (1947/63) tells how the Fascist Podestà often reduced the lists of welfare recipients as a false indication of the prosperity of a town.
25. BCUCEI f. 75: Cerrone to Unione, 21/11/1939.
26. CAHJP Eliezer Tritto's Diary.
27. Manduzio's Journal.
28. Ibid.

## Chapter Six: Falling into the Net

1. Sarfatti (2006) pp. 186–201.
2. Gribaudi (2005).
3. See Luzzatto (2007).
4. CAHJP Eliezer Tritto's diary.
5. Ibid.
6. Aron (1974) pp. 1–135.
7. See Wasserstein (1999) pp. 11–24.
8. NA WO 201, General Wavell to War Office 3/9/1939.
9. NA KV 5/33, Military Intelligence, Haganah.
10. NA FO 371, 147: P.M.'s personal minute.
11. Beckman (1998) p. 36: see also NA W.O-32/10874 1/5/1941. Cabinet-Memo 28/7/1944.
12. Aron (1974) pp. 1–6; Aron and Shilman-Cheong (1992) pp. 1–59: by a curious coincidence, Raffaele Cantoni had also drawn up a proposal for a Jewish legion recruited in Italy and Palestine which he presented to the British Ambassador in Rome in 1939. Needless to say, the Foreign Office in London rejected the proposal out of hand.

13. Aron (1974) pp. 63–4.
14. Ibid., pp. 98–102; Aron and Shilman-Cheong (1992) pp. 96–110.
15. See the reports by Rabbi Urbach in CAHJP Refugees P ii8/6 (Sicily) and in Pacifici (1993) pp. 70, 91–105. On Ferramonti Tarsia, DELASEM and Rabbi Riccardo Pacifici, see especially Stille (1992) pp. 191–236.
16. Aron (1974) p. 136.
17. Ibid., p. 163.
18. Della Seta and Carpi (1997) pp. 1348–51.
19. NA WO 32/10874 (JBG), Shertock to Major Gen. Seale 22/9/1944.

## Chapter Seven: A Hero Comes to Visit

1. On Sereni see Minerbi (1987) pp. 72–4 and Nahon (1973) pp. 191–5.
2. Nahon (1973) pp. 191–5.
3. CAHJP Eliezer Tritto's diary.
4. For the recollections of Lucia Giordano and Lia Cases see Nahon (1973) pp. 250–5.
5. Luzzatto (1939) in Luzzatto (1996) pp. 96–9.

## Chapter Eight: A Difficult Conversion

1. See the war diary of Bernard Casper, who served as military chaplain with the JBG: Casper (1947).
2. On the JBG and their activities see Beckman (1998) pp. 105–6 and Blum (2002). On Arazi see Minerbi (1987) p. 153, Sereni (1973) and Toscano (1990) pp. 35–40.
3. Beckman (1998). Wellesley Aron returned to Palestine before being sent to New York by the Jewish Agency where he successfully recruited American and Canadian volunteers for the war in Palestine. See Aron and Shilman-Cheong (1992) pp. 119–27 and Slaven (1970) pp. 210–18.
4. Casini (1986), 50–62 and Zuccotti (2007) pp. 160–8; Stille (1992) pp. 254–9.
5. Minerbi (1987) pp. 118–226.
6. Casper (1947) p. 59.
7. Minerbi (1987) and Sereni (1973).
8. See Newman (1945).
9. BCUCEI f. 79, Memorandum entitled 'San Nicandro Garganico' (no date).
10. Ibid., f. 79, Manduzio to the Union 22/4/1945.
11. Ibid., Manduzio to the Union 4/6/1945.
12. Ibid., Marrochella to the Union 11/7/1945.
13. Ravenna (1960) pp. 244–9.
14. BCUCEI f. 79, Manduzio to Nathan 27/8/1945.
15. Ibid., Manduzio to Nathan 27/12/1945.
16. Ibid., Relazione sul viaggio a S. Nicandro.
17. Ibid., Ravenna to Cantoni 16/8/1946.

## Chapter Nine: What Next?

1. BCUCEI f. 75, Manduzio to Cantoni 2/9/1946.
2. Ibid., Cerrone to Cantoni 5/9/1946.

NOTES to pp. 155–89

3. Ibid., Marrochella to Cantoni 16/8/1946.
4. Ibid., Marrochella to the Union 27/9/1946.
5. Ibid., Cantoni to Sezione della Communità Israelitica di San Nicandro 30/9/1946.
6. Ibid., Cerrone to Cantoni 3/12/1946.
7. Ibid., undated letter.
8. Ibid., Cantoni's reply (no date).
9. Ibid., Manduzio to Cantoni 26/2/1947.
10. Ibid., Cantoni to Manduzio 29/2/1947.
11. Ibid., Cerrone to Cantoni 25/2/1947.
12. Ibid., Manduzio to Cantoni 14/4/1947.
13. Ibid., Tritto to Cantoni 7/4/1947.
14. Ibid., Cantoni to Costantino (Chaim) Tritto.
15. Ibid., Cantoni to Pesach Cerrone, Tenuta di S. Marco, Cevoli (Pisa) 3/7/1947.
16. Ibid., Pesach Cerrone to Cantoni 10/7/1947.
17. Ibid., Cantoni to Manduzio 24/8/1947.
18. Ibid., Manduzio to Cantoni 10/9/1947.
19. Ibid., Manduzio to Cantoni 3/11/1947.

## Chapter Ten: After Manduzio

1. BCUCEI f. 75, Manduzio to the Union 5/1/1948.
2. See Segre (1978/2008) pp. 390–1 and Toscano (1990) pp. 40–3, 267–337.
3. BCUCEI f. 75, Manduzio to the Union 19/1/1948.
4. Ibid., 15/3/1948.
5. Ibid., Costantino (Chaim) Tritto to Cantoni 7/4/1948.
6. Ibid., Concetta di Leo to Cantoni 7/4/1948.
7. Ibid., Concetta di Leo to Cantoni 20/9/1948.
8. Ibid., Cantoni to Concetta di Leo 7/1/1949.
9. Ibid., Concetta di Leo to Cantoni 19/4/1949 (includes the typescript of her document).
10. Minerbi (1987) pp. 200–2; Toscano (1990) pp. 331–7; see also ACS Min. Interno DGPS f. 16 Ebrei Stranieri Attività Politica, 1948; PCM (1944–7), G. 3416.
11. BCUCEI f. 75, Concetta di Leo to Cantoni 9/5/1949.
12. Ibid., Cantoni to Concetta di Leo 11/5/1949.
13. Ibid., Concetta di Leo to Cantoni 13/5/1949.
14. Ibid., Cantoni to Concetta di Leo 13/6/1949.

## Chapter Eleven: The Promised Land

1. BCUCEI f. 75, Michele Bonfitto to Cantoni 23/3/1948.
2. Ibid., Michele Bonfitto to Cantoni 31/1/1949.
3. Ibid., Eliezer (Nazario) Tritto to Cantoni 31/1/1949 (see also Eliezer's diary, CAHJP).
4. Ibid., Michele Bonfitto to Della Seta 15/3/1949.
5. Ibid., Concetta di Leo to Cantoni 7/9/1949.
6. Ibid., Maria Frascaria to Cantoni 18/1/1949.

7. Pacifici (1993) p. 70. On the Pacifici family see also Stille (1992) pp. 236–9, 250–9.
8. BCUCEI 048, f. 75 Segre to President FSI Milan 21/6/1949.
9. Ibid., Cantoni to Anna Levi Minzi, Milan 29/6/1949.
10. Ibid., Judah Domnitz, Jerusalem, to Cantoni 27/7/1949.
11. Ibid., Pesach Cerrone to Cantoni 21/9/1949.
12. Ibid. The following list of families waiting to emigrate in 1949 did not include those who had already departed for Israel and so is not complete (for example, Cerrone and Marrochella). However, it gives a clear picture of the composition of the group and especially of their age and sex:

| Name | Date of Birth |
| --- | --- |
| Mugello di Salvia | |
| Incoronato | 7/4/1903 |
| Daniele | 3/3/1935 |
| Gemina | 17/7/1938 |
| Costantina | 24/3/1900 |
| Lea | 11/7/1936 |
| Gioele | 2/3/1939 |
| Colino-Tardio | |
| Angela | 1/1/1930 |
| Domenico | 27/1/1947 |
| De Sanctis | |
| Filomeno | 12/2/1884 |
| Frascaria Leone | |
| Maria | 14/1/1910 |
| Lucia | 20/2/1935 |
| Eliseo | 2/3/1939 |
| Leone | |
| Giovanni | 21/4/1930 |
| Palmieri Santelmo | |
| Rosa | 13/3/1914 |
| Giuseppe | 2/2/1939 |
| Soccio Leone | |
| Clorinda | 23/2/1933 |
| Tardio | |
| Leonardo | 8/8/1924 |
| Vicedomini | |
| Antonio | 1930 (in Israel since 1948) |
| Bonfitto | |
| Antonio | 1889 |
| Di Leo, Concetta | 1900 |
| Michele | 1925 |
| De Angelis | |
| Angelina | 1932 |
| Bonfitto | |
| Moshè | 1949 |
| Vincenzo | 1936 (di Michele) |

| Giuseppe | 1938 (di Antonio) |
|---|---|
| Lucia | 1941 |
| Levi | 1945 |
| Vocino | |
| Emanuela (widow Manduzio) | 1890 |
| Tritto | |
| Costantino | 1898 |

## Chapter Twelve: The Story's End

1. Cassin (1957/1993) pp. 11–15.
2. CAHJP Eliezer Tritto's Diary.
3. BCUCEI f. 75, Devora Bonfitto (Concetta di Leo) at Ras Laffimar to Cantoni. In October 1953, Eliezer Tritto also wrote for the first time to Cantoni to give him their news when they had just moved to *moshav* Alma at Dor Safed in Galilee. He said that at that time there were only six families from San Nicandro still in the *moshav* because in the previous year the others had moved to new settlements in the Negev region: ibid., Eliezer Tritto to Cantoni 2/10/1953 and 21/10/1953); for Cantoni's reply see 23/8/1950.
4. CAHJP P 252/13 (Leo Levi).
5. See Cassin (1994). The concern about the reactions of the Palestinian Jews to the immigrants may explain why in her account Cassin deliberately minimized the role of Cantoni and others in order to underline the spontaneity and unmediated nature of the conversion. But it has also to be remembered that at the time when she was writing few of the details of the Net and the organization of clandestine emigration to Palestine at the end of the war were known, and might have had serious consequences for those involved if made public. Ada Sereni's book, for example, was not published until 1973, and even then caused quite a stir.
6. BCUCEI f. 75, Giuseppe Corso and Matteo Russo (San Nicandro) to Cantoni 5/6/1949; Cantoni's reply 1/7/1949.
7. Ibid., Tritto to Cantoni 31/8/1949; Cantoni to Tritto 9/9/1949; Achille di Lella to the Union 12/1/1950.
8. Ibid., Tritto to Cantoni 28/8/1950.
9. Ibid., 1/6/1950.
10. Ibid., Tritto to Cantoni 28/8/1950.
11. The same Leo Levi who had acted as guide to the San Nicandresi in Israel.
12. BCUCEI f. 75; Cantoni to Tritto 16/10/1950.
13. See Ravenna (1960) p. 248.
14. BCUCEI f. 75, Luigi Israele di Seri (Palazzo S. Gervasio, Potenza) to President of the Union 16/8/1950.
15. Ibid., Francesco Giramonte (S. Giovanni in Fiore) 18/8/1950.
16. In his introduction to the 1995 Italian edition of Elena Cassin's book Alberto Cavaglion rightly concluded that Cantoni was 'the great puppet master who pulled the wires from Rome, Naples and the Tremiti Islands, the man who discovered the neophytes and was the moving force behind so many activities to bring help to the Jewish refugees in Italy'.

17. Leo Levi, for example, was unsparing in his criticisms of the 'falsification of facts as they appear in the book by Mr Lapide ... the facts presented are mostly invented and substantially changed ... it is a work of no documentary value whatsoever': CAHJP P 252/13.
18. See Levi (1947/1963) and also Marino (2003).
19. Segre (1979/2008) pp. 390-1.

# Sources

**Primary**

*Archivio Centrale dello Stato (ACS), Rome*

Ministero degli Interni, Direzione Generale Affari Generali, Direzione di Pubblica Sicurezza Affari Generali
    Ebrei Stranieri
    Ebrei Internati
Direzione Polizia Politica (fascicoli personali) 1927–1944
Casellario Politico Centrale
Presidenza Consiglio dei Ministrei (PCM) 1944–7

*Archivio Segreto del Vaticano (ASV), Rome*

Affari Ecclesiastici Straordinari (Italia) Pos 795 fascic 400 ('Protestanti')
Achivio della Segreteria di Stato, II Sezione 1938 Protocolli
171283, Riservato 2355

*Biblioteca Centrale della Unione delle Communità Ebraiche Italiane (BCUCEI), Rome*

Archivio Storico dell 'Unione delle Communita' Ebraiche Fondo Attivita dell'Unione delle, Communità Israelitiche Italiane dal 1934

Busta 75  Fascicolo 7: San Nicandro (missing)
          Fascicolo 11: Notizie su personalità e nuclei ebraici
          Fascicolo 12: Nuclei ed individui ebraicizzanti 1947

*Central Archives for the History of the Jewish People (CAHJP), Jerusalem*

| | |
|---|---|
| Refugees | P 118/6 (October 1943–February 1944) |
| Chaplains (Confidential) | P 119/5 (August 1943–February 1944) Sicily |
| Alfonso Pacifici papers | P 172/156 |
| Sergio Minerbi papers | P 262/7 Manduzio's Diary and summary |
| | P 262/6 Photographs Manduzio, Bonfitto and others |
| | P 262/8 Diary of Eliezer Tritto |

Leo Levi papers      P 252/13
Umberto Nahon papers   P 239/14/4

*National Archive (NA), Kew, London*
War Office
  WO 32/170 Jewish Brigade War Diary 201/214/219
  WO 32/10873–4 Jewish Brigade Group (JBG)
  WO 201 JBG
  WO224–8 War in Italy

*Security Service: Organization (OF series) Files*
KV 5/33 (OF 607) Haganah

*Colonial Office*
  CO 537/5371
  CAB/CO 80/98/33

*Foreign Office*
FO 371 Palestine and Transjordan

**Secondary**

Aron, Wellesley *Wheels in the Storm. The Genesis of the Israeli Defence Force* (Canberra, Roebuck 1974)

Aron, Wellesley and Silman-Cheong, Helen *Wellesley Aron Rebel with a Cause: A Memoir* (London, Valentine Mitchell 1992)

Bauer, Yehuda *Flight and Rescue. Bricah* (New York, Random House 1970)

Beckman, Morris *The Jewish Brigade. An Army with Two Masters 1944–5* (Rockville Center, NY, Sarpedon 1998)

Ben David, Joseph 'San Nicandro. A Sociological Comment', *Jewish Journal of Sociology* 2/2 (1960) pp. 250–8

Ben Ghiat, Ruth and Fuller, Mia (eds) *Italian Colonialism* (New York, Palgrave 2005)

Bettin, Cristina 'Identity and Identification: Jewish Youth in Italy 1870–1938', *Journal of Modern Jewish Studies* 3 (2005) pp. 323–45

Bevilacqua, P., De Clementi, A. and Franzina, E. *Storia dell'emigrazione italiana*, 2 vols (Rome, Donzelli 2002)

Blatt, Joel 'The battle of Turin 1933–6: Carlo Rosselli, Giustizia e Liberta, OVRA and the origins of Mussolini's anti-Semitic campaign', *Journal of Modern Italian Studies* 1/1 (1995) pp. 22–57

Blum, Howard *The Brigade: an epic story of vengeance, salvation and World War II* (New York, HarperCollins 2002)

Capuzzo, Ester *Gli ebrei italiani dal Risorgimento alla scelta sionista* (Florence, Le Monnier 2004)

Casini, Leto *Ricordi di un vecchio prete* (Florence, La Giuntina 1986)

Casper, Bernard *With the Jewish Brigade*, introduction by Brigadier E. R. Benjamin (London, Edward Goldston 1947)

Cassin, Elena *San Nicandro. Histoire d'une conversion* (Paris, Plon 1957). Translated and published in English as *San Nicandro. The Story of a Religious*

*Phenomenon* (London, Cohen & West 1959). A second edition of the original French edition was published with a 'Postface' by the author (Paris, Quai Voltaire 1993), followed by an Italian edition *San Nicandro. Un paese del Gargano si converte all'ebraismo*, introduction by Alberto Cavaglion and including the 'Diary of Eliezer Tritto' (pp. 141–53) (Milan, Corbaccio 1995)

Catalano, Tullio 'L'organizzazione delle communità ebraiche italiane dall'unità alla prima Guerra mondiale', in Corrado Vivanti (ed.) *Gli ebrei in Italia*, vol. II: *Dall'emancipazione a oggi* (Turin, Einaudi 1997) pp. 1245–72

Cavaglion, Alberto and Romagnini, Gian Paolo *Le interdizioni del Duce: le leggi razziali in Italia* (Turin, Claudiana 1988/2002)

Cividelli, Gualtiero 'Ritorno a San Nicandro', *La Rassegna Mensile di Israel* 39 (April 1973) pp. 226–36

Clark, Victoria *Allies for Armageddon. The Rise of Christian Zionism* (New Haven and London, Yale University Press 2007)

Colarizi, Simona *Dopoguerra e fascismo in Puglia (1919–1926)* (Bari, Laterza 1971)

Collotti, Enzo *Il Fascismo e gli ebrei* (Rome, Bari, Laterza 2003)

De Donato, Gigliola (ed.) *Verso i sud del mondo. Carlo Levi a cento anni della nascità* (Rome, Donzelli 2003)

De Felice, Renzo *The Jews in Fascist Italy: A History*, preface by Michael A. Ledeen (New York, Enigma Books 2001)

Della Seta, Simonetta and Carpi, Daniel 'Il movimento sionistico', in Corrado Vivanti (ed.) *Gli ebrei in Italia*, vol. II: *Dall'emancipazione a oggi* (Turin, Einaudi 1997) pp. 1323–66

De Martino, Ernesto *The Land of Remorse: a Study of Southern Italian Tarantism*, trans. D. L. Zinn, foreword By V. Crapanzano (London, Free Association 2005)

Ellwood, David *L'alleato nemico. La politica dell'occupazione anglo-americana in Italia 1943–1946* (Milan, Feltrinelli 1977)

*Encyclopaedia Judaica* ed. M. Berenbaum and F. Skolnik (Detroit, Macmillan Reference USA with Kerev Publishing House, 2007)

Franzinelli, Mimmo 'Nel retrobottega della polizia fascista' in Rossi (2000) pp. 7–116

Gribaudi, Gabriella *Guerra totale. Tra bombe alleate e violenze naziste. Napoli e il Fronte Meridionale 1940–44* (Turin, Bollati Boringhieri 2005)

Hametz, Maura 'Zionism, Emigration and Anti-Semitism in Trieste. Central Europe's 'Gateway to Zion'' 1896–1943', *Jewish Social Studies* 13/3 (Spring–Summer 2007) pp. 103–34

Herzer, Ivo (with Klaus Voigt and James Burgwyn) *The Italian Refuge. Rescue of Jews during the Holocaust* (Washington DC, Catholic Press of America 1989)

Hobsbawm, Eric J. *Primitive Rebels: Studies in Archaic Social Movements in the 19th and 20th Centuries* (Manchester, Manchester University Press 1959)

Kaplan, Steven *The Beta Israel (Falasha) in Ethiopia* (New York, New York University Press 1992)

Katz, Robert *Black Sabbath. A Journey through a Crime against Humanity* (Toronto, Macmillan 1969)

Kelikian, Alice A. 'The Church and Catholicism', in Adrian Lyttelton (ed.) *Liberal and Fascist Italy* (Oxford, Oxford University Press 2002) pp. 44–61

Kertzer, David I. *The Popes against the Jews. The Vatican's Role in the Rise of Modern Anti-Semitism* (New York, Knopf 2001)

Kertzer, David I. *Prisoner of the Vatican. The Pope's Secret Plot to Capture Rome from the New Italian State* (Boston, Houghton Mifflin 2004)

Kimche, Jon and David *The Secret Roads: The 'Illegal' Migration of a People 1938-48* (London, Secker & Warburg 1955)

Lapide, Phinn E. (Pinchas) *The Prophet of San Nicandro* (New York, Beechhurst Press 1953)

Lapide, Pinchas *Three Popes and the Jews* (London, Souvenir Press 1967)

Levi, Carlo *Christ Stopped at Eboli*, trans. Frances Frenaye (New York, Farrar, Straus 1947/1963)

Luzzatto, Guido Lodovico *Scritti Politici. Ebraismo ed anti-semitismo*, ed. Alberto Cavaglion and Elsia Tedeschi (Milan, Franco Angeli 1996). Includes 'Sei mesi di antisemitismo in Italia', *Il Nuovo Avanti* (Paris) 17/6/1939

Luzzatto, Sergio *Padre Pio. Miracoli e politica nell'Italia del Novecento* (Turin, Einaudi 2007)

Marino, Giuseppe Carlo 'Carlo Levi. Il meridionalismo, i contadini e la "rivoluzione italiana" ', in De Donato (ed.) (2003)

Martin, David *Forbidden Revolutions. Pentecostalism in Latin America and Catholicism in Eastern Europe* (London, SPCK 1996)

Martin, David *Pentecostalism. The World is their Parish* (Oxford, Blackwell 1992)

Martin, David 'In Tongues', *Times Literary Supplement* 19/9/2008

Marzano, Arturo *Una terra per rinascere. Gli ebrei italiani e l'emigrazione in Palestina prima della Guerra 1920-40*, introduction by Alberto Cavaglion (Genoa and Milan, Marietti 2003)

Michaelis, Meir *Mussolini and the Jews. German-Italian Relations and the Jewish Question in Italy 1922-1945* (Oxford, Clarendon Press 1978)

Minerbi, Sergio *Raffaele Cantoni. Un ebreo anti-conformista*, introduction by Giorgio Romano (Rome, Carucci 1987)

Molho, Anthony 'Ebrei e marrani fra Italia e Levante ottomano', in Corrado Vivanti (ed.), *Gli ebrei in Italia*, vol. II: *Dall'emancipazione a oggi* (Turin, Einaudi 1997) pp. 1014–48

Nahon, Umberto (ed.) *Per non morire. Enzo Sereni.Vita, scritti, testimonianze* (Milan, Federazione sionistica italiana 1973)

Newman, Lewis *A 'Chief Rabbi' of Rome Becomes a Catholic. A Study in Fright and Spite* (New York, Renascence Press 1945)

Ofer, Dalia *Escaping the Holocaust. Illegal Immigration to the Land of Israel 1939-44* (Oxford, London and New York: Oxford University Press 1990)

Pacifici, Emanuele *'Non ti voltare'. Autobiografia di un ebreo* (Florence, La Giuntina 1993)

Parfitt, Tudor and Trevisan Semi, Emanuela *Judaising Movements. Studies in the Margins of Judaism* (London, Routledge 2002)

Ravenna, Alfredo 'The Converts of San Nicandro', *Jewish Journal of Sociology* 2/2 (1960) pp. 244–9

Rochat, Giorgio *Regime fascista e chiese evangeliche* (Turin, Collana della Società di Studi Valdesi, Claudiana 1980)

Rossi, Ernesto *Una 'Spia del Regime Carlo Del Re e la provocazione contro Giustizia & Liberta* (Nuova edizione a cura di Mimmo Franzinelli (Turin, Bolleti Boringhieri 2000)

Russo, Giovanni *Baroni e contadini* (Bari, Laterza 1952)

Salvadori, Roberto G. *The Jews of Florence. From the Origins of the Community up to the Present*, trans. Ann Curiel (Florence, La Giuntina 2001)

Sarfatti, Michele *Jews in Mussolini's Italy. From Equality to Persecution*, trans. John and Ann Tedeschi (Madison, WI, University of Wisconsin Press 2006)

Sarfatti, Michele 'Characteristics and Objectives of the Anti-Jewish Racial Laws in Fascist Italy', in Zimmerman (ed.) (2005) pp. 71–80

Segre, Augusto *Memoirs of Jewish Life. From Italy to Jerusalem 1918–1960*, trans. with an introduction by Stephen Siporin (Lincoln, NE, University of Nebraska Press 2008). Originally *Memorie di vita ebraica* (Rome, Bonacci 1979)

Segre, Dan Vittorio *Memoirs of a Fortunate Jew. An Italian Story* (Northvale, NJ, and London, Jason Aronson 1995)

Sereni, Ada *I clandestini del mare. L'emigrazione ebraica in Terra d'Israele dal 1945 al 1948* (Milan, Mursia 1973)

Sereni, Clara *Il gioco dei regni* (Florence, Giunti 1993)

Slaven, Leonard *The Pledge* (New York, Simon & Schuster 1970)

Snowden, Frank *Conquest of Malaria. Italy 1900–1962* (New Haven and London, Yale University Press 2006)

Snowden, Frank *Violence and Great Estates in the South of Italy. Apulia 1900–1922* (Cambridge, Cambridge University Press 1986)

Stille, Alexander *Benevolence and Betrayal. Five Jewish Families under Fascism* (New York, Summit 1992)

Stille, A. 'The Double Bind of Italian Jews. Acceptance', in Zimmerman (ed.) (2005) pp. 19–34

Stretti, Eugenio *Il movimento pentecostale. Le Assemblee di Dio in Italia* (Turin, Claudiana 1988)

Stuart Hughes, H. *Prisoners of Hope. The Silver Age of the Italian Jews* (Cambridge, MA, Harvard University Press 1983)

Tancredi, Giovanni *Folclore Garganico* (Manfredonia, Armillotta & Marino 1938: republished Foggia, Claudio Grenzi 2004)

Tarrow, S. *Peasant Communism in Southern Italy* (New Haven and London, Yale University Press 1967)

Toscano, Mario *La 'Porta di Sion', L'Italia e l'immigrazione clandestina ebraica in Palestina (1945–1948)* (Bologna, Il Mulino 1990)

Toscano, Mario 'Italian Jewish Identity from the Risorgimento to Fascism', in Zimmerman (ed.) (2005) pp. 35–54

Trevisan Semi, Emanuela *Allo specchio dei Falascià. Ebrei ed etnologi durante il colonialismo fascista* (Florence, La Giuntina 1987)

Trevisan Semi, Emanuela 'A Conversion Movement in Italy. Jewish Universalism, Conversion and Gender in San Nicandro', in Parfitt and Trevisan Semi (2002) pp. 65–86

*Tribunale Speciale per la Difesa dello Stato – Sentenze 1931* (Rome, Ministero della Difesa 1987)

Ullendorff, Edward *The Ethiopians. An Introduction to the Country and People* (London and Oxford, Oxford University Press 1965)

Ullendorff, Edward *The Two Zions. Reminiscences of Jerusalem and Ethiopia* (London and Oxford, Oxford University Press 1988)

Varadi, Max *De l'Arno aux rives du Jourdain – Au revoir Italie* (Paris, L'Arche 1997)

Villa, Andrea *Dai lager alla terra promessa. La difficile reintegrazione nella 'nuova Italia' e l'immigrazione verso il Medio Oriente (1945–1948)* (Milan, Angelo Guerini 2005)

Violi, Roberto P. *Religiosità e identità collective. I santuari del Sud tra fascismo, Guerra e democrazia* (Rome, Edizione Studiorum 1996)

Vivarelli, Roberto *Dopoguerra in Italia e avvento del fascismo 1918–22* (Naples, Istituto per gli Studi Storici 1967)

Vivarelli, Roberto 'Le leggi razziali nella storia del fascismo italiano', *Rivista Storica Italiana* 121/2 (2009) pp. 738–72

Wasserstein, Bernard *Britain and the Jews of Europe 1939–1945* (London and New York, Leicester University Press 1999)

Zimmerman, Joshua D. (ed.) *The Jews in Italy under Fascist and Nazi Rule 1922–1945* (Cambridge, Cambridge University Press 2005)

Zuccotti, Susan *Holocaust Odysseys. The Jews of Saint-Martin-Vésubie and their Flight through France and Italy* (New Haven and London, Yale University Press 2007)

Zuccotti, Susan *Under his Very Window. The Vatican and the Holocaust in Italy* (New Haven and London, Yale University Press 2000)

# Index